UNDER SURGE, UNDER SIEGE

To the Pakenhan Group — with best regards & many thanks for being here in "The Bay"

ELLIS ANDERSON

Photography by Ellis Anderson and Joe Tomasovsky

University Press of Mississippi / Jackson

Ellis Anderson

UNDER SURGE UNDER SIEGE

The Odyssey of Bay St. Louis and Katrina

www.upress.state.ms.us

The University Press of Mississippi is a member
of the Association of American University Presses.

Designed by Todd Lape

Photographs are by the author unless otherwise specified.

First printing 2010
∞
Library of Congress Cataloging-in-Publication Data

Anderson, Ellis.
Under surge, under siege : the odyssey of
Bay St. Louis and Katrina / Ellis Anderson ;
photography by Ellis Anderson and Joe Tomasovsky.
p. cm.
Includes bibliographical references.
ISBN 978-1-60473-502-4 (cloth : alk. paper) — ISBN 978-
1-60473-503-1 (ebook) 1. Hurricane Katrina, 2005—Per-
sonal narratives. 2. Disaster victims— Mississippi—Bay
Saint Louis. 3. Disaster relief—Mississippi—Bay Saint
Louis. I. Title.
HV636 2005 .B3 A53 2010
976.2'14—dc22   2010003125

British Library Cataloging-in-Publication Data available

This book is dedicated to the people of

Bay St. Louis and the Mississippi Gulf Coast

and to the thousands of volunteers who

have worked toward our healing.

You've shown me that community spirit

is an animate and active essence, one that

can enrich a life beyond measure.

CONTENTS

PROLOGUE

The atmosphere of compassion that transforms a mass of alienated individuals into a caring community is created by countless acts of kindness . . . To
re-mind and en-courage myself in the practice of applied compassion, I collect
images and stories with which to create my personal pantheon of local heroes
and consecrated neighbors . . .
—SAM KEEN, "Hymns to an Unknown God"

The invisible net of fellowship that broke the horrific fall of my town was
woven long before Katrina. The knitting of that marvelous mesh was begun
three hundred years before by the mariners and merchants and fishermen
who first clustered their cottages on the Mississippi coast at the Bay of
St. Louis. During those three centuries, the hurricanes that periodically
hurtled in from the Gulf merely strengthened the weave, teaching hard
lessons about the benefits of solidarity. In "the Bay," the skills required for
a flourishing community—courage, tolerance, and humor in adversity—
were passed down to children like a legacy and taught by example to new-
comers like me.

Yet Katrina had to knock the stuffing out of the coast before I understood
community as a survival mechanism. During catastrophe, those neighborly
connections created lifelines of support for the individual—sometimes
literally. Here at ground zero, that supple safety net caught people during the full fury of the storm, even while the wind and tsunami-like surge
scoured the shore. Few gave way to the panicked mentality of every man for
himself. Seasoned and steeled by an ingrained concern for others, most of
my neighbors remained calm. Many risked their own lives to save others.
My serene little village was suddenly revealed as a hotbed of heroism. The
portly public official, the soft-spoken shopkeeper, and the zany artist were

transformed into real-time adventurers who faced down the most awesome storm in this country's history with grit and with grace.

In the days that followed, when the coast was shorn of electricity, communication, and law enforcement, "the Bay" didn't degenerate into chaos. Despite the pain, dignity reigned. In a darkness unbroken by any light, I flung open the doors of my house at night, hoping to catch a stray breeze, and then slept without fear of malice. Witnessing shell-shocked residents comforting each other, offering food and hugs and laughter, I began to understand that heroism didn't necessarily entail the risk of a life. It could be found in a small act of generosity in the midst of fear and loss.

Soon, the elastic boundaries of our community stretched as thousands of volunteers converged on the coast. Allies materialized from unlikely corners of the country, bearing supplies, fresh energy, and hope. As I write this prologue, it's been four years since Katrina upended the town, and still volunteers continue to come, realizing that our full recovery will take decades.

During these years of grinding aftermath, the journal I began to document a fleeting weather event took an odd turn: instead of recording the effects of a hurricane, my pen became possessed with the phenomenon of crafted kinship that sustained me—that sustained all of us in the town. I came to realize that in the Bay, community is a living web, one laced with the diverse fibers of my neighbors' courage and the bright threads of volunteer service.

This book introduces some of those unassuming heroes. In the first part, "Under Surge," I write of the storm and the immediate aftermath, when breathtaking bravery was the rule. The second part, "Under Siege," chronicles the perils that have threatened our town in the years since the hurricane, requiring residents to embody a more enduring kind of valor. The eight sections weave entries from my journal with the stories of townspeople and volunteers who serve so well as my source of inspiration. May they enrich your life as they have my own.

Welcome to Bay St. Louis.

BOOK ONE

UNDER SURGE

PART ONE
Storm Journal

THE LANGUAGE OF LOSS

THERE IS A MAN LIVING in my driveway now, and I don't find that at all unusual. He makes his bed in the back of his small SUV and sleeps there with his little dog. Many afternoons he can be found sitting behind the wheel, reading the paper, his shitz su nestled on his lap. He calls his car "home." It's part of the new vocabulary that's emerging on the Gulf Coast after Hurricane Katrina.

The man is the grandfather of Hannah, who's nine years old and one of my new residents. She and her parents stay at my house for now because the storm took their own. Hannah tells me that the shitz su is fussy and will pick fights with my dogs, so her grandfather would rather stay in his car than intrude. I've tried to insist that he come inside—we'd find him a bed to sleep in—but I think that now he'd rather be in the one place he can call his own.

He's not the only one. I have other friends living in tents in their driveways or in cramped travel trailers, rather than taking refuge with family in other towns. They want to stay connected with the place that has been their home, even if the structure is no longer standing. It may not seem very practical, but practicality flew out of the window along with everything else when Katrina tore through Mississippi two months ago.

The community that remains behind on the coast has evolved into a new animal—some fantastic creature I've never seen before. It's fiercely loyal, incredibly hardy, and deeply determined. It's developed a wicked sense of humor and doesn't whine very often. No matter your loss, too many others have lost more. It's bad form to complain.

And this new community is developing its own language, with an extensive and colorful vocabulary. There's "mucking out." That used to mean cleaning out a horse's stall. Now it's something you do to the inside of your house. "Gone-pecan" is used frequently—it's a designation for anything that got taken out by the storm—houses, businesses, cars, family photos. It's interchangeable with "got-gone."

Friends meeting in the meal tents or the FEMA lines will ask each other, "How'd you make out?" Too many times the answer is "I got slabbed," meaning nothing of the house remains except the concrete foundation. If one of them still has walls standing, the answer will be along these lines: "I came out pretty well—I only got six feet of water." The homeless friend will offer congratulations. This is the only place in America where having six feet of mud and water violently invade your house is considered lucky.

When we leave the region and go someplace that wasn't affected by the storm, we call it "the outside world." The outside world has cable TV and working phones. You can walk out your door and look at a neighborhood instead of rubble. You can drive to any number of gas stations and stores and they're actually open. You don't have to stand in line four hours to buy a washing machine or talk to a FEMA agent. A chain saw isn't a necessary household item. You can call an insurance agent and actually talk to someone. There isn't a ten o'clock curfew. And in the outside world, the word "Katrina" is just a name instead of an adjective.

Here, we have "Katrina-mind." That refers to blanking out, forgetting something absurdly simple, like your own phone number or the name of your best friend. We say "Katrina ware." That's the paper and plastic we mostly eat from now. There's the "Katrina cough," a persistent hacking from breathing all the silt brought in by the storm. This dust hangs in the air and coats everything with a fine, malevolent grit.

A portable toilet has become a "Katrina latrina." Fetid water that has hidden in corners and plastic boxes, a dark brew of multicolored molds

Photograph by Joe Tomasovsky.

that emits an unmistakable stench, is "Katrina juice." And my absolutely favorite new phrase is "Katrina patina."

Anything that survived the storm is coated with sludge, discolored, mangled at least to some degree. It's got that "Katrina patina." Jewelry, artwork, tools, photographs, furniture, clothes—all have been transformed by the storm into something vaguely recognizable, yet inalterably changed. Friends, at the end of a long day of mucking, covered with grime and sweat and a substance resembling black algae, will refuse an embrace. "Stay back," they'll warn. "I've got the Katrina patina."

Even after a scalding shower, scrubbing with soap and disinfectant, the Katrina patina remains, marking every one of us. It doesn't wash off. We, as well as our belongings, are vaguely recognizable, inalterably changed. We can only hope some of it wears away as the years pass.

Yet beneath that patina—under the sludge and the mud, the loss and the mourning—a bright determination flourishes. Our spirit as a community is evolving as surely as our vocabulary. We're fluent in the language of loss now, but we're also learning more about the language of love.

THE TIES THAT BIND

We're already forgetting our town.

A few days ago, I found a photo of Bay St. Louis before the storm. A friend had taken it last winter, during a sunset walk on the beach. I enlarged it on my computer screen and sat before it, staring.

Hannah, who's just turned ten, walked into the room with her mother, Kimberly. They've been living with me in the four months since Katrina destroyed their home. They were surprised to find me crying and checked out the photo causing my grief. Kimberly understood immediately. Their

A shot of my neighborhood after Katrina. Photograph by Joe Tomasovsky.

home had stood a block from where the picture had been taken. Now their house was gone. All the houses in the photo were gone. The image of our old, familiar town had already faded, and we were both stricken by a renewed sense of loss. But Hannah didn't get it. She peered more closely at the picture.

"That's beautiful!" she said. "Where is it?"

Her mother started crying, too.

Katrina robbed us. If you're not from here, you can't conceive of the damage. You may have seen pictures, but photos represent only a tiny window view of the disaster. A single image can't begin to convey the scale of the obliteration. Most of you have probably witnessed the aftermath of a tornado. Now, in your mind's eye, try to picture miles and miles of that same sort of splintered devastation. One can drive the coast for hours and find nothing that escaped harm.

The damage is unprecedented in three hundred years of recorded history. Katrina drove a thirty-five-foot wall of black water that barreled in from the Gulf like a gigantic bulldozer. Structures that had seen dozens of severe storms—buildings that had been standing solidly for over

a century—are simply gone. The old Spanish Customs House in the Bay, built on high ground in 1789, is scattered over a four-block area. Only the brick floor remains.

Mountains of debris will take years to completely clear. Most of my friends and neighbors lost everything they owned, many being without flood insurance because we lived in a "no flood" zone. Some of my friends are living in tents or trailers. Some have temporarily evacuated; others left for good. The ones that return sift through the remains of their lives and come back at the end of the day covered with mud, holding a small bag of odd items they've salvaged. They're happy if they found something like their mother's teacup.

The storm stole more from us than homes or personal possessions—it took a way of life. I don't want Hannah to forget that life. I don't want any of us who lived here to forget. And I want people who never knew this place to understand exactly what we lost. So let me tell you about Bay St. Louis before the storm. I'll try to paint the landscape that I loved so well, create a picture of this village by a sleepy sea.

Ancient oaks lined the coast, framing large and elegant houses—many of them built in the 1800s. Behind this dignified vanguard, cottages clustered along narrow shaded lanes. These neighborhoods were mixed in more ways than one. Professors lived next door to plumbers, young families next to retirees, black next to white, rich next to poor. That aspect delighted me—it flew directly in the distorted face most outsiders have pasted on the state of Mississippi.

The architectural styles of the homes varied as much as the people who lived in them. Cheek to cheek, the Creole cottage danced with the Victorian, the Greek Revival with the bungalow. In those lush yards, you could imagine the lingering ghosts from an era of ease. They didn't want to leave. Nobody who came here wanted to leave. This place pulled at the hearts of any who have them. It promised peace and made good on its word.

We were safe here. The simmering city anger that threatens harm was far away. Many of us casually left car keys in the ignition or forgot to lock our doors. That feeling of security was rooted in our sense of community. If you'd lived here, you wouldn't have known everyone in town, but sometimes it would have seemed like it. A trip to the grocery store or post office was a social outing. Checkout lines were always alive with chatter about kids and family. You would have heard the question "How's your mama?" several times a day.

Children of the Bay didn't realize it, but they lived in a Norman Rockwell portrait of a kinder time. Parents could take toddlers to the beach and relax their guard. They didn't have to worry about treacherous undertows and surf, because the shallow water lapped at the shore as if it were a placid lake. Older kids would walk down to the beach in groups or bike together down sparsely trafficked streets. If they recognized you, they'd wave and try to ride faster. They didn't want you to stop them and ask how their mama was doing. They were on a mission—to have fun and be free.

I'd feel like a kid myself when I'd go out for my daily bike ride. The freewheeling feeling of childhood, buoyant like a helium balloon, swelled in my chest when I'd pedal through the streets. I knew I must have looked strange—a middle-aged woman, sun hat shading my face, one dog riding in my basket, another trotting alongside—but it didn't matter here. A little eccentricity was welcome in the Bay.

Biking at night was even better. I could imagine that I was living in the 1930s as I silently glided past shuttered shops and cottages lit by antique lamps. The magic was palpable on soft, humid summer evenings. It was as if some alchemist had distilled the essence of a small southern town and poured it over the ground of Bay St. Louis. Our town motto is "A Place Apart," and it was.

Three mornings before the storm, I rode my bike to the beach for the last time. No premonition of doom followed me. The dawn was breaking and a diffused pink light tinted the town. It seemed like I moved through a fairy tale, one with a happily-ever-after ending. Would I have appreciated it more if I'd known it was my last time? I don't think so. I knew how lucky I was.

Despite Katrina, I still feel lucky. I'm learning new lessons every day. And of all the lessons I've learned since the storm upturned this idyllic coast, this seems the most important: a sense of community is the most undervalued asset in this country today.

In those first black days after the storm, we were cut off from the outside world, isolated and alone. Yet, I watched a couple who had lost all they

A "shrine" set up at the slab of a friend's house on Beach Boulevard in Bay St. Louis.

owned driving over from Pensacola repeatedly. They brought truckloads of needed supplies and distributed them around town. I saw the two elderly brothers on my block, the only ones in the area who had a generator, welcoming strangers in to charge cell phones and drills.

I witnessed the Miracle of the Shrines—neighbors would pick through the rubble from houses of friends and salvage the few personal belongings they could find. They would set these items up at the edge of the property. One could drive down the street and pass Irish crystal vases, family portraits, pottery or silver candlesticks, neatly arranged at the curb, awaiting the owners who had evacuated.

People are still stressed beyond comprehension, yet they continue to give. I've witnessed so many acts of kindness that my faith in the goodness of most humans has been restored. Yes, theft occurs, cross words are exchanged, hoarding happens. But overall, because we feel bound to each other, we've taken care of our neighbors.

No wonder so many of us want to stay and rebuild. Each day, we exist surrounded by destruction, and it's a hard, hard burden to bear. But this community possesses a spirit that the winds and the surge of Katrina weren't able to steal. The storm only strengthened those qualities that connect us.

I used to sing a hymn in church when I was a kid—"Blest Be the Ties That Bind." Now I understand that those ties can go beyond family, beyond religious affiliation, beyond political leanings or race or economic status. They're ties of the heart and can still be found in the remains of a little town called Bay St. Louis.

THE DETHRONING OF CAMILLE

MY INSURANCE ADJUSTER'S EYES bug out. "You *stayed* for the storm?" he says. He doesn't actually call me nuts, but his tone of voice says it for him.

After waiting two months to see a representative from my insurance company, I would lie down in front of a train to prevent his departure. "It's a Camille thing," I stammer. Even as I say it, I realize it won't make sense to someone from Ohio.

I am right. This answer does nothing to convince him of my sanity. He narrows his eyes and asks another question, and for this one, I can find no words. "What was it like?" he says.

For months, I've wanted to write about my storm experience, but procrastinate with persistence. I circle that mental minefield with suspicion and tread in tentatively, knowing one misstep will blow my carefully constructed composure to smithereens. So I'll cheat and sidle in the back way by starting with the history of Hurricane Camille. After all, she's the reason that I and hundreds of my neighbors chose to stay.

One of the best quotes I've heard since the storm is that Camille killed more people in 2005 than she did in 1969. If your house survived that

The Merchants Bank building on the Bay St. Louis bluff had overlooked the Gulf for nearly a hundred years. Photograph by Joe Tomasovsky.

storm, it could handle the worst nature could throw at you. After all, Queen Camille broke every record in the book.

Here are a few statistics: Camille was the most intense storm to hit the mainland U.S. in modern history. Sustained winds were 190 mph, gusts to 220. The lowest storm pressure (909 mbs) ever recorded on the mainland was measured in Bay St. Louis. The tidal surge was estimated at twenty-two to twenty-seven feet, an all-time record for our country.

Camille was our town's yardstick for catastrophe. Before Katrina, when guests asked me how I felt about living in a hurricane-prone area, I had blithe and confident answers. "Bay St. Louis is on a high ridge of land," I'd explain smugly. "This neighborhood didn't even flood in Camille." If I was shopping for real estate, the first question I'd ask is "Did it flood in Camille?" If the answer was no, I rested easy, knowing that it would be eternally high and dry.

Insurance agents were equally as confident. They'd tell you, "If your property didn't see water in 1969, don't waste your money on flood insurance." Lots of my friends heard the same line, but no one really blames the agents. We were all insurance poor, paying vast amounts just for the windstorm policies. Why not save the money if you were located on some of the highest ground on the Gulf?

The numerous historic houses on the coast bolstered our community confidence even higher. Homes that were 100–150 years old lined the shore. The sturdy Spanish Customs House, right up the street from me, had stood overlooking the beach since 1789 and faced off countless storms. These buildings were monuments to indestructibility, daily reminders to keep the faith.

Camille was called a "hundred-year storm." What were the chances of another striking in our lifetime? And if another monster storm were to occur in that hundred years, could lightning possibly strike twice in the same place? Throw in the astronomical probability of a worse storm making landfall in the same area within thirty years and you have odds that would be the dream of any bookie. It's a bet the most timid gambler would have taken in a heartbeat. I certainly did.

In the days before Katrina hit, the name Camille became a mantra while the community prepared for a "bad one." Everyone on the Gulf Coast takes hurricanes seriously, but many of my neighbors were Camille veterans. While we were boarding up, filling our bathtubs, checking our batteries, I heard over and over, "The weather people are alarmists. They're predicting a twenty-foot surge, so maybe it'll get to fifteen. And even if it's twenty feet, we didn't take water in '69. We'll be fine."

Outsiders may not understand this mentality. Before any storm, the weather stations and public authorities screech in strident tones, "Evacuate now!" But while coast residents pay attention to the wind speed of storms, we know from generations of experience that tidal surge will present the most danger. If your roof blows off (and it's happened to me in the past), it's dramatic, but not usually life-threatening.

My neighborhood after Katrina. Photograph by Joe Tomasovsky.

If you have sturdy shelter on high ground, you have two choices when a storm approaches: you can fight bumper-to-bumper traffic which crawls along—and it can take six hours to move fifty miles—hoping to find a motel room two states away. Or you can trust the surge predictions, batten down the hatches, and stay put.

As Katrina moved into the Gulf, family and friends around the country pled with me to evacuate. I invoked the name of Camille, holding it up like a banner, a bright talisman to ward off my fears. I was too exhausted to attempt a long drive and resisted last-minute pressure to retreat to Diamondhead—a community five miles north. I trusted my own stout historic house more than any new and untested structure. "The only thing I'm really worried about is the water and this property has never flooded—not even in Camille. They're predicting a much lower surge for Katrina," I declared again and again.

Now, when people ask me why I stayed, my standard line is "If I'd known we were going to be hit by a thirty-five-foot tsunami, I would have been in Nebraska." Despite the advances in science, weather forecasts are not infallible. My neighbors and I had trusted that a twenty-foot surge would be the worst-case scenario. I should have remembered that my thesaurus lists an interesting synonym for "prediction." That word is "guess."

The afternoon of the storm, when the waters had receded from the coast and the winds had relented somewhat, I picked my way through the rubble and gazed in shock at the splintered, unrecognizable remains of my historic neighborhood. In a single morning, hundreds of years of heritage had been erased. Elegant houses and quaint cottages were crushed or left twisted in the middle of streets. Even the Spanish Customs House had vanished completely, the lot filled with tangled heaps of debris. Worse yet, we knew without doubt that beneath the mountains of timbers and trees lay bodies of our neighbors and friends.

Queen Camille has been dethroned. It turned out she was just the dress rehearsal for loss, a dry run for true disaster. Katrina took our homes, our livelihoods, members of our community—but my friend Kat pegged one of the most important things: the storm stripped us of our illusion of security.

So when my insurance adjuster asks his final question, I have a final answer. "Would you stay again?" he asks.

"No" is my very short reply.

THE DOMINOS OF DENIAL

AT FIRST, I THOUGHT THE STREET was flooding from the hours-long downpour of rain, but the thin film of water covering the road quickly became a seething stream. An orange cat bounded pell-mell across the yard, headed to higher ground. A cooler sailed by at a fast clip, followed by a sheet of tin from someone's roof. When the trunk of a large tree careened past—looking like a kayak caught in rapids—adrenaline began

The view from Joe's front porch as the storm surge charged up Citizen Street. Photograph by Joe Tomasovsky.

to roar through my veins. The roots of my hair rose up in a futile effort to desert the rest of my body. Denial wasn't possible any more. I was watching a storm surge charging in from the Gulf of Mexico.

I'd always prided myself on being cool in a crisis, yet now, only one thought ran through my head, repeating like a record on an unbalanced jukebox: "You idiot. You should have gone to Diamondhead."

Diamondhead is a community five miles north of Bay St. Louis. Friends who had evacuated to ride out the storm there had begged me to join them. I had resisted. "I'll be fine," I said. "No surge will make it back to my house—I'm a quarter mile from the beach," I assured them. "It can't be worse than Camille."

But now, Katrina had me feeling like I was trapped in the Alamo, surrounded by an enemy whose strength had been vastly underestimated. No reinforcements would arrive, no escape was possible. If the walls were breached, my survival would be in doubt. How did I find myself in that precarious position? The decisions had fallen into place like dominos of denial, ending with my resolution to ride out the storm.

Three days before I'd been packing for a trip to North Carolina for my dad's eighty-fourth birthday celebration. Katrina was already in the Gulf, but our town was well outside the cone of the predicted path. How could the storm alter course enough to affect my plans? After fretting through the morning, I packed my car and hit the road that Friday afternoon. I drove for six hours and was on the far side of Montgomery when my cell phone rang.

"The storm's changed course and it's headed straight here," said my friend Lori. "You've got to come back." To someone in another part of the world that might sound like advice from a madwoman, but it made perfect sense to me. I had to prepare my house. I pulled off the interstate, sat in the parking lot of a fast food joint, and made calls to several other friends. After an hour of listening to conflicting reports, I regretfully turned the car south and headed home, just to be on the safe side.

Late that night, I stopped in a motel and slept for a few hours, continuing the drive at dawn on Saturday. When I neared Mobile, I was struck by a sudden resentment that my vacation had been cut short. I veered off the interstate and headed down to Dauphin Island, slightly to the south and west of Mobile. I'd always loved the place and wanted to play tourist for a few hours.

Once I crossed the causeway onto the island, the atmosphere changed. An eerie sense of doom hung in the air like a thick fog. I drove to the west end of the island and saw that it was already underwater, although the storm was still two days from landfall. Waves had engulfed the pilings of several raised houses, giving them the appearance of abandoned oil rigs. A few crews were out boarding up windows, but for the most part, it looked as if residents had given up any attempts at protection.

I stopped for breakfast in the only open café. There were few diners, and, while I ate, I listened to the local waitresses terrorize the tourists with stories of past storms. It was amusing, but the sense of crisis was contagious. I didn't linger for more coffee. Knowing the stores at home would be mobbed, I shopped at an Alabama grocery store, stocking up with gallons of water, some canned goods, and a large bag of dog food. I also filled the tank of my car with gas, blissfully unaware that it would be for the last time. On the road back to the Bay, an escalating urgency made me ignore the speed limits.

My home in Bay St. Louis is a renovated schoolhouse—the Webb School—built in 1913. My contractor friends assure me that it's as strong as a fortress. It's a raised building, set on solid concrete pilings that are ten feet tall. I'd already had the largest of the many windows boarded over, but there was still a lot of work to be done. The next twenty-four hours blurred by as I put my hurricane preparation system into effect.

The list is long: take down every piece of art and store it in the most protected closets (a strong storm can vibrate the walls so much, paintings will crash to the floor). Move all the potted plants and outdoor furniture to safety beneath the house. Ditto the car. Cover the important furniture with tarps in case the roof blows off. Pack up all the pottery and sacred books in plastic crates. Fill up the bathtub. Check the battery supply and make sure all the flashlights are working. Make backup discs for the computer.

By Sunday afternoon, I was utterly exhausted. The squalls were beginning to roll in, with thin bands of clouds hurling through a sky tinged with a freakish yellowish cast. As I worked, images from *The Wizard of Oz* kept flashing in my head. I saw myself as Dorothy, racing for the root cellar while a relentless tornado bore down on her. The wicked witch cackled in the background.

I checked the Internet for the latest information on the storm. It looked bad, but not as bad as Camille. My house hadn't taken any damage with Camille. My property hadn't flooded in Camille. Another domino fell and I made the decision to stay. After all, in thirty years of living on the Gulf Coast, I'd ridden out numerous tropical storms or hurricanes. What could be different this time?

My ninety-two-year-old friend Mimi agreed. Through the years, she and I had ridden out four storms together. She'd recently been confined to a nursing home in the Bay, which was busing all their patients to Jackson, where they'd sleep on a gym floor. She felt like the journey would kill her and commanded that her son Jimmie—another good friend—bring her to my house. A Camille veteran, Mimi was not afraid of this hurricane.

As we were helping her into my house, I jokingly asked her, "Where's the family silver?" Usually, when she'd evacuate her low-lying house, she'd bring a little carpetbag crammed with sterling heirlooms. I'd always thought it the epitome of southern charm. This time, it'd been forgotten in the rush and there was no going back. We both made light of the oversight, assuming it'd be safe. But Mimi had seen her home and her silver for the last time.

When Jimmie and his mother were comfortably settled in, I walked next door to ride out the storm with Joe Tomasovsky. He'd moved in as my neighbor just three months before, after retiring from a long career as a photography teacher in Florida. We'd been friends for years and had only started "seeing" each other that spring.

Joe has lived most of his life on the Gulf Coast where hurricanes are part of the package. After considering the weather reports, he'd decided to stay in his house. It wasn't as high off the ground as my own, but it'd weathered many storms in the past century—the previous owner had told Joe she'd only sustained thirty dollars' worth of damage in Camille. Joe made a last-ditch attempt to send me packing to Diamondhead, but my mind was made up. I was convinced surge wasn't an issue and felt safe in his time-tested house. Besides, it might even be a "bonding experience."

In Joe's living room, Cleo the squirrel leapt around in a large cage. Joe rehabs baby squirrels and Cleo had been his latest orphan. He'd released her as a mischievous adult into his yard shortly after he'd moved from Florida, but she still showed up from time to time, performing antics and begging for nuts. That afternoon, she'd appeared on his porch after a long absence. She was completely wet, leading Joe to believe she'd returned from afar to take refuge. He'd interrupted his work to assemble a cage and brought her inside. Cleo didn't seem to resent her lapse into captivity. She darted around the inside of the cage with a manic energy, pausing only to accept a peanut from my hand.

All preparations complete, we tried to make phone calls, but the lines were overloaded. We couldn't get through to Joe's daughter Robyn, who lived in New Orleans. We only hoped that she'd evacuated to Baton Rouge as planned. When I finally connected with my parents in North Carolina, I urged them not to listen to the news. "They always make a catastrophe out of any storm," I said. "You may not hear from me for a few days because the lines will be down, but don't worry. I'll be fine."

We spent the rest of the evening on the computer, pulling up every weather site we could find. They were all still predicting a local surge of twenty to twenty-two feet, although one or two doomsday sites warned it could be as high as twenty-five. A friend called from Florida and reported the news that buoys in the gulf were registering waves fifty-five feet high, giving me my first real burst of alarm. But waves aren't the same as surge, I told myself. I wasn't going to allow alarmists to cause me extra anxiety. Fatigue finally overcame foreboding, and we fell asleep to the sound of fitful winds slamming through the trees.

We woke about two in the morning with gusts hitting the house like the fists of ogres. Rain tore at the windows. The light in the kitchen went out and we knew we'd seen the last of electricity for what we naively imagined would be a few days. The rest of the night was punctuated by sharp cracks as trees fell and heavy oak limbs snapped. When something hit the house, one of us would leap from bed to make sure the roof hadn't been compromised, then we'd drift back into an uneasy sleep.

The morning brought dim light, but no letup in the winds. My cell phone rang at about eight o'clock. Lori, hunkered down with friends in Diamondhead, had managed to get through. "Heads up," she said. "We just heard on the weather radio that the storm surge is supposed to be worst in Waveland and Bay St. Louis. It's going to hit between eight-thirty and nine. They're saying it could be twenty to twenty-two feet." Her voice sounded calm. She didn't tell me that she'd dreamed both Joe and I had perished in the storm and thought it was a premonition.

Joe and I patrolled the house aimlessly, looking for leaks, trying to keep busy. The walls were shaking from the force of the storm. Curtains billowed into the rooms, so I kept checking the windows to make sure they were closed. I found none open. Despite the extra protection of storm windows, the thundering winds still penetrated the house. Cleo hid in her nesting box, only the tip of her tail visible. It looked like an enviable place to be.

At nine o'clock, I began to feel more at ease. According to Lori's report, the surge should have already hit and was probably receding. That would mean we were halfway through the storm with no major mishaps. I could see many sheets of tin had blown off the back of my own roof, but wasn't terribly concerned. It'd be a little wet inside. Mimi and Jimmie would be fine. This was going to be just another bad storm. We'd probably forget its name in a few years.

Then around quarter past nine, Joe called me into the front room where he'd managed to force open the door. Erratic gusts slammed against him and he gripped the doorframe to remain upright. He was looking up the street towards the beach. I fought to join him as sharp blasts of air ripped through the house like psychotic poltergeists on a rampage.

"The street's flooding," he shouted to be heard over the wind. "Has it done that before?" I shrugged. "No, but we must have had seven or eight inches of rain in the past few hours." Joe pointed out that the grass in his yard was beginning to be covered by water, too. "My yard floods some-times, too," I said, a little more doubtfully. But ten minutes later, when the water had already reached a foot and was rising steadily, the awful reality of the situation was clear. The last domino had fallen. I was about to spend the longest two hours of my life.

THE FOURTH STEP

THE FIRST STEP   My cell phone became a high-tech rosary. My fingers fumbled as I punched number after number into the keyboard. Even when I managed to enter a correct number, I'd only hear a busy signal. Lines were either down or overwhelmed. I rehearsed the one question I'd ask if I was lucky enough to make outside contact: *Where is the eye of the storm?* If it was passing, the surge was peaking. If the hurricane was still at sea, we were experiencing just the beginning of a tsunami.

View of Joe's yard from his kitchen door before the storm. Photograph by Joe Tomasovsky.

Phone in hand, I paced from room to room, unconsciously looking for a way to escape. In Joe's office, I eyed the attic pull-down, remembering the old New Orleans adage about keeping an axe in the attic. Yesterday, I'd joked about the tradition. Joe had never heard of it, so I had to explain that people who retreated to an attic because of rising waters could be trapped there and drowned. If an axe were in the attic, they could at least hack a hole in the roof. It had seemed funny the night before—now I wondered if I'd be climbing up there soon.

My pacing took me to the kitchen door and I peered out into the storm. The Gulf of Mexico covered the patio and yard, but it looked more like the Amazon River. Sinister, dark eddies swirled against the stairs to the house. Five steps rose from the ground level to the porch landing. The first was already submerged, the second was under attack.

View of Joe's yard from his kitchen door while the surge was rising. Photograph by Joe Tomasovsky.

Mesmerized by the sight, I almost dropped the phone in surprise when I heard a voice. I'd somehow gotten through to my friends Regan and Mark, weathering the storm at their house several miles inland. Regan had no new reports. Their radio had gone out, and the last they'd heard was that the eye should have passed at nine.

Regan suggested that we try to make it back to my house. I moved to another window and looked longingly towards the massive white building. Through the sheets of rain, it beckoned like a lighthouse. But the short path between Joe's house and mine had disappeared beneath muddy rapids, seething with debris. The current ran against us.

"Ahh, honey," Regan said, her tone heavy with pity. She put Mark on the line, but our call was cut short. Their roof was blowing off. It was the last phone conversation I'd have for three days.

THE SECOND STEP   Still working the phone, I joined Joe on the back porch. He seemed unperturbed by the gusts of wind pummeling him and held his camera to his eye as he framed shots of his yard. The raging river was rising—the second step had been overtaken and water lapped hungrily at the third.

A flying sheet of tin sent us scurrying for cover, and, once inside, I put my hand on his arm. In a shaky attempt at humor, I asked Joe if he'd put the axe in the attic. "Ellis," he said, a hint of irritation in his voice, "you've already asked me that three times. No. The axe is in the garage."

I realized then how addled I was. I had no recollection of asking before. We gazed at the garage, only twenty feet away, separated from the house now by a rushing torrent.

Joe explained that if the water rose much higher, the house could float off the pilings. "When the water comes into the house," he said, "we have to get out."

Some details stick in my memory like glints of glitter. He used the word "when" instead of "if." Another wash of raw terror slid through my body. I looked out into the raging winds and across the expanse of black, pitiless water. An incredulous voice in my head protested: *Are you crazy? Just shoot me in the head right now and get it over with!*

I hadn't spoken aloud, but my face must have registered horror. Joe's teacher persona took control. Suddenly, he was directing students during a bomb threat or fire drill. "We need to look for floatation devices," he said. "See what you can find."

I salvaged the remains of my composure and began roaming the rooms on the bizarre hunt. It's amazing how few things in most houses will double as life preservers. Furniture, books, beds, toilet seats, computers— nothing offered any buoyancy. The voice in my head shouted as I searched: *There are no frigging floatation devices in this house!* Then I remembered the Tupperware stash in the kitchen cabinets. I actually laughed aloud at the image of Joe and me swimming for our lives clutching plastic leftover containers.

THE THIRD STEP   I returned to the kitchen to make my report and noticed the water had overtaken the third step. Joe had continued shooting while I'd searched and didn't seem surprised at my failure. I understood then that he'd given me the job to focus my attention and disperse my panic.

He decided that I was calm enough for swimming lessons. Joe's an avid kayaker and knows the ways of wild water. His measured voice commanded my attention—he might have been in a high school classroom lecturing students on darkroom technique. He began with a reminder about the futility of fighting currents. I already knew this from experience, but his next piece of information surprised me.

"Don't try to reach out and grab something in front of you. The water can push you into it and hurt you—you could go under. Turn around in the water and try to catch something that's going by or already passed." He noticed my skepticism. "I know it sounds crazy, but it's really important you remember that."

My inner movie theatre began projecting a surrealistic film. *An Esther Williams version of myself backstroked across Joe's lawn. I wore a bathing cap, accented with a spray of hibiscus flowers. I avoided the pecan tree in front of me. Instead, I gracefully wrapped my arms around the palm to the side, embracing it like a lover.* Joe must have wondered why I smiled. I assured him I wouldn't forget his advice.

THE FOURTH STEP   I looked at the battery clock on the kitchen wall. It read 10:15. The hands had not moved in hours. I decided it was broken, but a glance out the door proved that time had passed. The water had marched past the fourth step and was relentlessly working up towards the landing. A few more inches and it would begin to invade the house.

The water surrounding the house reminded me of the Mississippi River during spring flooding. When I lived in New Orleans, I used to walk my dogs on the riverfront and watch the malicious, writhing currents hurl freighters around the bends as if they were paper boats in a whirlpool. I'd be in that water soon, with 150-mile-an-hour winds screeching overhead.

I decided to take a break and collect myself before entering the maelstrom. The safest place in the house seemed to be Joe's office. He'd screwed plywood over the storm windows that, in turn, protected the inner windows. Three degrees of separation made the room feel very secure. I collapsed on the sofa and tried to meditate.

The rational, Zen part of myself began a deep breathing routine. The hysterical, screaming part repeated the warning from the night before—*fifty-five-foot waves in the Gulf!* The rational part of me curled into a fetal position when my head did the math: *we were at twenty-five feet of elevation. The remaining thirty feet would more than cover the roof.* Suddenly, I wanted to vomit.

I struggled to get a grip. A phrase from the sci-fi novel *Dune* popped into my head. "Fear is the mind-killer." Whatever was to come in the next few hours, I knew that panic would paralyze me. I'd need every iota of self-possession if I wanted to survive. My eyes closed and I called serenity to me, repeating a phrase from my old-hippie lexicon: *Be Here Now.*

My pulse slowed, the adrenaline abated. Feeling at peace with the universe, I opened my eyes. In front of me, the bank of boarded windows afforded a sense of security. Then a blast of wind hit the side of the house so hard that the entire wall of glass actually bulged into the room, undulating like a sail of a boat. I leapt up and fled into the kitchen. Apparently, there was a hurricane version of the secret to inner peace—*Be Somewhere Else Now.*

Joe was checking on Cleo in the living room. I wondered how she would fare if we had to release her into the storm. How could either animals or humans survive that fury without shelter? Many of my neighbors had stayed in their homes and those houses closer to the beach would be underwater by now. All over town, families would be struggling for their lives.

Calling 911 wasn't an option. Even if the phones had worked, no one would have answered. The people who might have helped us needed help themselves. Later, I would learn that the entire Waveland police force—twenty-seven officers—was hanging on to a tree in their parking lot. At the Emergency Operations Center, thirty-five people were trapped in a dark building with water rising. They passed around a flashlight and a marker, writing their names on their arms to make body identification easier.

I checked the step gauge. The water hung at the four-plus mark. The clock seemed to be working again, and I watched its second hand revolve with a speed that mimicked three-hundred-year-old tortoises. Five eternal minutes passed before I allowed myself to look back at the steps. A tiny twig had been stranded on the top of the fourth step by the retreating surge.

"Joe! Joe!" I shouted. "It's going down!"

Joe joined me at the kitchen door and forced it open. He stepped out onto the landing and examined the water line. For the next ten minutes, we watched silently until the surface of the third step was revealed. Our hands slapped together in a spontaneous high five as I danced a jig of joy around the kitchen. The eye had passed and the tide had turned. Luck had saved us from the surge. The worst was over. But I should have remembered the lesson I'd learned in Joe's office: security is simply another illusion.

THE PASSING OF THE EYE

THE EYE MAY HAVE PASSED, pushing the surge back to the sea, but the storm was only half over. The clock read 11:30. Katrina had been raging for over six hours, with at least six more to go.

Joe and I were checking his front rooms for leaks when we heard knocking at the kitchen door. Our eyes widened in disbelief. Who would be politely visiting in the middle of a hurricane? But the rapping came again, insistent and much too rhythmic to be caused by the fitful winds that shook the house. I hurried into the kitchen and found Jimmie and my neighbor Paul patiently waiting on the landing.

I pulled them into the house, where they shook the rain off themselves like big dogs climbing out of a pond. I had lots of questions, all fighting to be first in line. The winner was one about Mimi.

Jimmie assured us that she was fine. "The boat people are watching her," he said. I couldn't quite get my head around that. *Boat people?* Jimmie began to reel off a jumble of details, but they bounced off my exhausted brain like children on a taut trampoline:

My house had become a shelter for the neighborhood. The first arrival was Paul. Paul's apartment across the street from me had lost the roof and then began to flood. He'd grabbed his kitten and waded to my house to take refuge with Mimi and Jimmie. The two men had tried to minimize the damage inside by patching broken panes of glass and putting out pots to catch the numerous leaks. In the frenzy, Jimmie had been blown from a ladder while trying to secure a transom window in the living room. He'd landed solidly on his hip, but could still manage to walk.

Then a boat had floated to my house with four people clinging to the sides. Jimmie helped the sodden survivors inside and made them as comfortable as possible. The new arrivals said they were neighbors of mine from down the street, but Jimmie couldn't remember their names. When the water had gone down, he and Paul decided to cross the yard to Joe's house to check on us. The boat people agreed to keep an eye on the sleeping Mimi while they were gone.

Jimmie reported that my two dogs, Frieda and Jack, were safe and seemed to be enjoying the adventure. The night before I'd made the hard decision to leave them at my house for the storm. I was worried they'd add to Cleo's anxiety if I'd brought them to Joe's. Both dogs loved Jimmie, who had sat for them before, so this good news relieved me of a nagging guilt.

But the house hadn't fared as well as I'd imagined. Jimmie said that water poured through the ceilings and cascaded down the walls. Light fixtures had filled with rain and smashed to the floor, scattering glass everywhere. Four transom windows had blown out, and hurricane force winds whipped through the interior. Jimmie and I had parked our cars beneath the house for protection. Both had been submerged in the surge and were certainly totaled.

The afternoon before, I'd mentioned to Joe that I'd taken the precaution of putting my musical instruments and family photos in the trunk of my car. It was part of my normal hurricane routine. If the roof came off, at least my most sacred possessions would be safe. "I think you should put them upstairs," he said. His tone of voice had a peculiar resonant quality when he spoke that single line, as if he were an oracle channeling a warning. I didn't argue, although reason was on my side. Hedging my bet, I had moved the guitar and violin and half of the family photos upstairs. I was suddenly very grateful to Joe.

Jimmie finished his recital and then raided Joe's ibuprofen stash for his pain. He and Paul set out back for my house. Almost as soon as they'd left, water began invading Joe's living room. The limbs that had hit his roof in the night had caused more damage than we'd first thought. We worked without pause for the next few hours. I handled the bucket brigade inside—mopping, emptying the many containers, catching new leaks as they sprang from the ceiling. Part of the ceiling eventually collapsed. Meanwhile, Joe sorted through his garage, which had flooded and lost the roof. He worked frantically to save the photography equipment he'd stored there, but it was mostly wasted effort.

Around midafternoon, the gusts and rain began to slacken. I slid on my raincoat and began the trek back to my own house. The well-worn path had become an obstacle course. I leapt over branches, lumber, roofing tin, and railroad ties. My three huge oaks still stood, but they'd lost half their branches and were stripped of leaves. The yard was a thicket of cruelly amputated tree limbs.

Coming in through the back door, I didn't recognize my own kitchen. A grim confetti of glass shards covered every surface. The entire ceiling dripped water, so it appeared to be raining inside. Pots and pans placed to catch the leaks had been outnumbered and sat overflowing in the shallow pool that covered the floor. I sloshed through to my living room.

Frieda was napping on a wet sofa, but Jack met me with his normal exuberant welcome, hoping it was time for a bike ride. In typical doggie fashion, he seemed unaware that anything was out of the ordinary. I found Mimi in bed, nested in the one relatively dry corner of the house. She held a radio to her ear and waved me off when I asked what she needed. Her only complaint was that "the blasted news only talks about New Orleans. There's not one word about the Gulf Coast." We didn't know that this would be a permanent trend.

I forced one of the front doors open and looked over the railing. The boat below canted to one side, the bow nosed into my azaleas. A dirty cotton rope secured it to my porch railing. I leaned over the rail, scanning the neighborhood. Most of the surrounding houses still stood, though many had been shorn of their roofs. The cabinet shop across the street had been completely demolished by the winds. When I looked up the block to the west, my view was obstructed by an entire house resting in the middle of the street.

I went looking for the "boat people" and found two of them in the dining room. I recognized them as neighbors who lived on Citizen Street, about a block closer to the beach. Augusta Acker and her daughter, Augusta-Inez, had houses next to each other. Both were soaked through and shrouded with towels. Jimmie had served them cheese and crackers on a blue glass plate. The refugee kitten played hide-and-seek with my dogs beneath their chairs.

Tired to the bone, we sat passively around the table, indifferent to the blasts of wind tearing through the broken windows and around the high ceilings. I offered them some water and we drank from the plastic bottles, while Augusta gave me an abbreviated version of their escape.

She, her daughter, and two grown sons had been floundering in the rapidly rising water in the middle of Citizen Street. They'd been on the brink of drowning, trying to make it to higher ground. A boat had floated by and they'd grabbed hold, managing to steer it to my house—the only raised building in the neighborhood. It was an astonishing tale, but I didn't realize then that it was actually a ghost story. I wouldn't hear the full account until more than three weeks had passed.

We were quiet for a few minutes. Finally, to make some conversation, I said, "It's got to be over soon." Both women nodded their heads. We didn't understand that our ordeal was just beginning.

LIONEL'S BOAT

MY HOUSE IS A QUARTER MILE from the Gulf, yet five months after Katrina, there's still a boat beached in my front yard. It's an ugly boat. The fiberglass is flaking and dark stains mottle the lackluster hull. It's the sort of small power skiff that's used to fish in bayous or in our shallow bay. There's no motor now. The interior—where fishermen used to land their catches, swap tales, and drink cold beers out of coolers—is filled with branches, leaves, and mud. This boat's been around the block a few times. Literally.

The boat didn't arrive at my house in the normal way—on a trailer. It sailed the streets of my town, borne by the greatest storm surge in American history. Coming to rest at my porch like some battered gondola from Venice, it carried four souls to safety, four names that would have been added to the long list of Katrina's dead. Augusta thinks it was steered by a spirit.

Though some might call it a useless eyesore, it has a new life ahead as a shrine. Augusta has given me permission to make a planter out of it. She thinks it's a fitting end to Lionel's boat.

I didn't even know who Lionel was until the end of September, almost a month after the storm had passed. Hungry for a hot meal, I went to the food tent in my neighborhood that'd been set up by volunteers. I'd gotten my lunch and was looking for a seat when I ran into Augusta and Augusta-Inez. I embraced them with joy, but Augusta seemed confused at first. Her daughter had to remind her that I was "the Webb School lady."

I could understand the confusion. Even though they'd stayed with me for three days after the storm, they'd probably never seen me with my hair combed before. Augusta's face lit up once she made the connection. We talked about the day of the storm. I admitted how frightened I'd been.

"You know," Augusta said. "I never was scared, that whole time. I'd prayed beforehand that the Lord would keep me from being afraid. Some people get heart attacks they get so frightened. I didn't want that happening to me."

She asked me what I was going to do with the boat. I explained that I wanted to make a planter out of it to commemorate the event. Although the boat seemed ruined, I was trying to track down the owners for permission. All I had to go on were the barely legible registration numbers.

"Why, honey, that's our boat," Augusta said. This was news to me. I had thought it was a stray.

"Let me tell you," she said. "The morning of the storm, Donald came and got me from my room. He said we got to get out now. I didn't understand until my feet hit the floor and I was standing in water." Donald works for the local power company. He and his brother, Steve, stayed with their mother during the storm. Donald's teenaged son and nephew, Otis, were next door with Augusta-Inez.

At first, Donald thought the street flooding was from the heavy rains. He decided to move the company truck to higher ground. He began to put on his shoes, but by the time he got them tied, the water outside had risen over the tires. In moments, it began to seep through the floors of the house. Donald alerted Augusta and then swam across to his sister's house to help them evacuate. There, he had to break down the front door—the six feet of water had created a vacuum. Donald and Otis made their way back to Augusta's, fighting a heavy current and driving rain that felt like "needles in the eyes."

Meanwhile, Steven helped Augusta down the front steps of her raised house, now covered with several feet of water. "He was going real slow," Augusta said. "Just like I was a baby. Then Otis came back with Donald. He yelled, 'I'll give my life for my grandma!' He grabbed me around the waist and tucked me under his arm like I was a piece of wood. He dragged me next door to my daughter's house so fast, I still can't believe it. It was like he was running across the top of the water."

Reunited for the moment on Inez's submerged porch, the family of six decided they had to set out for higher ground. Donald told his nephew and son to go on ahead, and the two boys swam towards Third Street. The four adults thrashed and struggled in the current, the water well above the heads of the two women. Then Augusta looked back towards her house.

"That boat was tied to the trailer in my yard," she said, "but somehow it got loose and came out of the driveway. Then it made a sharp turn right towards us. It wasn't on one side of the street or another. It came right up the middle, just as smooth as you please. We all grabbed hold tight to the sides—we couldn't get in, the water was too deep. Then Donald turned around and saw a big wave headed our way. He was shouting, 'Go, go, go!'"

"We made it to the school," Augusta told me. "The boys had beat us there and were up on the porch. We got up the steps, then the door flew open and this big man said, 'Come in! Come in!'"

Jimmie ushered them into the house, while Donald stayed to tie up the boat in case the water kept rising and they'd need it again. He didn't see his

Augusta Acker and her son Lionel's boat planted with flowers.

family go inside. He admitted later that he had a moment of panic when he reached the top of the stairs and they had all disappeared. The winds were so fierce, he wondered if they'd blown off the porch. Then the door opened again and Donald was pulled in to join his family.

But there was more to the story.

Augusta continued. "That boat belonged to my son Lionel. He used to come over from New Orleans when he was free and use it out on the bay. He loved to fish. He'd just graduated, got his Ph.D. in business from Vanderbilt and was headed over one weekend. That was in 1981. He was bringing his three-year-old daughter—a beautiful child. They were driving across Lake Pontchartrain when a drunk ran them off the bridge and into the water. They both drowned. That was in February, on Friday the thirteenth. It was thirteen days before they found his body, too. Thirteens all over the place.

"I just never had the heart to get rid of that boat. It stayed in my yard for twenty-five years. Then when we were drowning in the street, water up over our heads, that boat floated right to us. Now how did that boat get untied off that trailer and come directly to us? I think my son Lionel did that."

Goosebumps rose on my arms in salute to the story. I wiped at my eyes with a rough paper napkin. People moving around us in the food tent ignored my tears. Public weeping wasn't unusual these days.

"So you keep that boat, honey," Augusta said. "You go ahead and make your planter out of it. That'd be good, real good."

THE EDGE OF THE ABYSS

IN BAY ST. LOUIS, at the intersection where Hancock crosses Washington, my life changed forever. Reality shifted like a plate in the earth and I suddenly found myself teetering on the edge of a chasm. The force of the storm ripped open that same dark abyss for everyone on the coast, so I'm not alone. But for me, it happened in a heartbeat, the moment I saw that Katrina had stolen my town.

The afternoon of the hurricane, when the winds began to die down, I still felt fortunate. Everyone who'd taken refuge in my home was safe. Both Joe's house and mine were standing, although damaged. Some of the houses around us had flooded and most had taken a beating, but the neighborhood seemed intact. A few months of cleanup, and life in the Bay would return to normal. I'd forgotten that our houses were on the edge of an "island." We're on the fringes of the old town, built on some of the highest ground on the Gulf. Less than a block away, the elevation drops off dramatically.

Joe brought his camera and we ventured into the streets. Before we began our expedition, Joe took a photo of me in front of my house. I look at it now, hardly recognizing myself. The woman in the picture is at least seventy and has been hanging out in a wind tunnel. There's a wry smile on my exhausted face, but there's relief there, too. I thought the worst was over. I was wrong.

We wanted to get to the waterfront, but our routes were limited. Roads were blockaded by uprooted trees or houses that had been shoved off their foundations. Our closest option was Washington, one street back towards Old Town. As we walked the two blocks to the beach, occasional bursts of rain pelted us and leftover gusts hurtled past. The damage we saw increased with every step. The street was covered with power lines and roofing tin, lumber and mangled cars. A few of our neighbors had emerged from hiding. Every face wore the same dazed expression, as if they were waking from a long and tangled nightmare.

Shortly after turning onto Washington Street, I saw a brightly painted table blocking the driveway of a house. I paused. It was hand-crafted from a fine, light wood and in excellent condition. It looked as if it'd been placed at the curb for trash pickup. I couldn't understand why someone would be throwing such a nice table away. In fact, hadn't I seen a similar table at my friend Keith's house? But Keith lived two blocks away on Citizen, close to the beach. Suddenly, a little bomb of horror detonated in my throat.

As we approached the intersection of Hancock and Washington, we found it impossible to go further. We were still a block from the beach, but an enormous pile of rubble barricaded the road. Joe climbed onto the heap and began shooting photos, while I strained to see over the top. Finally, I summoned the courage to follow him up the mountain of debris. I clambered onto someone's front door and gazed out at the apocalypse. The only word that came to mind was "Hiroshima."

The intersection of Hancock and Washington streets, taken on the afternoon of the storm. The ruins of Dave and Alison's house can be seen on the far right. Photograph by Joe Tomasovsky.

On the corner, I saw the home of my friends Alison and Dave. The stately historic house was oddly distorted, as if it were melting. Doors and windows had been punched out of their frames. Someone else's roof had crashed into the porch, one corner resting in what used to be their living room. The yard was heaped head-high with entire walls and floors from other houses, large appliances and furniture, cars, and riding mowers. Worse yet, theirs was the only house standing on that side of the street. On the other side, just three battered shells remained. Everything else had been crushed.

From memory, I began to count the houses that had once lined the block. I got up to sixteen before my tears began. Washington Street boasts some of the highest elevation on the Gulf of Mexico, twenty-five feet above sea level. If this neighborhood had been destroyed, I knew the rest of the coast didn't have a prayer. Waveland would be gone. Pass Christian would be gone. Long Beach, Clermont Harbor, Lakeshore, and Cedar Point, gone, gone, gone. I was looking at the tip of an incomprehensible iceberg. Thousands of homes had been completely obliterated. Bay St. Louis had been three hundred years in the making and had survived dozens of direct hits by storms. Katrina had annihilated most of the town in the span of a single morning.

I heard a voice call my name. I shakily climbed down from my perch and saw my neighbor Betsy. She stood in front of the collapsed remains of her house, yet seemed unconcerned about her own loss. She asked if I knew where our friend Phil was. I hadn't talked to him in several days. Betsy said that he'd planned on riding out the storm in his Hancock Street house, a few doors down from hers. We looked over at the building. It had floated off the foundations. No one who stayed would have survived. Betsy had somehow commandeered some firemen who were searching the ruins for his body.

I'd seen enough. I looked around for Joe, but he'd disappeared while I was talking to Betsy. Stricken to my core, I headed for home. Although I'd walked that route hundreds of times, it had never seemed so long and lonely.

At the corner by my house, a fire truck was parked in the middle of the street. Several of my neighbors gathered around two stunned firemen. A pack of skittish dogs, loosed by the storm, circled the small crowd, hopeful of finding their owners. I heard a young fireman trying to reassure a man with a gashed lip. "This isn't as bad as Camille," he said with bravado. I didn't have the heart to correct him.

Jimmie met me on the front porch. His mother was sleeping comfortably. Mimi may have been ninety-two and frail, but she was hardy. We discussed the gravity of the situation and decided that she needed to go to the hospital. She had a catheter, and sanitation would quickly become an issue with no running water. Jimmie alerted the firemen, who'd promised they'd send someone to pick her up shortly. None of us knew that the hospital— almost two miles inland—had been destroyed as well. Three more endless days would pass before help of any kind arrived.

A woman I didn't recognize came to the foot of my steps and asked if I had any water. The man with the gashed lip was her boyfriend and she wanted to get him cleaned up. I invited them both inside. He was an older man and climbed the steps with difficulty. Blood covered his face and the front of his shirt, but he seemed unaware. His girlfriend explained that they lived around the corner and the house had caved in around them. The man was a diabetic and had lost his insulin in the mayhem. He silently sipped the orange juice I brought him, while his girlfriend tended his wounds with bottled water and a paper towel. "Baby, baby," she crooned as she cleaned off the crusted blood. She told me that the firemen had promised to take them to the hospital. They both thanked me as they walked back to the fire truck. I never saw them again.

The light was fading and so were the dregs of my energy. I put out flashlights, snacks, and the last of the dry bedding for Augusta and her family and went over to Joe's. He'd cooked a hot meal on his camp stove and insisted that I eat. I forced a few bites down, commanding myself not to retch. Joe had opened all the windows that weren't boarded, allowing the remnants of the storm to air out the house. He told me to enjoy my last cool night for a long while—tomorrow we'd be sweltering, with no fans or air conditioning to diminish the heat.

I must have slept at last, for when I woke it was as dark as the desert. At first, I didn't remember the storm. When I did, I tried to convince myself it'd been a bad dream. The night told the truth. I heard no cars passing, no trains, no crickets or frogs or sweet-singing mockingbirds. No street or porch light cast a shadow. I stared out the window, hoping to spot even a flicker of light, but the blackness was unrelenting. The only thing I could see was the vision of my town in ruins. Homes and lives, hopes and dreams, an idyllic way of life—all gone with the wind. Margaret Mitchell had thought that the Yankees were the ultimate force of destruction, but she hadn't imagined a Katrina. None of us had.

"Are you awake?" Joe whispered.

"Yes," I answered. "I'm crying."

THE GOOD LIFE

BEFORE THE STORM HIT BAY ST. LOUIS, the first thing I'd hear in the morning was a rooster crowing. He lived a few doors down and would get started well before dawn. It could be a charming way to wake, but lots of times I'd want to strangle him. It wouldn't have done any good. As the sky grew light, he'd be joined by a variety of wild birds. Flocks of them would gather in the trees around my house, and the volume of their chattering made it hard to sleep late.

The morning after the storm, I woke in a very different world. If the rooster hadn't drowned, he was depressed. The other birds had either died or fled. The only thing I heard were the beating blades of a helicopter.

The first thought in my head was, *Help is here! It's the National Guard!* Joe and I looked out the window and spotted a chopper circling low, but it had no official markings. After a few minutes, we realized it was probably a news helicopter, photographing the destruction below. Joe predicted help would be a long time coming. "They'll be focused on New Orleans and forget about us," he said. I didn't believe him at the time.

Then Joe launched into what would become a morning ritual and listed the day's priorities. As a high school teacher, he'd had a lifetime to hone his organizational skills. I accepted the direction gratefully because a dense fog had settled over my own mind. Joe didn't sugarcoat the situation: *life as we knew it was over.* If we were to survive with sanity, we'd need to take extreme measures.

The first extreme measure was to abandon our toilets. The water and sewage systems would be down for the foreseeable future. If we used the bathroom inside and flushed manually, sewage might back up into our houses. We'd need to set up a latrine, and the only available place was the dark storage room beneath my house. The floor was covered with a dense, rank-smelling slime left by the surge. I shoved debris away from the storage room door to make space for the five-gallon bucket Joe gave me. He removed a toilet seat from one of my real bathrooms and placed it over the rim of the bucket. I hung a roll of tissue from a nail on the wall. The new bathroom was ready for business.

The next point Joe tackled was the fact that our homes were some of the few standing buildings in town that hadn't flooded inside. We'd need to house and feed people—maybe lots of them—and that would take some planning. Over the next few days, we'd set up an emergency shelter. We had plenty of dry bedding and enough food and water to last several days, even with a crowd. Joe guessed the propane for his camp stove, used sparingly, would hold out for a week. He pointed out that hot meals every evening would boost morale. We'd share cooking duties.

My first priority, however, was to see if anything could be salvaged from either my retail shop or jewelry studio. Joe loaned me a backpack and a bicycle—mine had been ruined by the surge. I whistled for Jack and he trotted beside the bike, eager for adventure. He was in a great mood. The stench that rose up from the mud-coated streets may have distressed me, but Jack found it invigorating.

It was slow going. I stopped frequently and splashed water from puddles onto the bike tires to remove mud that clung to the wheels like heavy mortar. Many times I was forced to carry the bike over and around fallen trees or sections of houses that blocked the route. The only moving vehicles I saw were the trucks of Georgia Power and an Oklahoma tree-cutting company. Amazingly, their crews were already at work clearing the streets. Their chain saws roared in the still heat of morning.

Six blocks and half an hour later, I reached the Lumberyard. It's a renovated arts center owned by my friends Vicki and Doug. Just three weeks before, I'd moved my office and studio into an inviting space on the ground floor. Nothing looked inviting now. The gate to the center was blocked by a massive fallen tree. I climbed over it and trudged through the thick mud, shouting for Doug. The last I'd heard, he'd planned to ride out the storm there. He didn't respond, so I guessed he'd left for Jackson with Vicki. Later, I'd learn that he'd evacuated, all right—from the frying pan into the fire.

It was obvious that a wall of water had crashed through the arts complex. It was located closer to the beach than my house, but on higher ground, so I was astonished at the damage. I peered into my studio through the plate glass windows. The room had been ransacked. My cherished tools had been churned with an evil black silt dredged from the bottom of the sea. Office equipment and files had overturned in the frenzy, while books and personal memorabilia had been hurled around the room. The shock of the sight almost brought me to my knees. Then, to ward off self-pity, I repeated a phrase that was already becoming a town maxim: *no sniveling.*

I biked the two blocks to Main Street, where the debris field became too treacherous for riding. Main Street runs straight to the beach along the highest ridge of land in the Bay. On the first block from the front, I'd owned a Creole cottage built in 1850. I'd painstakingly renovated it, and for ten years, it had housed my gallery, studio, and apartment. The older people in town called it "The Monkey House." In the 1940s, an eccentric woman had run a small, feisty newspaper in the front part of the building.

Photograph by Joe Tomasovsky.

She'd lived in the back with her large pet monkey that would periodically escape and terrorize the neighborhood children.

A month before, wanting to downsize my business, I'd sold the building. I'd signed over the deed, but not my heart. The Monkey House had never flooded in a 150-year lifespan of serious storms, and, together, Mimi and I had safely weathered three hurricanes there. I held my breath as I rounded the corner. When I saw that it still stood, I was overwhelmed with gratitude. It'd lost part of the roof and taken on four to five feet of water, but the sturdy cottage shone like a beacon of hope.

That hope dimmed as Jack and I continued towards the waterfront. A thick hedge of wrecked cars, beams, furniture, and utility poles made it impossible to even carry the bike. I left it behind and walked forward into the nightmare. The gallery building where I'd recently rented a retail space was toast. Much of the roof had caved in, burying my display cases and jewelry. After twenty years, I couldn't find enough left of my business to put into a backpack. I wouldn't be alone—most of the old downtown had been demolished.

The waterfront itself was unrecognizable. Main Street used to end at Beach Boulevard. Now, it abruptly dropped off to the Gulf below. The beach road was gone. Every structure on the beach side of the road was gone. The buildings on the near side hadn't fared much better—the few surviving shells looked as if they'd been bombed. The entire front of one brick building had been sheared away. A fully furnished living room on the second floor was exposed to the street, looking like a bizarre set for a Fellini film.

The railroad bridge bisecting Old Town was no longer a bridge. Concrete pilings rising out of the water were all that remained, while the track itself twisted crazily into the Gulf, a roller-coaster ride gone berserk. I looked towards the four-lane bay bridge in the distance. Only scattered supports bore witness to the fact it had even existed.

A few of my neighbors joined me at the literal dead end of Main. They slouched against the edge of an asphalt slab like worn shipwreck survivors. I nodded and they nodded back. There wasn't much to say. We surveyed the absolute eradication of our town in silence.

Walking back towards my bike, I came upon a wedding photo face up in the mud. I studied the eager, hopeful faces, but didn't recognize them. Where were these people now? Tears ambushed me again. Like some madwoman, I carefully worked to dislodge the picture from the mud, ignoring the magnitude of the ruin around me. I somehow hoped to save the photo and return it to the owners, but it fell to pieces in my hand—a shredded symbol of the countless losses around me. I wailed aloud from rage and frustration. Jack was the only witness to this tantrum, and he burrowed his head beneath my arm. He didn't know what was wrong, but he wanted to make it better. I pulled him tightly against me and cried into his fur.

I headed back up Main Street and saw my friend Doug. My spirits lifted immediately as we greeted each other with enthusiastic hugs. Doug always exudes a relaxed humor, and that morning was no exception. He's a Hurricane Hunter by profession—flying planes into the heart of storms for a living probably gives him a certain immunity to anxiety.

As I'd guessed, he'd evacuated the arts center before the storm. He'd stayed with six friends at the Bay Town Inn, a historic bed-and-breakfast on the beach. He reported that all had survived. I wouldn't find out until later exactly *what* they'd survived: the Bay Town Inn no longer existed. When I pressed Doug for details that morning, he answered with characteristic understatement: "It was one heck of a ride."

Further up Main, the houses had flooded but were still mostly intact. I met a truck inching through the debris towards the front. The driver was Ernie, owner of a popular beach bar. Ironically, he'd named it the Good Life—something we'd all had a shot at in the Bay. "Have you been down there?" he said, pointing to the Gulf. I nodded my head, knowing what he was going to ask next. I didn't want to break the news to him, but I was trapped. "How is it?" he asked. Tears came to my eyes when I said, "Ernie, it's all gone."

He shook his head and choked for a moment. Then he smiled. "Cheer up, baby," Ernie said, patting me on the shoulder. "There'll be another Good Life."

I knew he wasn't talking about his bar. Before he left, Ernie offered his help. "Honey, let me know if you need anything," he said. He drove away to look at the eroded bank where the sea had devoured his dream.

I didn't have time to escape before another friend pulled up with her two teenaged sons in the back seat. I was both glad and horrified to see them: their home had faced the beach. "What's it like?" she asked. I didn't want to lie. "The whole front's gone," I said. She looked stricken, so I started to be evasive. "But I haven't actually been down to your house. . . ." My neighbor took a deep breath, looked back at the impassive faces of her sons, and attempted a smile. I wished her luck as they left. It didn't do any good. Later, I'd see for myself that only the pilings of their home remained.

I'd always understood why messengers got shot, but now I wondered why more messengers didn't shoot themselves. I had to get off Main before I ran into anyone else. Jack and I navigated back streets the rest of the way home. The temperature was in the high nineties and even Jack was dragging. By the time I arrived, I was drenched with sweat and liberally spattered with mud.

Augusta and most of her family had gone to see what they could salvage from their houses, while Donald had walked to his job at the local power company. He'd been teamed with some Georgia Power linemen, and they'd dropped off juice and bottled water for the household. I helped myself to a juice while I rested in the shade of the porch.

Jimmie joined me and we discussed his mother, Mimi. On my ride, I'd heard from a neighbor that the hospital had been destroyed. It was clear to us now that no ambulance would arrive, no medics. Mimi was bedridden for the most part, and Jimmie was concerned about sanitation. He'd been helping clean her, but she was understandably mortified. I was mortified myself—I hadn't understood the situation fully. I'm not a nurse, but agreed to try my best.

I went into the bedroom where Mimi lay atop the sheets, listening to the news on her battery radio. She'd kept it pressed against her ear since the storm began, even when she slept. With no air conditioning or fans, the room was stifling, but Mimi never complained. I asked how she was feeling.

She didn't waste time with niceties—she knew why I'd come. "Oh darling," she protested. "I don't want you to do this. I feel so useless. I want to get up and help you, but all I can do is lie here and be a burden. Just give me some water. I can take care of myself."

Pretending to be stern, I told her to quit fussing. I spread out garbage bags across the bed and cleaned her with water from my bathtub reservoir and a pack of disinfectant wipes. I was terrified I'd do something wrong; if her catheter became infected, her life would be at risk without antibiotics. Mimi kept trying to apologize, and I chattered to distract her until we were finished. For lack of other disposable options, I cut up some old T-shirts and swaddled her with them, joking about the new fashion statement. I helped her into a clean gown and then, with fresh water, sponged off her face and hands. "Thank you," she said. "That feels wonderful!" Then she asked, "Do you have any perfume?" We both laughed and I gave her a spritz of my favorite.

Mimi dozed off listening to the news of her hometown, New Orleans. It wasn't good. The levies had broken; most of the city was underwater. I only

The corner of Main Street and Beach Boulevard shortly after the storm, reputed to be one of the cell phone "hot spots" in town. Photograph by Joe Tomasovsky.

hoped Joe's daughter Robyn was in Baton Rouge with her sister. Briefly, I thought of my other friends who lived in the city, then slammed that mental door tightly shut. There was nothing I could do for New Orleans, and I needed to focus on the troubles at hand.

I took two more treks on the bike that day. The first was to the foot of the bay bridge pilings, two miles away. Doug had told me that it was the one place in town where cell phones would work. A small crowd had gathered, but few people actually talked on their phones. I tried my own cell phone and dialed several numbers, frustrated when the signal would die before I'd connect. Finally, I asked one woman whose phone was working if I could make a quick call to my parents. She kindly agreed, but the signal died before I could enter the number.

Around sunset, Joe and I biked to Saint Stanislaus, a school close to my house. The campus overlooks the beach, and we'd heard it was another cell phone hot spot. The sun was beginning to set, and it was the time when many residents used to exercise along the beach. That evening, people had come only with the hope of making a simple phone call to let loved ones know they were alive.

No one was having any luck, but I saw several people I knew, including my friends Grady and Sally. They'd evacuated with their three children to Grady's office at Stennis International Airport, more than six miles north of the coast. Even there, the water had risen over six feet. I was staggered at the news—that meant the entire southern part of the county had been inundated by the surge.

Grady and Sally were both shaken. Not only had their home been destroyed, but they'd also had an ugly run-in with some would-be looters. While they were picking though the rubble of their house, two men had confronted and threatened them. The incident ended without violence, but my idealistic bubble burst when I heard their story. Although Bay St. Louis was an extraordinary community, apparently it wasn't perfect.

I can't remember eating dinner that night. Between the heat, the exhaustion, and the stress, I'm sure I didn't care. The final defeat of the day came when I realized I'd lost the new prescription glasses I'd gotten three days before. Somehow, the case had popped out of my pocket while I'd been biking. Finding it in the debris and mud would be impossible. It was a relatively small loss, yet utterly disheartening.

Joe chose to camp out in his driveway, to escape the heat inside. I crawled into my loft bedroom in the center hallway of my own house. I'd covered the bed with plastic before the storm, so it was still relatively dry. Jimmie and his mother slept in rooms to one side of me, and Augusta's family spread out on the porch, where it was cooler.

Despite the story of the looters, I left the windows and front doors open for cross-ventilation. I don't have screens anywhere in my house, because I don't need them. I have bats. A small colony nests between two beams under my house. They're my secret treasures, patrolling my yard in the evenings, devouring every bug that dares come near. That night, two bats somehow got into my room, something that had never

The site of the Good Life bar after the storm. Before Katrina, a small auxiliary bar called Day Dreams was located beneath the building and overlooked the beach. Residents resurrected the bar just days after the storm, decorating it with a disconnected pay phone and a salvaged "No Tank Tops" sign. The handwritten sign on the upper left proclaims, "Katrina won't keep us down!" Photograph by Joe Tomasovsky.

happened before. At first I was anxious, wondering if they'd accidentally land on me as I slept. Finally, I decided to be grateful I had personal guardians for the evening. No surviving mosquito would draw my blood this night. In the eerie silence, I heard the membranes of the bats' wings fluttering, felt swift movements in the air close above my face. The darkness wrapped the house like a thick cloth. The entire coast was stripped of artificial light, and through the open windows, I looked out at stars I'd never seen before.

As I lay in bed, the bats winging overhead, I thought about the Good Life. The neon sign for the bar had always amused me. It rarely worked perfectly, although Ernie had tried many times through the years to fix it. Sometimes, it said "The _____ Life." Sometimes it just read "Good," and occasionally just "The." It seemed like a metaphor for our lives in general. Years before, I'd written a poem about the sign. It wasn't a very good poem, but it seemed prophetic when I remembered it that night:

THE GOOD LIFE

The "Good" part is burned out
What remains is "Life."
It glows a steady phosphorescent blue
against the dark sky over the Bay

The red border flashes
off and on
with typical neon anxiety.
The caption underneath
blinks as well:

"live entertainment"

E. A. 1996

PART TWO

The Story of Bay Town Inn

SOLID AS A ROCK

When I ran into my friend Doug Niolet the day after the hurricane, he told me that he'd ridden out the storm with six others at the Bay Town Inn, a beachfront bed-and-breakfast. That morning he didn't elaborate—his only comment was "it was quite a ride." At the time, I didn't even know that the local landmark had been completely demolished during the storm. It would be weeks before I heard some of the jaw-dropping details. Then in late October 2005, Nikki Nicholson, owner of the Inn and one of the survivors, asked me if I'd write up an account of the story.

All seven of the people who chose to stay in the Inn are my friends and neighbors. I don't need a writer's imagination to fill in the details—I'm simply recording their story, interweaving five of the individual accounts. Two survivors declined to be interviewed. I've changed their names to Kay and Pete Stevens to respect their privacy.

The experience of this group is riveting because they barely escaped with their lives. Yet they overcame what must have been an imperative to panic and took care of each other, offering what they could despite their personal peril. While this account may be extraordinary, it's not unusual—I've heard dozens of others that are similar. It's actually a typical example of the way people on the coast helped others—both during and after the storm. This is the story of Bay Town Inn, but it's also the story of our town.

Nikki Nicholson holds her dog, Maddy, in the lot where the Bay Town Inn once stood. Photograph by Joe Tomasovsky.

AUGUST 29, 2005   Nikki Nicholson straddled the oak branch, lying face down and hugging it with all her might. Her small dog, Maddy, was tucked beneath her stomach like a baby. She pressed the dog closer to her, wondering how they'd possibly survive. Each wave that washed over the tree threatened to tear them from the limb and drag them into the seething surge. Nikki had always figured she'd be killed in a plane crash. Now, it looked like all those hours of airport anxiety had been wasted. In a bizarre twist of fate, she was caught in a tree, facing death by hurricane. It seemed like a very strange way to die.

Doug Niolet reached up from his perch on the branch below and held on to Nikki's boots for dear life. As a professional Hurricane Hunter, he'd piloted a plane through the eye of the storm forty-eight hours before. Now, he was in the center of Katrina again, hoping his branch wouldn't break. Doug wasn't sure he was going to die, but he wasn't sure he'd make it either. He'd seen the others disappear.

After the Bay Town Inn disintegrated around them, the seven friends had been forced into the fury of the storm. In the chaos, they'd been separated. Three of them made it to a large oak. The other four had vanished. Doug had watched in horror as Kay Stevens was pulled under the Gulf's raging waters. She didn't resurface. Her husband, Pete, had made it to a cluster of smaller trees nearby, but soon after he'd disappeared as well. The elders of the group, Dick and Nadine Stamm, had floated away together on a small section of roof. They'd actually waved good-bye as they sailed past on the makeshift raft. Doug waved back and started praying the rosary. It had been his grandmother's favorite prayer.

Kevan Guillory had been the last person to make it to the tree. His branch faced the Gulf, so he'd warn Nikki and Doug when a breaker was about to hit. The three friends were trapped for the duration—they couldn't go higher and they couldn't go down. Whenever the sea slammed into them, Kevan would bury his face in the resurrection ferns that grew on the branch and ask himself one question: "What in the cornbread hell led us to this?"

Nikki and Kevan became worldwide celebrities the day after the storm when CNN repeatedly aired a short interview with them. But the network missed the best parts of the story. Exactly who are these people? What kept them all from panicking in the worst of circumstances? And the question that Kevan asked of himself is one of the most compelling—what led seven mature, intelligent people to ride out the storm in a beachfront bed-and-breakfast?

As with most Katrina stories, this one begins with Camille. Thirty-five years before, the "storm of the century" had charged directly into Bay St. Louis with a twenty-seven-foot tidal wave and gusts of over two hundred miles an hour. Heeding evacuation warnings, Dick and Nadine Stamm left their home in the lower elevation Cedar Point neighborhood. They took refuge in the 2nd Street Elementary School. The school was only a block from the beach, but it'd been built on the "bluff" of old town—some of the highest ground bordering the Gulf of Mexico.

It was a good decision. The Stamms' own house on Cedar Point flooded, but the couple weathered Camille at the school with no problems. When the storm relented at daybreak, Dick walked to his boss's house, which faced the beach. He found his employer, wife, and three children unharmed, their stately historic home high and dry. The monster storm had broken only a few windows of the sturdy building. This was the house that would later become Bay Town Inn. This was a house the Stamms thought they could count on.

Decades later, when Katrina took aim for the Bay, the Stamms again considered their options. Nadine was now in her late seventies and Dick was eighty-one. Although they were both active and vital, they were concerned about attempting the drive to their daughter's house a hundred miles north. News reports warned of impossibly clogged highways. The Stamms debated and then called their friend Nikki Nicholson, owner of the Bay Town Inn. Nikki assured them of a warm welcome at the bed-and-breakfast. The last of her paying guests departed Sunday morning, so she had plenty of room. They'd all be very comfortable, even if they lost electricity.

Nikki had no qualms about staying in her house or in sheltering others for the storm. She'd purchased the Bay Town Inn three years before from Ann Tidwell, Doug's mother-in-law. Nikki knew the house was a Camille veteran, but she also understood the principles of structural integrity.

Built in 1899, the Inn had been constructed to withstand storms from the Gulf. Large beams ran the length of the building—it was solid as a rock. They don't make houses like that anymore.

So when Pete and Kay Stevens called, she didn't hesitate to offer them refuge as well. Kay's an artist who worked part-time at the Inn. The Stevenses' house was located a few miles west of Bay St. Louis in Waveland. Although their home was well back from the water, Kay wanted to be on the safe side and move to higher ground. Since their large dog limited evacuation options, the Bay Town Inn seemed the perfect solution.

The chain of events that led Doug Niolet to stay began three days before the storm. When he reported to work at Keesler Air Force Base on Friday, August 26, he wasn't slated to fly; however, the scheduled pilot couldn't take the nighttime mission, so Doug volunteered. For six hours, he flew in and out of Katrina's eye. When he entered the hurricane, it had just passed over Florida and had weakened to a Category 1. By the time he headed back to Keesler early Saturday morning, the storm had intensified to a Category 3.

Saturday afternoon, Doug was back in the Bay boarding up his various properties. His old friend and partner, Kevan, worked alongside. The two men moved around town, securing doors, screwing plywood over windows, stacking sandbags where heavy rains might cause drainage problems. At one point, Kevan asked Doug's opinion of the storm.

"Well," Doug said. "It's not the worst storm I've ever flown into, but somebody's world will never be the same." He didn't realize he was talking about his own.

Doug finally slept Saturday night, assuming he'd be flying again the next morning. But by Sunday, the base had decided to move operations to Houston. Relieved of work obligations, Doug was inclined to stay through the storm. He'd be able to help Kevan with final preparations and then get a jump start on the cleanup afterward. At the same time, he was uncomfortable with the thought of his wife, Vicki, remaining with him. He urged her to evacuate. Vicki wasn't really worried about her husband's safety if he chose to stay—several times a year, he was required to attend survival training exercises—but she wasn't as confident with her own emergency skills. She and her mother, Ann, packed and headed for Jackson early that afternoon.

Doug and Kevan spent the rest of the day boarding up several buildings and houses, including the Bay Town Inn. They were old hands at the procedure, and by the end of the day they'd completed most of their goals. They still had a punch list of last-minute tasks, but since the storm wasn't predicted to hit until late Monday morning, they figured they'd have time the next day. The group of seven gathered at the Inn. Kevan, a native Cajun and an excellent cook, baked a crawfish pie for dinner.

After the meal, they retired early. Pete and Kay slept in the small guest cottage directly behind the main house. Kevan went next door to keep watch on Ann Tidwell's building at 200 Beach, a solid brick structure that had also made it through Camille unharmed. He moved into the second floor for the night. Doug had originally planned on staying at the Lumberyard, the Niolets' arts center, but in the end, he decided that the Stamms and Nikki might appreciate some extra moral support. The die was cast. Doug, Nadine and Dick, and Nikki took rooms on the first floor of the Inn. The seven friends had made a seemingly simple decision without any suspicion that their lives would soon be in peril.

When Nikki got up at three in the morning, she found Doug listening to storm reports on the television. The hurricane had moved faster than expected; already wind and rain pummeled the house. She made a pot of coffee for him and then headed back to bed, her Scottish terrier, Maddy, trotting dutifully behind. Doug eventually returned to his room as well, but was too disturbed to sleep. Forecasters still predicted surges to peak at eighteen to twenty feet, yet one announcer had made a comment that kept replaying in his head: *no one really knew for sure.*

Doug lay in bed wondering if it was too late to leave. He tried to reassure himself that no matter what happened, the building would still be standing after the storm. The house sat on land that was over twenty-five feet above sea level. It'd been built an additional five feet off the ground. Even if the surge rose to an unheard-of thirty feet, the house wouldn't flood. It hadn't in 1969. And this storm would never match the ferocity of Camille.

At five in the morning, Doug gave up on sleep. Nikki joined him in the kitchen for coffee. The pot she'd made earlier was still warm, although they'd lost electricity an hour or so before. Frustrated that the television didn't work, Doug remembered a battery-operated TV that he had at the Lumberyard Arts Center, four blocks away. He decided to get it and called on Kevan to ride shotgun. His friend grumbled at being roused so early, but agreed it might be a good idea to travel as a team. The Stamms were still sleeping, and since Nikki was reluctant to be left without company, she joined the men for the expedition. She kept her notepad in hand as they climbed into Doug's truck, determined to keep a thorough record of events.

They drove along the beach road, which was built a good twenty feet above sea level. Water lapped across the top of the pavement, so the three assumed they were seeing the peak of the predicted surge. Power wires flailed like streamers in the wind, tree branches tumbled across their path. Turning onto Main Street, Doug answered a phone call. It was his daughter, Courtney, demanding to know where he was.

Doug answered as a nearby building blew away. "Whoa!" he said. "Look at that roof going off!"

Courtney was livid when she realized her father was still in the Bay. She began shouting at him, "Dad, you're not qualified to hunt hurricanes on the ground!"

Doug tried to reassure her and signed off. He continued slowly down the treacherous roads. It took the group almost thirty minutes to retrieve the television, but they made it back to the bed-and-breakfast without mishap. Kevan returned to his post next door, while Doug tried to get more news. It had been a wasted trip. The battery TV worked, but stations were no longer broadcasting.

In a last-ditch attempt for information, he called his headquarters in Houston to ask when the eye of the storm would pass. The mission commander, Roger, was incredulous to hear that Doug was still in the Bay and asked his exact location. The answer turned out to be another inadvertent prophecy.

"Why, we're diving off the first floor of the bed-and-breakfast," Doug cracked. "And we're getting ready to go up to the second floor and do high dives."

Roger wasn't amused, but promised to call back shortly with the information.

About seven o'clock, conditions began to deteriorate rapidly. The wind peeled plywood away from some of the windows and rain started pushing beneath the exterior doors. Doug called Kevan and asked for help at the Inn. He also tried calling his commander back for the all-important location of the eye. There was no answer. His cell phone wasn't getting through.

To get back to the Inn, Kevan had to wade across a lawn now covered with ankle-deep water. Several times he had to stop and crouch down. The thundering gusts threatened to carry him off. Directly across the street, he saw that the Dock of the Bay, a popular restaurant built on the bluff overlooking the beach, was beginning to show signs of defeat. Bit by bit, the building was being dismembered by the wind.

Once inside the Inn, Kevan helped the others take emergency measures. The group built a "nest" in the most sheltered part of the building, a nook in the center of the house, behind the massive staircase on the first floor. They furnished it with blankets and pillows, flashlights and water. Everyone sealed their most valuable belongings—wallets, laptops, personal papers—into plastic bags and piled them in the nest. Nikki even protected her current needlepoint project.

Her last contact with the outside world for the next twenty-four hours came when she answered a phone call from a friend at about 8:00 a.m. As Nikki talked, she looked out the back windows and noticed the water rising on her patio. When her friend asked if the worst had passed, she saw her grill begin to float. "I don't think so," she said.

At 8:30 the Stamms took a coffee break and sat at the kitchen table. They were calm—in fact, according to Dick, "dumb and happy." Through the windows, they could see DeMontluzin Street, which ran along one side of the house. It was quickly becoming a river. Suddenly, they saw their car cruise by, floating away down the street. Kay's car had been parked in front of the guest cottage. Now it butted against the walls of the small house repeatedly, riding a rising surf. The headlights flashed as the car alarm signaled an emergency.

Nadine retreated to the nest and took over the job of news gatherer. She pressed the portable radio to her ear and searched the airwaves with quiet composure. Dick went into the dining room off the kitchen to check for leaks. A renegade gust of wind broke a window, blasted through the house and slammed the door behind him. When he struggled to open it, the air pressure in the house worked against him. The rest of the group came to his rescue. Together, they were able to force back one of the giant pocket doors leading from the dining room to the hallway and finally release Dick.

The guest cottage in the back had its own problems. It had been built at ground level. When the water first started slipping under the doors, the Stevenses decided to make for the main house. Together, they struggled across the patio in chest-high water, important papers held high. Kay managed to somehow hang on to her dog's leash as he swam.

They burst in through the kitchen door of the house, grateful to have reached refuge. But the air pressure was still playing tricks. When the back door opened, the tremendous suction broke open the massive front door, which had been boarded over. Doug and Kevan raced to wrestle it back into submission. They used a portable drill to screw the door shut. While the Stevenses dried off in the kitchen, the rest of the team worked furiously as the storm found new ways to breach the walls. Dick barricaded off the laundry room, which had lost part of the roof. Nadine reluctantly made the sad report that the storm was intensifying, while Doug wedged various utensils against the kitchen windows to keep them shut.

Kevan and Nikki decided to check on the second floor. Upstairs, rain was being forced through the windows, so the two grabbed some towels. When they tried to secure one window, glass exploded into the room. Shards sliced into Kevan's chin and foot. They gave up and pushed a heavy armoire in front of the opening. Nikki found some hydrogen peroxide to put on Kevan's cuts, and they joined the others on the first floor.

Downstairs a new battle was being waged to fortify the front door. The water now swamped two feet over the level of the porch, and waves beat furiously against the house. The men used a shutter from an upstairs closet to wedge against the door, then overturned a table and braced it against the shutter. To complete the emergency barricade, they jammed a cutting board between the table and the foot of the stairs. In the end, they had a contraption that exerted considerable force against the door.

Kevan became the official lookout. The enormous front and side windows of the house had been boarded over, but the plywood left a small gap at the top. He dragged a stool around the rooms, standing on it to peek over the boards. After looking through one of the front windows, he quietly called Doug over to him.

"Don't say anything to the others," he said. "But you've got to see this. The Dock of the Bay is in the front yard."

ROOM NUMBER FIVE

DOUG PEERED OUT THE WINDOW, straining to see through the sheets of rain. The building across the street had vanished. Large sections of the restaurant churned in the water covering the front yard. Frenzied waves drove the debris against the foundations of the Bay Town Inn, shaking the house with every slam of the surge.

Kevan and Doug announced it was time to move the nest to the second floor. Room number five was the obvious choice. It was centered in the back of the house, directly at the top of the stairs. The room was flanked on one side by a walk-in closet and on the other by a bath.

The group began hauling their possessions and supplies up the stairs. The Stamms depended on several medications, and Nadine made sure she had them all with her in a black garbage bag. She also carried up the portable radio, even though the reception had been reduced to static.

Nadine knew they were in for a "very challenging time." She settled on a daybed, with Kay at her feet. Kay chanted a soothing mantra, while Nadine repeated more traditional prayers. When Nikki commented on their composure, Nadine smiled. "It's in God's hands now," she said serenely.

The men remained below trying to brace the doors against the Gulf of Mexico. The waves pounded against the front of the house as if an outside army sensed victory and had taken up battering rams. Doug took a last look through the cracks in the plywood. The front porch was no longer attached to the building. "That's extreme," he thought. He shouted over the thunderous noise, warning the other men that it was time to go. They fled up the steps, crowding with the women into room five.

Kevan was the last to leave, racing behind the others. "Just as I turned to go upstairs," he said, "the water broke through. A gush raged through the house. At the same time, water poured in the back from the kitchen. I'd taken my glasses off, but could see the waves coming up the stairwell. They just slashed against the back wall where the nest had been. Then the entire staircase broke loose. It went crashing through to the back of the house. I wondered, now how we are going to get down from the second floor? That's when I first realized we really had a problem."

At the top of the stairs, Kevan veered off into the doorway of a bedroom directly to the left. He could see the rest of the group huddled in room five, but he could also look down into the gaping chasm below. Breakers smashed through the bottom floor, hurling antique furnishings against walls that were beginning to break apart. Wave after wave mauled the house with a feral ferocity, ripping away sections as he watched. Finally, the entire front of the building groaned in surrender and fell away into a gorging sea.

The doorway to number five suddenly opened directly onto an ocean writhing in fury. The front rooms no longer existed. The floor of the hallway had been sucked into the surf. The room behind Kevan began to distort as it pulled away from the back of the house. Nikki screamed when she saw Kevan's danger. He vaulted toward the others from the crumbling remains of his perilous perch. Propelled by adrenaline, Kevan cleared a six-foot rift that dropped away to certain death below. He made it to the threshold of room number five and was pulled by the others into the last safe haven.

But it wasn't a haven for long. Number five became the only survivor of the house when the remaining back rooms on both sides were pulled away. As the final supports of the first floor gave way, number five settled onto the heaving surface of the sea. The walls and ceiling of the room began to cave in on the group. The men struggled to keep it from collapsing onto them while the floor rippled beneath their feet. They weren't able to save the front wall. The churning water inexorably devoured their last protection from the elements.

Now seven people and two dogs found themselves in a shifting shell, open to the fury of the storm. "Hello, Gulf of Mexico," Doug thought. He realized that the room had become a little boat—and one that was about to sink. Gusts blasted them with bullets of rain. As they fought to keep the ceiling from falling onto them, the room twisted in the water. The open front of number five now faced towards the rear of the lot. A large oak tree that grew in the backyard came into view.

Doug shouted to be heard over the wind, urging his friends to enter the water and make for the tree. Nadine, still calm, answered resolutely. "I'm not going into the water," she said. "I can't swim." Dick held her close against his side. He was going nowhere without his wife.

The group faced imminent death, but the Cajun in Kevan couldn't resist the opening for a good line. As he strained against the ceiling to hold it in place, he looked at Doug and grinned. "Houston, we have a problem," he yelled.

Kevan and Doug didn't need to speak next to determine their roles. Doug ushered Nikki into the dark, raging surge with Kay and Pete, while Kevan stayed with the Stamms, waiting for a miracle.

Pete persuaded his wife to release their dog from its leash. He led Kay into the water, and, together, they fought their way to the tree. Pete helped Kay grab hold of a sturdy branch, then was pushed ahead by the current. He finally managed to catch a clump of smaller trees further up the street.

Nikki held her dog close to her. She scuttled crablike across the debris floating on top of the water, using it like a series of rafts. When she arrived at the tree, she saw that Kay was pinned against the trunk by the same tide of wreckage. Yet Kay took Maddy into her arms, allowing Nikki to climb onto a limb. When Nikki was secure, Kay handed up the dog.

Doug kept his head above the water, but the mass of floating debris knocked against him with every swell of the sea. When he reached the tree, he was able to pull himself above the deadly layer of lumber. Once anchored on a branch, he grasped the hand of Kay, who was still pinned. Each undulation of the water pinched her between the debris and the trunk of the tree, threatening to cut her in half. He couldn't manage to pull her from the water, so hung onto her arm in desperation.

Meanwhile, Kevan and the Stamms got their miracle. A section of roof floated by and began to butt up against the open part of room five, as if beckoning them. Kevan struggled to hold back the last remaining walls as Dick helped Nadine slide into the water. Her husband encouraged her as she did the unthinkable. "You can do it," he said. "You can do this. I'm right here with you."

Nadine later said that she "felt miraculous guidance with every step. Our bodies were not harmed in any way. I didn't step on nails. Nothing even caught our clothes. We tried to catch a tree trunk, but the Lord didn't want that, so we floated on a little branch. The water doused over me once and then went down to my waist. When we got to the piece of roof, Dick said, 'I'll help you up.'" Once onboard their makeshift raft, Nadine lay down. Dick spooned against her back and covered her body with his own to protect her from the cold and rain. He couldn't see where they were going, but it didn't matter. He was with his wife.

As they drifted away, Nadine lay against the shingles, still clutching the plastic bag that held their medications. Dick's arms surrounded her as if they were nesting birds. Their friends noticed the extraordinary expression of peace on both faces. Nikki later recalled, "The Stamms were together and that was all that counted—the two of them were ready to face anything, even death." "They may have been floating away to never-never land," Doug recounted, "but it looked like they'd be all right with that as long as they died together."

Kevan had entered the water right behind the Stamms and made it to the tree in time to wave good-bye as they passed. He joined Doug in more attempts to pull Kay from the water, but even their combined strength couldn't free her. Kay was in agony from the heavy debris battering her torso. If the brutal beating continued, the men realized she would soon die. Finally, in a desperate effort to save her, they shoved at the debris pile with all their strength, trying to push it away from her body. But Kay was impossibly tangled in the mass of lumber. As she moved away with the debris, they were forced to release their hold on her. Kevan was the last to let go of her hand. He watched in horror as she lost consciousness and her face slipped beneath the water. He was certain she was dead.

The island of debris carried Kay up the street towards where Pete clung to the top of a flimsy crepe myrtle bush. To get his attention, the three in the oak screamed together, "loud enough to be heard in Biloxi." But the gusts whipped away their cries and the pile washed past Pete unnoticed. The friends saw it move swiftly up DeMontluzin Street, following the path of the Stamms. Kay's head did not break the surface again. Shortly after, Pete disappeared from their view as well.

For the next two hours, Nikki, Doug, and Kevan clung like barnacles to the oak. At times, Nikki would reach over to Kevan and touch him for reassurance. He encouraged her by shouting, "Just hang on! As long as you don't lose your grip, you'll be OK." Maddy squirmed beneath her with typical terrier impatience, but Nikki only tightened her grip. After all they'd been through together, she wasn't about to lose her dog now. She thought about her brother the priest and her mother, who had passed away. She wondered if her mother was watching her from the other side.

To steady her, Doug held on to Nikki's boots dangling from above. He tried to watch the storm, but it was difficult to see anything. When he opened his eyes, the rain drove into them. If he shut them, the salt stung ferociously. He silently continued praying for his own life and those of his companions, yet he felt a quiet acceptance. He ended his prayers the way he always did: thy will be done.

Kevan spent the long hours "kissing the tree" and contemplating his surreal situation. He marveled over the events of his life that had led him to that particular place and time. Kevan wasn't sure why he'd ended up hanging on to a tree in the middle of a monster hurricane, but he had a sense that he was fulfilling an odd destiny. His humor never failed him. After one particularly violent round of waves had submersed the trio, he shouted to Doug. "Niolet, next time you want to go hunting a hurricane in a tree, don't call me!"

Finally, Kevan noticed the wind shifting to the south. Nikki watched as the water began to recede slowly. Suddenly, she felt as if she had regained the ability to breathe. It began to look like they might just make it after all. The group waited another endless hour before they thought about leaving their roost. As the surge retreated back into the Gulf, a new problem emerged—how were they going to get down? Doug was on the lowest branch, which was still at least eight feet from the ground. He'd lost a shoe in the escape, so was reluctant to jump into the muddy water that still covered the yard. While it looked fairly shallow, he could see part of a picket fence directly beneath him, strung out like a line of punji stakes. Doug realized that for some reason, he was wearing a towel around his neck. He supposed it had been white at one time—now it was completely brown. He draped it over his branch and lowered himself tentatively into the water below.

As Nikki readied herself to go next, she looked in the direction of State Street, the next block over. She spotted two figures waving to get her attention. They shouted across the debris and the wide lake of standing water that separated them from the tree. No one could hear their words over the wind, but Nikki was jubilant when she recognized one of the men as Pete. Pete and the stranger were dragging a makeshift ladder and apparently wanted to help. However, the group agreed that crossing "the lake" would be too risky and simply signaled to Pete that they were safe.

Nikki handed Maddy off to Kevan, and using Doug's towel technique, scrambled down with his assistance. Kevan gently lowered the dog and followed. They turned in the direction of the only high ground in sight—an enormous pile of sand. It had been deposited by the surge at the foot of DeMontluzin, where the street had once met the beach road.

Exhausted, the three friends rested on the mound for several minutes and tried to get their bearings. The sense of disorientation was overwhelming. They could barely recognize each other under the sticky, black silt covering them head to toe. Even the landscape around them was no longer familiar. They might have been standing on the surface of another planet. There was no sign of the Bay Town Inn, nothing even to mark where it had stood. The stretch of beach road, once lined with shops and restaurants, was now barren. The street itself had been eaten away.

It was early afternoon when they picked their way across the shredded remains of their town to a neighbor's house that was somehow still standing. The bottom floor had been demolished, but the upstairs had survived intact. In the kitchen, the group found Cokes and V-8 juice, which they gulped down. On the second floor, they rummaged through closets, hunting for clothes. Doug and Kevan were delighted to discover new men's bathing suits in their sizes. Everyone changed out of their wet rags, then collapsed onto beds that were miraculously dry. Storm-force winds hammered the house, ripping off sheets of metal roofing overhead. Kevan was kept awake by the racket, but Nikki and Doug were asleep in minutes.

Just a block away, the Stamms were sleeping, too. Their raft had floated up DeMontluzin, passing over a large oak that had fallen across the street. When the water began to recede, the tree acted as a roadblock, preventing the raft from being swept out to sea. The roof section had settled gently onto a thick layer of mud. Dick helped Nadine down and they slogged across the street to a row of standing houses. Dick chose one that looked as if it had only flooded a few feet inside. He broke in through a side window and gallantly opened the front door for Nadine. The food in the refrigerator was still cold, so they ate for the first time since early morning. In one of the bedrooms, a four-poster king-sized bed provided a luxurious resting place. The antique had been set up on wooden blocks, so even the bedding was dry. They lay down and both slept soundly, despite the winds still raging above them.

By midafternoon, they were wakened by a call from the front door. A trustee from the county jail was making a house-to-house search for survivors. He introduced himself as Jeff and told the Stamms he'd escort them to the sheriff's office and jail a few blocks away. Nadine had lost her slippers in the surge, so Jeff rooted through the closet until he found a pair of men's shoes she could wear. The jail had been converted to a makeshift MASH unit, and when they arrived, the Stamms were relieved to find Pete and Kay already there. Kay was alive, but in grave condition. During a search of the neighborhood, two deputies had found her battered and barely conscious and carried her back to the jail.

Semiconscious, she lay on a thin bed under layers of blankets, shivering from exposure and shock. Everyone was concerned about internal injuries she'd almost certainly sustained from the battering. Her breathing was labored. Powerless, Pete sat by her side as she gasped. The local hospital was in ruins, and the roads leading there were impassable. Medical help would have to come from the outside world, and it wasn't going to come quickly.

Pete wasn't in such good shape himself. At first, he'd made his stand against the surge by hanging tenaciously on to the flimsy crepe myrtle bushes. Finally, he found refuge in a wind-beaten house on State Street, about half a block from where the Inn had stood. A man who had stayed there for the storm helped him inside. When the water went down, the neighbor went with Pete to search for Kay. Shortly after, the two had spotted Nikki, Doug, and Kevan climbing out of the tree and attempted a rescue. By the time the Stamms arrived at the jail, Pete had been reunited with his wife. Dick and Nadine draped themselves with blankets and remained with the Stevenses until the storm was spent.

Kevan found them all there, late in the day. When the winds had slackened, he and Doug had left their temporary refuge to check on other neighbors. They made their way further inland to a friend's house. It had flooded on the ground floor and lost a major part of the roof, but it could still provide shelter. They decided to make the home emergency headquarters. The two men broke in without guilt, then found the key to a truck parked in the driveway. The old truck surprised them by starting immediately. They commandeered it and were even able to drive part of the way back to the beach to pick up Nikki.

Doug and Kevan were on a roll—etiquette took second place to survival. They raided friends' freezers for ice and food, taking it back to the "headquarters." Then Kevan picked up the Stamms and the Stevenses from the jail. He settled them for the night into another house Nikki owned on Carroll Street, a few blocks away. It had been battered and flooded, but the upstairs beds were dry. Kay was in a very fragile state. Despite the warm evening air and bundles of blankets, she shivered uncontrollably.

Kevan "borrowed" a grill on the way back to meet Nikki and Doug. They'd been joined by two other friends, who'd ridden out the peak of the surge in the cab of their floating pickup truck. Kevan lit the charcoal and cooked a feast of fried baloney, which he rendered down to a crisp. Food had never tasted so good. The meal at the Inn the night before seemed a million years ago, in a fractured past. They ate in total blackness, the glow of the coals their only illumination. They didn't talk a lot. Adrenaline had been replaced by shock. Each was absorbed by the new reality. Their beloved town was destroyed. Friends and neighbors had perished or, like Kay, teetered on the brink. Communication was impossible; loved ones far away most likely presumed them dead.

Yet this new reality contained gold as well as grit. Friendship had new meaning and community had become something more than just a word. Courage wore a different face, one that could be lined with age. And faith had broken past the bounds of any church. It roamed freely like a spirit through the dark and broken streets of Bay St. Louis.

EPILOGUE—APRIL 2006   *Kay Stevens was flown to a Jackson hospital the next afternoon. She remained hospitalized for several weeks with multiple injuries and respiratory problems. Months later, she was finally given a release from medical care. Pete and Kay's home in Waveland was destroyed, and they lost everything they owned. Seven months after the storm, they moved out west.*

Nikki bounced between different friends' houses for months after the storm. In February, repairs were completed on her Carroll Street house, and she was able to return to the Bay. At this writing, she's working part-time for the New Orleans Convention and Visitors Bureau. She'd retired from there after twenty-five years, but after the storm returned to her job on a part-time basis.

She's hoping to build another Bay Town Inn when the major infrastructure of the town is back in place. "I'd love nothing better," she says, "although I might build it back a little bit further from the beach." Maddy misses all the treats and pats she got from doting guests when she was a bed-and-breakfast pet. The only obvious change in the dog since her traumatic experience is that she's more cuddly. "She lost everything, too," Nikki says. "It's not been easy for her either."

Kevan's cottage is located in the highest section of Bay St. Louis. Although it lost part of the roof, it sustained little damage in comparison to the rest of the houses in town. He claims he'd stay for another hurricane, although nowhere close to the beach. He also says that he's in the Bay to stay. "After making love to a tree for three and a half hours, you kind of feel connected to a place."

In the spring of 2006, Doug Niolet remained an active Hurricane Hunter, planning retirement later in the year. He says his co-workers had a universal reaction the first time they saw him after the storm. First, they'd embrace him and tell him they were thankful he was alive. Then they'd say they were going to knock the shit out of him for staying. His daughter, Courtney, finally forgave him, but made him promise that next time he'll evacuate. Doug and his wife, Vicki, plan to remain in Bay St. Louis and help rebuild.

L to R: Doug Niolet, Kevan Guillory, Nikki Nicholson (holding Maddy) stand beneath the tree that saved their lives. The sign reads, "God Bless This Tree." Photograph by Joe Tomasovsky.

Vicki Niolet heard from her husband the day after the storm when he managed to get a call through on a borrowed cell phone. She returned to town on Wednesday. Their living quarters at the Lumberyard Arts Center had been wrecked, as well as her own art studio. But Vicki doesn't need a studio to produce art—she began taking photographs immediately. Her photo study of Bay St. Louis after Katrina, titled "Parting Shots," was published in March 2006.

Dick Stamm says he heard that Jeff, the trustee, received a pardon for his heroic efforts the day of the storm.

Nothing remains of Dick and Nadine's house or any of their belongings. Since October 2005, they've lived in a house next door to their daughter, in the countryside of south Louisiana. As of this writing, they have no plans to rebuild in Bay St. Louis. They say they miss it dreadfully. They always loved the community, but the storm brought new appreciation. Dick says that after the hurricane, there were no strangers in town, only family.

They both credit their faith in God for their survival. When I asked Nadine how she remained so calm during life-threatening circumstances, she evaded the question at first, praising the entire group for being cool and levelheaded. She *said that none of them had time to be scared. She told me that thinking back over events, she gets "spiritual goose bumps."*

At last, Nadine handed me the answer in a nutshell. She quoted, "'I will give my angels charge over thee.' And there's another scripture that reads, 'Let not your heart be troubled.' I believe that you're only given what you can bear."

PART THREE
Storm Journal

ON OUR OWN

THIS PARTICULAR KATRINA LEGEND is short, but it speaks volumes for our town. It begins four long days after the storm, when the National Guard finally arrived in the Bay. The commander strode into the fire station to find Eddie Favre, the mayor of Bay St. Louis. Eddie's cousin is the famous football player Brett Favre, but Katrina hadn't cared about connections with celebrities, nor had she shown respect for authority. Our mayor's house had been flattened by the storm like thousands of others. He'd moved into the fire department and camped out on the floor.

The commander and his entourage must have made a formidable impression, dressed in their fresh camouflage uniforms and carrying rifles. They formally presented themselves to the mayor. Then the commander explained why they had come, announcing, "We're here to prevent looting."

An irate Eddie snapped back an order. "You leave my looters alone!"

Or so the story goes. I hope it's true. It's a reply that everyone who was here in those first desperate days appreciates and applauds. My favorite version has our mayor adding, "If you see somebody carting off a TV, shoot 'em, but if you see a person carrying away water or food, help 'em out, for Christ's sake."

I ran into the mayor at a city council meeting a few months after the storm and asked him if this was an accurate account. He neither confirmed

nor denied it. Eddie just grinned and said, "We [the city workers] were having to loot ourselves. We had nothing. What were we supposed to do?"

What were we supposed to do? It's a question I'm still asking. As an
American, I grew up with a sense of entitlement. I had confidence that if
my community were ever in trouble, my government would be there like
a shot to help out. I'd seen the immediate national response to the 9/11
disaster, when the entire country leaped to its feet and was on the scene
in a heartbeat. I expected the same response when Katrina destroyed my
town.

But by the time government help began to trickle in on Thursday—
three endless days after the storm—I felt angry, betrayed, and forgotten.
The Biloxi *Sun Herald* published an editorial on Wednesday, August 31,
voicing the same disappointment:

> [O]ur reporters have yet to find evidence of a coordinated approach
> to relieve pain and hunger or to secure property and maintain order.
> People are hurting and people are being vandalized . . . Yet where is
> the National Guard, why hasn't every able-bodied member of the
> armed forces in South Mississippi been pressed into service?
> . . . [R]eporters listening to horrific stories of death and survival at
> the Biloxi Junior High School shelter looked north across Irish Hill
> Road and saw Air Force personnel playing basketball and perform-
> ing calisthenics.

Calisthenics? On Wednesday?

The fact that no one had arrived on Tuesday was almost understand-
able. Twenty-four hours after the storm, communications were still cut
off, roads were blocked by fallen trees and debris, bridges were severed.
Katrina had blown us back into the Dark Ages. Yet somehow a crew from
CNN—that Maserati of mobilization—managed to make it into town.
They briefly interviewed two of the Bay Town Inn survivors before they
raced off to cover more dramatic happenings in New Orleans.

I also wondered how the crews of Georgia Power had arrived before the
armed forces or the Red Cross. Less than twelve hours after the storm had

passed, legions of them were everywhere, armed with chain saws, clearing the streets. But hey—maybe they were on the coast before the storm.

However, Wednesday morning, I woke up certain that soon men in uniforms would be at my door, asking what they could do to help. They would offer food and water and whisk Mimi away to a hospital. My ninety-two-year-old friend may have been tough, but the heat was wicked enough to wilt the hardiest athlete.

As I tried to orient myself to a new day in the apocalypse, I wasn't surprised to hear knocking at the front door. I raced to throw it open for the troops. Instead, I found my friend Hugh Penn, looking very disheveled. At first, he misread my shock as dismay.

"I know I stink," he explained. "I just got in from Lucedale last night. I've been sleeping in my car and haven't had a shower in three days."

Smelly or not, I had never been so glad to see anyone in my life. Hugh was the first friend from the outside world who'd made it back in. He must have been surprised when I threw my arms around his neck and burst into tears.

Hugh owned both a cottage in the Bay and a house in New Orleans, where he worked as an environmental lawyer. On the Sunday morning before the storm, he'd evacuated from his home in the Bay and headed east with a convoy of friends. The vehicles became separated, and Hugh's car began to overheat from the stop-and-go traffic. Every motel was full. "Clerks would just laugh at me when I'd stop and ask for a room," he said.

The night was closing in when the storm began in earnest. Hugh took an exit towards Lucedale, a small town just to the west of Mobile, Alabama. He pulled into a private campground and eased his car against the back wall of the office, hoping the building would afford some protection from the winds. Hugh and his dog spent the long night together, riding out the hurricane in his car.

In the morning, he was wakened from a fitful sleep by a rapping on his windshield. He opened his eyes and saw a man standing in the rain by the driver's-side window, dressed like a farmer in overalls and a straw hat. Hugh rolled down the window, and the man asked where he was from.

"I'm a refugee from New Orleans," Hugh answered.

"That'll be fifteen dollars," the man said, matter-of-factly.

But for Hugh's fifteen dollars, he also received hot meals—the owner of the RV park was not completely without mercy. Hugh ended up staying at the campground on Monday night as well. There was no place else to go.

Before dawn on Tuesday morning, Hugh struck out for the coast to check on his house in the Bay. He ignored warnings from his host that marshal law had been declared and authorities were arresting anyone driving at night. He worked his way southwest using back roads that had become debris-strewn obstacle courses. Although he traveled less than a hundred miles, the trip took him most of the day.

In the afternoon, Hugh finally made it to Highway 603. That's the main route that runs from the north directly into Bay St. Louis and Waveland on the coast. He traveled south on the road until he reached the point where Interstate 10 crosses the highway, several miles north of the two towns. The east and west lanes of the interstate above him appeared to be open, but the road ahead was blocked. A large group of vehicles had pulled over, and about forty people waited outside their cars. When Hugh joined them, he saw the problem. An enormous lake of water still covered Highway 603, and no one wanted to chance flooding their cars by driving through.

At the interstate overpass where Hugh stood—*seven miles* from the coast—the surge had risen over ten feet. The hurricane had slammed the coastline with a record-breaking wall of water, but it had also driven an impossibly high surge up any body of water *leading* to the Gulf. The Bay of Saint Louis itself—along with every river and bayou—had channeled the raging tides far inland. For the first time in recorded history, the briny waters of the Gulf had covered most of southern Hancock County.

Hugh joined the crowd and waited, wondering when the water would recede enough to continue. Then a red sports car pulled up to the scene.

"It was a shiny little convertible and this beautiful woman was driving," Hugh said. "She was all dolled up, like she was out for a Sunday drive—nice clothes, earrings and makeup, perfect hair. When she heard what the problem was, she shrugged and said, 'Oh, I'm not worried about that.' Then she gunned her engine and peeled out of there at about a hundred miles an hour. That car just flew across that water. When she got to the other side, the whole crowd spontaneously broke out into a big cheer. It was like she'd made a touchdown. She just waved back at us and then tore off down the road."

The "babe in the sports car" gave the rest of the group courage to slowly creep through the impasse, and Hugh made it back to his house before dark. He was surprised to find that the water had stopped inches before it invaded his house. And although every large tree in his yard had been felled by the winds, none of the fifteen had directly hit the building. Even his new roof was miraculously intact. He'd collapsed onto his own dry bed and slept soundly.

When Hugh had finished filling me in on his adventures, he asked about the beached boat in my front yard. I told him the story of Augusta's family, but he wouldn't meet them until later—they'd already left for the day, hoping to salvage a few more mementos from their house. Hugh already knew Jimmie, so I introduced him to Mimi. Jimmie had helped her into her wheelchair, and she sat at the dining table eating a breakfast of bananas and bottled water. Mimi may have been trapped and frightened, yet her courtly sense of dignity set the bar for the rest of us. She welcomed Hugh as if he were a gentleman arriving for high tea.

The three of us listened as Hugh relayed more news from the outside world. Joe came over from his house and joined us. He didn't comment—he'd already heard most of the grisly tales from New Orleans on his pocket radio. As Hugh talked, I watched Joe's face. His features were firmly set in a stoic mask, yet I knew his mind must be whirling with anxiety, plagued by the possibility that his daughter Robyn might still be in the city.

As Hugh wound down, Joe gave us the latest weather report. Severe storms were predicted that afternoon. Both of our houses had been ripped open by the hurricane and were extremely vulnerable. I could stand in my kitchen, look up and see blue sky. If we wanted to minimize further damage, we'd need to start immediately. Joe headed home to cover the worst parts of his own roof with some camping tarps he had on hand. Jimmie, Hugh, and I collected sheets of battered tin from the street. There was no shortage of it—pieces of my own roof and from many other houses littered the ground. The challenge was to find sheets that weren't too mangled or torn to be recycled.

The two men climbed up on my roof and perched high in the air. Although it was early morning, the heat was already stifling. I knew Jimmie must still be in great pain from his fall during the storm, but he and Hugh began to piece the crumpled tin over a few of the tremendous holes. To me, the project looked hopeless—they were trying to put Band-Aids on a land mine victim. Since I'm a silversmith and had hammered metal for a living, I figured I'd be able to work alongside the men. I was wrong. I'd swing down the hammer with all my strength and the nails would just bounce around on the surface of the tin. Rarely in my life have I felt such frustration at being a woman.

Finally, the guys grew tired of watching my ineptitude and suggested I try working on communications. They both gave me a list of numbers to try, to see if I could get a call out. I grabbed my bike and headed for the bridge, about two miles away. Jack wanted to come, but I sternly ordered him to stay behind. Under the murderous sun, even my tireless dog would be at risk for heat stroke.

The Georgia Power crews had already cleared most of the main arteries, so the going was much easier than the day before. I ran into two other friends biking with the same mission, and we pedaled on together. They're members of the Baptist church in Old Town and told me that a relief center was already being set up in the building. We marveled at the fact that the churches and the power companies had hit the ground running, while there was still no evidence of government help anywhere.

At the foot of the destroyed bridge, a crowd had already gathered. People held up phones like antennae, walking around trying to get a signal. Someone would call out, "I have three bars!" and everyone would flock to the lucky spot. Frustrated and hot, I punched in number after number without result, my anxiety level rising as the battery level ran down. Finally, the Washington, D.C., number of my friend Lucy began ringing and I crossed my fingers. When she answered, we both wept with relief.

She told me that my call to her the day before had actually connected for a moment without my knowledge. Lucy had heard my voice briefly, so knew that I was alive. Now she wanted details, but not knowing how many minutes we'd have before the tenuous connection was severed, I began to rattle off phone numbers. Lucy agreed to call a long list of strangers and let them know their loved ones had survived. Her top priority would be trying to get through to Joe's younger daughter, Andrea, who lived in Baton Rouge. Joe and I had been trying to imagine Robyn there, safe with her sister, but we needed confirmation for peace of mind.

Then Lucy asked me an odd question. "What do you guys need?" she demanded. "I need a list."

"We need everything," I answered wearily.

She persisted. "Give me specifics," she said. I was confused. How could Lucy, a thousand miles away, possibly get us supplies? The Red Cross couldn't even manage it. I vaguely promised to call her back with a list and signed off thinking that she'd been affected by some sort of delusional hysteria.

Before the battery ran out, I tried calling my parents' house in North Carolina again. Their phone had been busy the first time around. For three days, I'd been tortured, imagining the fear my eighty-four-year-old parents must have been experiencing. I visualized them sitting in front of the television, wringing their hands as they watched the mayhem, wondering if I'd survived. I snagged a connection and my mother answered the phone. Just hearing her sweet voice asking, "Hello?" triggered a stream of tears that poured down my cheeks.

"Mom, Mom! I'm alive, I'm OK!" I shouted into the phone.

"Well, yes," she said serenely. "Of course you are. Is anything wrong?"

I had to laugh. It turned out that my parents had obeyed the command I'd given them the night before the storm. Neither of them had watched the news. They'd believed my warning about how the media tries to turn every hurricane into a major catastrophe.

My sister, Diane, lives in a neighboring town. She kept our folks abreast of the basics, but she hadn't been particularly concerned about my well-being either. All the news reports were about New Orleans, with a few snippets covering Gulfport and Biloxi. Since my town was never mentioned, my sister assumed it had come through unscathed. None of my family knew enough about coast geography to realize that Bay St. Louis had been just east of the eye—the worst possible place. For once, I blessed the media for ignoring the Bay. I told my parents not to worry and recommended they continue their news boycott. Before my battery gave out, I

Lori Gordon at the slab of her Clermont Harbor house. For weeks after the storm, she went almost daily to sweep the intricate tile floor she had installed herself—the only part of her home that had remained intact. One day when she arrived, she found that an insurance adjuster had spray-painted it with claim information. Photograph by Joe Tomasovsky.

promised to call again soon. It was a promise I wasn't sure I could keep, but I wanted to reassure them.

I biked towards home and paused to look at the steeple from the Methodist church on Main Street. It had been neatly amputated and lay sadly on its side. A car suddenly screeched to a halt beside me. Lori leapt out, and we stood in the middle of the muddy street, embracing.

"I thought you were dead!" she cried. She confessed that on the night of the storm, she'd dreamed that Joe and I had both drowned. While Lori's an incredible artist, I was relieved to learn she was a lousy psychic.

The cottage crossing Sycamore Street that Jan and I passed through. My dog Jack stands in the foreground.

I greeted her husband, Cairo. The two of them had managed to make it down from Diamondhead, the community five miles north where they'd ridden out the storm. She told me that my other friends who had taken refuge there were safe as well. Because of blocked roads, Lori and Cairo weren't able to reach their Clermont Harbor neighborhood further west on the coast. She'd given up hope though. After seeing the utter defeat of the Old Town bluff, she knew that her house and studio built on lower elevation hadn't stood a prayer. She was right. When they finally made it back to Clermont Harbor two days later, not a single wall remained standing in the entire neighborhood.

By the time I got back to the house midmorning, another of the Diamondhead crew had arrived. Jan was a friend who owned a cottage a few blocks away on Sycamore Street. She'd fallen in love with Bay St. Louis two years before, purchased and renovated a small house on the bluff, then moved down from Pittsburgh that spring. Katrina was her first hurricane experience. She asked me if I'd walk with her to check on her house. Mimi was napping, while Hugh and Jimmie still worked on the roof, so I agreed to go.

I called for Jack and pushed my bike beside Jan. Half a block from her house, a small cottage sat skewed across the street, looking like a prop from *The Wizard of Oz*. We paused, wondering if we should change our route. Then we saw that others were actually passing through the house to get to the other side. I hauled my bike up and across the splintered porch. Jan apologized to the couple who moved around the doorless and exposed rooms. They were trying to salvage some of their belongings even as their home had become a pathway for strangers.

We were both delighted to find Jan's house still standing, and, at first glance, it appeared to be relatively unharmed. She heaved a grand sigh of relief and gratitude. I remember making some stupid, inane comment about how sometimes things turn out better than you think. Then Jan noticed that furniture from her dining room was strewn around her front yard. The dining room had been at the rear of the house. The yard was piled high with debris; we couldn't pick our way back to see that the rear walls of the house had been blown out. We peered through the muddy front windows and saw that six feet of water had torn through the rest of the cottage, ruining everything.

Unable to enter her house, we were drawn towards the beach, a block away. A few doors down, we ran into one of Jan's neighbors. Bob smiled as he greeted us, and then gave an account of how he'd survived by hanging on to a magnolia tree. After listening to his story, I couldn't believe the man could even talk, much less be in good spirits.

We slogged ahead. The closer we got to the front, the more my heart bled. Several houses past Jan's, the neighborhood simply vanished. I stood in front of the slab that had been the house of my friends Al and Mark. A few weeks before, I'd enjoyed a dinner party on their patio. Afterwards, we'd lounged in the pristine pool that had been perfectly landscaped. It was softly lit on that warm night. We'd all joked about synchronized swimming, then jumped in and given it a go ourselves. Al had "directed" the small group of friends, making me laugh until I cried. Now I just cried. Absurdly, all that remained of the 1920s bungalow was the tiny Spanish-style pool house. The pool itself was filled with an evil concoction of black sludge and debris, the stuff of nightmares.

In shock, Jan continued walking along the waterfront alone, while Jack and I turned towards home. My nostrils stung from the acrid stench that rose out of the steaming mud. There was no respite from the midday sun— all leaves had been torn from every tree. I biked slowly, but the four blocks back in the blinding heat exhausted us both. Jack panted desperately, and I felt smothered by a coating of thick, sticky sweat. We stopped briefly at the home of two retired brothers who lived on Citizen Street. They had the only generator in the neighborhood and had opened their house to anyone who needed to charge cell phones. I plugged mine in for round two at the bridge that evening.

Back home, I found that Hugh had gone to search for more drinking water. He and Jimmie had completed what temporary repairs they could under the circumstances. A few of the gaps in my roof were now covered and just in time—thunderheads gathered on the horizon. Jimmie and I used the last of our energy to haul in the furniture and bedding we'd put out to dry.

When the rain began in the early afternoon, torrents poured from what was left of my roof onto the back deck. Jimmie and I were quickly soaked as we worked to position every available container under the eaves, catching it for later use. Then the cascades of rain beckoned to me irresistibly. I hadn't had a shower in four days and didn't know when I'd have another chance. I grabbed soap, shampoo, and conditioner and stood beneath a gush of water. Modesty took a back seat to necessity as I scrubbed furiously to remove the layers of dirt. Never had a shower felt so good.

Jimmie had the same idea and bathed at the other end of the porch. My deck is built ten feet above the ground, so I could look down and see Joe showering in his own backyard. We laughed and waved. Later, I found out that people all over town had taken advantage of the same downpour and had happily rinsed the grime from their bodies.

Suddenly, I was struck by a bizarre idea. I may have been living in a Road Warrior environment, but my feminine genes would not be denied. I grabbed a razor from inside, came back out, and began to shave my legs in the rain. When I was finished, I felt like a new woman. Invigorated, I raced around the house for the next half hour, mopping up water and emptying buckets. The patches had done little to stop the water from pouring back into the house.

The storm ended, and I realized that Mimi would probably enjoy a real bath as well. Jimmie helped her into the wheelchair, rolling her onto the tiled kitchen floor. We set up her walker in front of it. Then Jimmie borrowed my bike and rode towards the hospital, hoping to bring back medical help for his mother. When he'd left, I helped Mimi undress. I brought in pots of water from the sacred bathtub reservoir and started from the top down, washing her hair first. It didn't matter how much water got on the kitchen floor; it was already a new pool from the thunderstorm. While I bathed her, she alternated between sitting and standing with the support of her walker.

After drying her off, I helped her into a "gown" I created from one of Joe's old soccer shirts. I'd cut out the arms and slit it down the sides so it'd be cooler. Once her hair was combed, she asked for more perfume and some lipstick. I chose a color that complemented the red soccer shirt. Mimi liked the fact that her new gown was emblazoned with the name "Patriots."

When I had settled Mimi into bed for a nap, I walked next door to check on Joe. He was up on his roof working. Cleo the squirrel raced up and down the brick chimney as easily as if it'd been a tree. She'd gotten restless after being confined in the cage for three days, so Joe had released her. A branch the size of a large tree had fallen beside his living room window, and Cleo had already made a nest there. From that vantage point, she could see through the window into the house. She liked to keep an eye on Joe.

Suddenly, a formation of military helicopters began roaring overhead. One after another, they passed low across the yard. The deep slapping of the blades reverberated through my body.

"They're finally here!" I shouted to Joe, hoping to be heard over the racket. "The cavalry's arrived!"

Joe shook his head. "Nope," he yelled back over the thundering engines. "I heard on the radio that Bush is doing a flyover on his way back from vacation. This is probably just his military escort."

I thought about Mimi, who was one of Bush's biggest supporters, and shook my head in disbelief. The president of the United States might be flying right over us, but he was light years distant from the suffering below him.

The surprises continued as we watched an SUV pull up in front of Joe's house. We both gaped as his brother Jerry climbed out and greeted us casually, as if he were dropping in for a friendly visit. He'd driven 250 miles from Kosciusko, Mississippi, his home north of Jackson. A retired military man, he hadn't been daunted by the warnings about roads being closed. He'd taken the back routes, stopping often to cut his way through with the chain saw he'd brought. Along the way, Jerry had joined many locals who were busily clearing their own sections of road, not waiting for the National Guard.

Jerry was planning to return home that evening and agreed to take Mimi and Jimmie with him to Jackson. Certainly there, she'd have access to medical care. That crisis resolved, Jerry revved up the chain saw and went to work clearing the driveway. Joe's truck had escaped damage, but it was impossibly blocked in. Massive limbs of live oak had broken off in the storm and created a heavy barricade. Meanwhile, Joe and I teamed up to unload the boxes of food, water, and ice that his brother had delivered. When we were finished, I went home to gather Mimi's belongings for the trip.

Later in the afternoon, Hugh returned to my house and found me resting in the shade of the front porch, hoping to catch a breeze. He offered me a ride to the bridge for another communications attempt, and I gratefully accepted. My legs ached. Hugh wove through back streets towards the bay. Georgia Power crews were still hard at work. It seemed like their trucks blocked every turn, but we were grateful. In just two days, they'd become my heroes, working tirelessly and efficiently. I couldn't help but wish that FEMA was a subsidiary.

On one narrow ribbon of road, the SUV in front of us stopped short. A slip of a woman got out and waved to some people sitting on the remains of their front porch. She signaled them over to the car, opened the back, and began handing out gallons of water, bottles of bleach, and bags of fruit. When I recognized her as my friend Denise, I leapt from Hugh's car and ran to greet her and her husband, Mark, who was driving.

Denise told me that on Sunday, she and Mark had evacuated their beachfront home in Waveland, finally finding refuge in a Florida panhandle hotel with their four dogs and four cats. Wednesday morning, they filled their car with emergency supplies and drove the two hundred miles back to the Bay, knowing they'd be returning to a bare lot and a beaten town. I'd caught them in the process of distributing the goods door to door, giving freely to anyone they came across. Denise told me that they'd be back on Friday and asked what she could bring me.

Then this woman who had lost everything she owned—all of her worldly possessions—gave me a bag of apples. This simple act of generosity rocked me to the marrow. Never had a gift meant as much. As we drove away, Hugh and I devoured the fruit. It seemed like months since I'd had fresh food. The tart taste of my apple was mixed with the salt of my tears.

We joined the other cell-phone hopefuls at the water's edge, but I only managed to connect with Andrea before my battery died. My heart shriveled when she told me that Robyn was not with her in Baton Rouge. The last Andrea had heard, her sister had intended to stay in New Orleans. She'd been unable to contact Robyn since Sunday night.

The ride home was depressing and seemed many miles long. I rehearsed the way I'd deliver the bad news before I came to a conclusion: there is no good way to tell a father that his daughter is trapped alone in a city gone berserk. However, I got a reprieve when we returned. Jimmie had found the only area hospital emergency room in a state of emergency and in no position to accept new patients. He and Mimi would be leaving shortly with Jerry. My household was overtaken by a flurry of activity as they prepared for departure.

We'd saved one clean housedress for Mimi. I helped her change out of the soccer shirt, combed her hair, and looked on as she used a small hand mirror to carefully reapply the lipstick. I tucked the tube in her overnight bag and we hugged tightly. I didn't want to let go, afraid this could be the last time I ever saw her.

"Darling, you're such a friend," Mimi said to me. "I'm so sorry I couldn't help more." The men carried her down the steps and helped her into Jerry's truck. They drove away while I waved good-bye from the front porch, wondering if it was possible to run out of tears.

I was still sniffling when Jan trudged up the stairs, exhausted from her marathon walk. She'd spent the rest of the day wandering through the town on foot, and her skin was sunburned to the point of blistering. Jan's a retired therapist and had used her skills to comfort anyone she came across. Hugh and I listened as she repeated some of the stories she'd heard. The most tragic was that of a family who'd clung to a tree in the swirling surge. The wife's strength gave out and with her last words, she charged her husband with the care of their small children. Then she let go of her branch and was carried away forever.

Joe brought over a meal he'd cooked on his camp stove using the groceries that Jerry had brought. The four of us ate on the front porch. None of us had much of an appetite, despite the enormous amounts of energy we'd expended in the grueling heat. Yet the ritual of a meal with friends provided an unexpected comfort.

After dinner, I caught Joe alone and relayed my conversation with Andrea. His expression didn't change, but something smoldered behind his eyes.

"Are you OK?" I asked.

Even as the words formed, I understood how ridiculous the question was, and Joe didn't answer. Instead, he told me that Robyn could take care of herself. "I've got faith in her," he said. "She's tough and she's smart." Then he bid me goodnight, turned away, and walked back across the yard alone. Since the inside of his house was as hot as a furnace, I knew he'd spend another night on the lawn chair in his driveway.

Augusta, Augusta-Inez, and Donald returned after dark to pack up their few belongings. Donald had secured them a place with friends in the country—one that featured the luxury of running water. We swapped news before they left, talking first about Augusta's friends who had died in their house just a block away. The roof had collapsed, crushing them as they slept. Donald told us that many of his power company colleagues had spent the day in the low-lying Lakeshore area, using cherry pickers to pluck bodies from the trees.

Then Augusta captured our attention by using the soft drawn-out tone of an elder telling a ghost story to children around a campfire. The candles burning on the front porch heightened the eerie effect.

"Well, now," she said. "I heard today that they found a body right here in this house. People are saying that they pulled a corpse from the attic of the old Webb School."

All eyes widened and rolled towards the ceiling. Augusta chuckled at our reaction. She said, "I told them, stop being silly. My family and I have been staying there for three days. We would've been the first to know."

Augusta left with hugs and thanks. Donald promised to drop by more drinking water in the morning. Hugh headed for his house, leaving Jan and me alone on the porch. I pulled out a bottle of wine I'd been saving for a special occasion, and we each downed a glass. Bats zipped across the porch, illuminated only by the flickering candles. Breezes brought welcome relief from the lingering heat, but they also carried something new, an ominous odor I didn't recognize. I wondered if it was the smell of death.

We decided to leave the doors open for the night, even though there was no sign of any law enforcement. This was still Bay St. Louis, and we weren't worried about personal safety. As for the danger of looters, I was too exhausted to care. I'd witnessed so much pain and loss in the past few days, defending possessions seemed petty. I climbed into the loft and both dogs leaped up beside me. Jan made her bed on the sofa directly below. We blew out the candles.

The total blackness was something I'd only experienced before camping out in deep desert—it was unsettling to have it surround us in my home. The silence of the town was palpable. There were no cars passing, no hum of electricity, no night creatures chirping. We talked softly while we shared our doubts in the darkness, but our voices resonated through the house.

"Why haven't they come?" Jan asked.

I knew who she was talking about. She meant the National Guard or the army or the Red Cross—somebody, *anybody*. Where was our country?

I thought about Iraq. I thought about communication and transportation problems. I also thought about Mimi. If Jerry hadn't arrived, she'd still be in the next room waiting for help. There were thousands of other Mimis who weren't as lucky. None of the flimsy excuses I invented for my government that night offered any true justification. A balloon of abandonment swelled in my chest.

"I don't know," I finally answered. Then despite the heat, I pulled the warm bodies of my dogs closer to me for comfort, shut my eyes, and tried to sleep.

PART FOUR
Robyn's Story

WIND IN THE WILLOW

When you're in pain or afraid, the hours stretch. Time distorts, extending itself in a way that both astonishes and horrifies you, like a snake coming out of a coil. For five days after the storm, Joe and I didn't know if his daughter Robyn was alive or dead. Each of those days seemed like a year. I couldn't even bring myself to listen to the harrowing news reports. While Joe seemed confident in the resourcefulness of his daughter and her ability to survive, I privately wondered how anyone could escape that pit of chaos unharmed.

Although Bay St. Louis had been crushed, it's a tightly knit community where neighbors helped neighbors in the aftermath. The media made it sound as if the fabric of community in New Orleans had completely unraveled and it was each man for himself. That turned out not to be entirely true. Robyn's strength, resourcefulness, and flexibility did save her, but she was helped along the way by the "kindness of strangers."

Imagine a woman alone. She's trapped in her apartment by poisonous floodwaters with a cat as her only companion. Communication isn't possible, so she can't call for help. The one radio station she can tune in tells stories of desperate people around her dying from starvation or bullet holes or from drowning in their own attics. She believes her father in a nearby town may have been killed by a tidal wave. The sounds of helicopters relentlessly remind her that she's smack in the middle of a war zone. She's caught in a city that's been wounded so badly that some lash out at hands trying to help.

This woman is no character created for a horror movie. She's real and her name is Robyn Tomasovsky. When people describe her, they're likely to use adjectives like "wispy" or "willowy." Sometimes she jokingly refers to herself as a "skinny white woman." But her fragile appearance belies the strength she possesses. The five perilous days she spent in New Orleans after Katrina prove the point.

SATURDAY, AUGUST 27   Robyn didn't intend to ride out the storm in town. Like so many others, she was prodded into that dark corner by circumstance. The first she heard of Katrina was on Saturday night, a day and a half before the hurricane washed away her world. She was packing for a move and updating her resume when the mother of a friend called and asked what she was doing for the storm. Alone in her apartment, she'd been focused on her tasks, listening to CDs instead of the news.

"What storm?" Robyn asked.

The rest of the night she continued packing while monitoring weather reports. Her plan was to wait until Sunday afternoon before evacuating to her sister Andrea's house in Baton Rouge. Maybe the storm would turn, as most before it had. If it didn't, evacuation would be easier without having to fight the main exodus leaving Saturday. Normally, it took just over an hour to reach Baton Rouge, but standstill traffic on Saturday had stretched the trip to seven or eight hours at best.

SUNDAY, AUGUST 28   She was right. The next day, the city seemed nearly deserted. Only a few cars darted through the rain-drenched streets as the storm's vanguard of feeder bands moved in. Robyn's truck was low on gas and one of the tires dangerously low, so she made a circuit around town looking for an open service station. Unfortunately, most businesses had already closed. Finally, she came across a single open station and filled both her tire and her tank. On the way back to her Mid-City apartment, she passed an open corner store and obeyed an impulse to stop. The shelves had been stripped. She made her selection from the dusty remains of stock and purchased cookies, candy, water, and cat food.

At home, she gathered her belongings and prepared her cat for the trip. Robyn began loading her truck, then paused to speak to her landlords, Hal and Charlie (names have been changed). The two older men lived on the other half of the raised duplex and had heard the latest report: the storm had been reduced to a Category 2. They were staying put.

Knowing the two older men would be next door in case of emergency and believing that the storm was no longer a major threat, Robyn decided to ride it out. To be on the safe side, she went through her normal hurricane preparation routine. She filled her bathtub and all available pots and pans with water. She readied her batteries and candles—even if the storm was only a 2, she knew that the power would probably go out for a day or so. She parked her truck on the sidewalk across the street, under the eaves of a large metal warehouse. Even though that "high ground" was only six inches above street level, experience had taught her that the added elevation would probably save her vehicle from street flooding caused by heavy rains. She noticed that her landlords had taken the same precaution by pulling into a neighboring driveway.

About 10 p.m., Andrea called, wanting to know why her sister hadn't arrived yet. When Robyn explained her decision and the reason behind it, Andrea's voice rose with fear.

"Robyn," she said. "The storm is back up to a 5!"

The rains poured down outside and winds already buffeted the house. At that point, Robyn realized that whatever number the storm was, she was now committed. The highway would be the worst place to be caught during a hurricane. Andrea wished her luck, begged her to stay in touch, and they disconnected. They wouldn't be able to speak again for five days.

Robyn's exhaustion overpowered the anxiety from her sister's warnings, so she headed for bed. Before she went to sleep shortly after 11 p.m., the power went out. Her cat, Day, snuggled against her in the dark as high winds shook the walls and rattled the windows. Robyn slept through what she imagined then was the worst part of the storm.

MONDAY, AUGUST 29   In the morning, it appeared that she'd made the right decision. The rains were still pelting down and gusts soared down the streets, yet the damage in her neighborhood seemed minimal. Once again, New Orleans had worked that hoodoo magic that sent most storms veering off at the last moment, sparing the city. While she was concerned about her father on the Mississippi coast where Katrina had actually hit, Robyn knew his house in Bay St. Louis was on high ground. He certainly wouldn't be having any storm surge problems.

She busied herself tidying up the apartment. Robyn was transferring ice from her freezer to her refrigerator to preserve food, when two friends from around the corner surprised her. They'd decided to stay in town as well and had walked over to check on her. She hadn't eaten yet, so accepted at once when they invited her back to their house for a Mexican lunch. Together the three sloshed around the corner through ankle-deep water, avoiding debris in their path.

After a celebratory meal of quesadillas and chocolate brownies, Robyn left for home, escorted by her friends. The time was around one o'clock. They were stunned to find that in just one hour, the water had risen to their knees. The rains had ended, so they couldn't imagine where the water was coming from. The direct route home was blocked by debris that had been blown onto the streets and was beginning to float. They were forced to detour around the block.

By the time Robyn arrived at her apartment, her heart raced as she bounded up the flight of stairs to her door. The relief she'd felt earlier had turned into a panicky urge to flee. She quickly kenneled her cat and gathered her essentials to load into the truck. Stepping out onto her porch less than an hour later, she saw that the water had risen even higher—it would have been up to her waist. While the engine of her truck hadn't been submerged, driving anywhere would be impossible. She waded up to the corner of Bienville Street—a main thoroughfare that ran from the French Quarter towards the suburb of Metairie. Bienville had become a canal. Water covered the street as far as she could see in both directions. A man slogging his way through the flood told her that towards the Quarter things were even worse. He said he'd heard the water was as high as sixteen feet at one major intersection.

Dumbfounded, Robyn returned to her apartment and dried off. Her land line was dead and her cell phone wasn't getting out. The only station on the radio still broadcasting was WWL, a talk show station in normal times. Now it had become a switchboard, fielding calls from rescue workers and officials and desperate people trapped around the city—some calling from their attics. Robyn remembers how one couple spoke while watching their own death approach, the water around them inching up their bodies. They left their names and address with the announcer so that their family could be notified. Evening approached, and, as Robyn lit candles, the enormity of the disaster began to filter through her shock.

From her back window, she could look down into the backyard of a neighboring house. In the garden stood a statue on a pedestal. Robyn thought the bust was the likeness of some ancient Roman official—the laurel wreath crowning its head made it look like a "Caesar with hair." She picked this statue to be her flood gauge. When she went to bed, she promised herself she wouldn't worry unless the water came up to his chin. In the middle of the night, she peered down from her window and, aiming her flashlight at the statue, could see that the water was up to his nose. She upped the stakes, telling herself it wouldn't really be bad unless the water rose to his eyes. When she woke close to dawn, his eyebrows were covered. She decided to quit playing that game. It was obviously time to worry.

TUESDAY, AUGUST 30   The news the next morning brought no comfort. The only word from the Mississippi coast was one ominous statement on the radio that Bay St. Louis had been completely wiped off the map and was "gone." Robyn's spirits sank, thinking of her father being washed out to sea. He didn't feel gone to her—they still seemed psychically connected—yet how could he have possibly survived?

Shortly later, a conversation with her landlords brought more distressing news. The radio had warned that during planned levee repair attempts, the water could rise as much as nine additional feet in parts of the city. So far, the upstairs of the duplex had remained uncompromised, and only the vacant apartment and storage area downstairs had flooded. But nine more feet would bring the water close to the ceilings on the second floor. They needed to find a safe refuge and find it fast.

Robyn's apartment is what people in New Orleans refer to as a "shotgun." The rooms are lined up one after the other with no hallway. Supposedly, you could shoot a gun through the front door and the bullet would go out the back without hitting anything—if no one was in the way. Robyn began pacing through the rooms, from front to back, making laps as she tried to burn off nervous energy. The sensation of being trapped like a mouse in a cage brought with it an overpowering feeling of desperation. Soon, even her small sanctuary would be inundated. She tried to imagine swimming through water, holding the cat carrier aloft. It'd be an impossible feat.

Finally, she sat on the bed, totally overwhelmed and on the point of giving up. She struggled to gather her wits and order her priorities. If her worldly possessions were going to be submerged, she first needed to protect important papers and sentimental treasures. She'd shaken off the paralysis of panic and had begun sealing her valuables in plastic food-storage bags when her landlords approached her with an idea.

Hal and Charlie may have been on the far side of middle-aged, but they were active and resourceful. The two men had devised a plan to evacuate to the flat roof of the warehouse across the street. Charlie had already carried over an extension ladder and positioned it against the warehouse wall to provide access. If they all went up to the rooftop, they'd be safe even if the water rose an additional fifteen feet. Robyn didn't hesitate to join them.

Together, they ferried supplies across the street in water that came to Robyn's chest (she measured herself later and found that the depth must have been fifty-two inches). Pets were included in the evacuation—Hal and Charlie brought their two parakeets and their own cat. Robyn easily moved Day in the carrier, but her landlords' dog presented another problem. Boots was a large lab mix and no one would be able to carry her up to the roof. Robyn's facility of communicating with animals came to the rescue—she patiently taught the large dog to climb the ladder. Robyn pushed from behind while Charlie pulled on Boots's leash, and together they coaxed the dog up the rungs, one by one.

Their new refuge turned out to be a series of connected roofs—most of the entire square block was covered by various commercial and industrial structures built with adjoining walls. The roof was wickedly hot—the afternoon sun beat down ruthlessly and they had no place to hide. The two men created a lean-to from tarps, while Robyn made repeated trips back to their apartments, shuttling more supplies up to the roof.

In between trips, she explored the territory and photographed the neighborhood below. Growing up with a photography teacher as a father, she'd learned the importance of recording history. Robyn's the sort of person who manages to find beauty in the most unlikely places. She took pictures of the iridescent patterns created by the oil suspended on the surface of the flood.

Late in the afternoon, the stranded trio hailed a motorboat passing below. Spirits soared as two people in scrub suits steered the boat towards the warehouse. They identified themselves as staff from a nearby medical center and offered to take the trio to safety. At first, the group was jubilant and prepared to board the boat. Then their would-be rescuers told them that no pets would be allowed—only people. There was a long silence.

The three didn't have to discuss the option—none of them was willing to abandon their animal companions. The man and woman in the boat must never have owned any pets themselves, because they became impatient and then irritated at the group's refusal to leave their animals behind. Without further discussion, they shrugged their shoulders and turned the boat away. The group was stunned when it became apparent that they were being left for good. Apparently, the sight of the dismay on their faces moved the man on the boat to act with a little compassion. Wordlessly, he hurled three small bottles of water towards the rooftop before the boat motored out of sight.

As evening approached, swarms of ravenous mosquitoes attacked, hungry enough to bite through clothing. When the radio announced that the water was probably not going to rise dramatically, the men decided it'd still be prudent to stay in their new campground. Robyn had concerns about Day overheating in the carrier, so opted to take a chance and return to her apartment for the night. It might flood, but at least it had screens.

The heat inside was maddening and no breeze penetrated her open windows. The gasoline coating the surface of the floodwaters emitted a noxious smell that filled her room. Periodically, she spritzed herself with a spray bottle to keep cool. Outside, the normal night noises of the inner city had changed. Boats and refrigerators that had been stored in a nearby lot floated freely, clashing and clanging as they collided against each other. Robyn was reminded of her childhood, when she'd spent the night dockside at a river community.

Drifting into an exhausted slumber, she took a final precaution. She draped one arm over the edge of the bed and rested her hand on the floor, hoping she'd wake in the night if water invaded her house.

WEDNESDAY, AUGUST 31   Robyn woke to the sound of a helicopter, the first of many. The number of flights overhead escalated throughout the day until it became a constant stream. The noise grated against her tattered nerves. A quick inventory of her supplies didn't help matters— she'd finished the last of her drinking water. The rest of the food in her refrigerator had gone bad, and she'd eaten most of the nonperishables she had on hand. Cleaning out her fridge, she threw out some bread that was beginning to mold. Later she retrieved it from the trash for lunch.

Hal and Charlie descended from their rooftop camp, and Boots proved how adaptable she was by backing down the ladder with a little help. The two men still had some food, yet their drinking water was gone as well. While Robyn had lost most of the water in the tub she'd filled before the storm because of a slow leak, she still had a good supply left in her pots and pans. It wasn't very appealing to think about drinking water that'd been sitting in the open for three days, but neither was eating moldy bread.

Other emergency measures included going to the bathroom in a bucket. She lined the container with a garbage bag, tying it up and placing it into a covered can when she was finished. Plastic was proving to be a valuable commodity. She spent much of the morning debating which of her possessions deserved the chance of survival in one of her precious ziplock bags. Like a squirrel hiding nuts, she shuffled contents, then moved the bags around her apartment again and again, hoping to find a high place that would be safe. She tried to observe her behavior objectively and realized that she must have looked like a madwoman rearranging deck furniture on the Titanic.

Feeling stir-crazy, she returned to the roof of the warehouse, where at least she had a bird's-eye view of the neighborhood. The water that she crossed had developed an unpredictable character—sometimes it ran with a current and at other times it was as still as a lake. It was fouled with debris and trash and emitted a rank odor. She worried about the chemicals that it carried. The radio had warned of major toxic wastes that had been freed by the flood.

Once she'd made the circuit of the roofs, she returned to her apartment, inspired by an idea. She began to create a perch on her own roof, so she wouldn't have to wade across the river to see what was going on. Hal and Charlie helped her place boards across the railing of their porch onto the one next door, less than ten feet away. A ladder was placed atop this impromptu scaffolding. Using this method, Robyn was able to climb onto her own tiled roof. Over the next three days, the few neighbors who remained in the neighborhood would call out when they spotted her there. "Hey, Cat Woman!" they'd cry.

It became a day for visitors. The first was a neighbor she'd never met previously, Bobby. He was wading through the chest-high water, checking on people from house to house. He chatted amicably and they swapped rumors and news. She learned that Bobby was a Vietnam vet who lived just a few streets over. He assured her that he'd check in the next day just to see how they were doing.

Even from her porch, Robyn could see down to the Bienville Street intersection. Boats cruised up and down Bienville as easily as cars. Most of them seemed to be fishing boats, the shallow, flat-bottomed kind used for navigating bayous. Since her block had more commercial buildings than houses, no one even looked her way. But later in the afternoon, a boat cruised up to her house, manned by two men in their early twenties. They introduced themselves as Peter and Danny (names have been changed) and explained that they were running a free delivery service for stranded neighbors, using the boat they'd commandeered. They were distributing supplies they'd pilfered from nearby grocery stores. The stores had already been looted, but still had a good selection of needed items. These modern-day Robin Hoods stocked her with water, batteries, a lighter, matches and candles, Band-Aids, and antibiotic ointment before they left, promising to return the next day.

That evening, she sat alone in her apartment with her cat. Day was behaving strangely and refused to leave the post she'd established by the front door. Day was an indoor cat, but she seemed to know that the apartment was no longer a safe haven. Robyn lit some of the candles that Danny and Peter had given her. The setting of the sun hadn't done much to relieve the heat, and the stench worsened by the hour. Now the air she breathed carried much more than the odor of gasoline. Every molecule of oxygen she drew in seemed tainted with a vile blend of decay from the dead bodies of people and animals, human waste, and the colorful assortment of chemicals floating below. Helicopters still rumbled overhead—there'd been no letup in the racket all day.

Sleep evaded her at first. Robyn worried about her father. If he were still alive, he would be frantic about her safety. She worried about her sister. Andrea would be in Baton Rouge, feeding her newborn son, wondering if he was going to have a chance to know his aunt. She looked around her rooms, at her furniture and possessions illuminated by the candlelight. She wondered which things would survive the water and which would perish. Finally, her natural optimism took a playful turn and she came up with a new game. She tried to imagine various belongings and furniture after they'd been immersed in water. Some of her possessions would be ruined, but the rank baptism might actually improve the looks of others. A good soaking might leave behind an interesting patina and give her newer pieces a little character.

Her sleep was punctuated by nightmares that would continue to plague her for months. Most of the dreams had the common theme of rising water. Her mind spun out a series of vivid images from all the desperate calls she'd heard on the radio. One call had especially distressed her—it'd been from a mother trapped in an attic with several children, including a newborn. Robyn's still uncertain about their fate: "The announcer begged anybody with a boat to go to that area and help them. I imagined them in the dark with the water and the bugs and the children and it just kills me still. I don't know what happened to them."

THURSDAY, SEPTEMBER 1   Thursday morning, Peter and Danny arrived in the flatboat with their daily delivery, just as they'd promised. Robyn and her landlords had been placed on their list of regular "customers." Robyn told them that she was determined to leave, but everyone she'd been able to talk with had assured her it was impossible. She wanted to see with her own eyes.

"If it's true, put me on your boat and show me," she demanded. The young men obliged and rode her around the neighborhood towards the interstate. By the time they returned to her house half an hour later, she'd been convinced of the futility of escape.

Robyn took one more trip across to the warehouse roof to retrieve more of the supplies the group had left behind. She was more cautious this time—during a previous venture to Bienville Street, she'd heard a frightening story. A man on his porch had shouted down a warning to her. He said he'd heard on the radio that a three-foot shark had attacked a deputy. When she'd repeated this incredible rumor to her landlords, they said they'd seen a small alligator swim past the house, eyes emerging from the dark brew.

While she was crossing over to the warehouse, she noticed a yellow substance floating on the surface of the water. When she returned home, she found that her elbow was capped with a dark brown paste that was beginning to burn her skin. A putrid yellow slime also covered her shirt. She quickly shed all her clothes and was horrified to see that her whole body was covered with an oily film. She used a bottle of rubbing alcohol to scrub herself. The brown stuff on her elbow didn't want to come off, even with the alcohol. Robyn didn't go into the water again.

Bobby came by on his regular rounds later, and she voiced her concerns for his health. She was worried about what effects the constant immersion in the toxic waters might have on him. Bobby shrugged it off. He reassured Robyn that he was a vet, he'd been through worse. He wasn't about to stop checking in on his neighbors.

She still dreamed of rescue. From her roof perch late in the afternoon, Robyn tried to flag down some of the helicopters flying over her house. An unremitting stream passed overhead, and now she noticed that many of them were military aircraft. She had counted four basic types of choppers being used for rescue efforts and had already learned to identify them by their sound alone. From listening to the radio, she realized that these rescuers weren't taking pets, but she hoped to persuade them to send someone who would. A few of the aircraft flew so low, she could clearly see the crew members, yet no one paid attention to the slender blond woman signaling them from her rooftop. At last, she gave up and climbed down from her post.

The evening hours approached, but the long light of summer was still in the sky when WWL anchor Garland Robinette began broadcasting an interview with New Orleans mayor Ray Nagin. Robyn was instantly caught up by the mayor's raw pleas for help. Later, outside sources would label the interview as sounding "rambling," but she could relate to the disjointed despair. Nagin voiced the same sense of futility, the same frustration, and the same heartbreak that she and thousands of other New Orleans residents felt. The following text was taken from a transcript found on the CNN Web site.

You know the reason the looters got out of control? Because we had most of our resources saving people, thousands of people that were stuck in attics, man, old ladies . . . You pull off the doggone ventilator vent and you look down there and they're standing there in water up to their freaking necks.

And they don't have a clue what's going on down here. They flew over one time two days after the doggone event was over with TV cameras, AP reporters, all kind of goddamn—excuse my French everybody in America, but I am pissed . . .

. . . one of the briefings we had, they were talking about getting public school bus drivers to come down here and bus people out here. I'm like, "You've got to be kidding me. This is a national disaster. Get every doggone Greyhound bus line in the country and get their asses moving to New Orleans.". . . They're thinking small, man. And this is a major, major, major deal. And I can't emphasize it enough, man. This is crazy . . .

. . . We're getting reports and calls that are breaking my heart, from people saying, I've been in my attic, I can't take it anymore. The water is up to my neck. I don't think I can hold out. And that's happening as we speak . . .

. . . Now you mean to tell me that a place where most of your oil is coming through, a place that is so unique when you mention New Orleans anywhere around the world, everybody's eyes light up—you mean to tell me that a place where you probably have thousands of people that have died and thousands more that are dying every day, that we can't figure out a way to authorize the resources we need? Come on, man . . .

. . . And I don't know whose problem it is. I don't know whether it's the governor's problem. I don't know if it's the president's problem, but somebody needs to get their ass on a plane and sit down, the two of them and figure this out right now . . . Don't tell me 40,000 people are coming here. They're not here. It's too doggone late. Now get off your asses and do something and let's fix the biggest goddamn crisis in the history of this country!

As Robyn listened to the interview, river sounds drifted up, sounds that didn't belong in a neighborhood miles away from any normal waterway. The humid summer air used to carry the scents of jasmine and honeysuckle. Now it reeked of death. She was one woman, alone in this new world of sorrow, tapping into the emotion of the voices on the radio. The willow bent. For the first time since Katrina came to town, Robyn cried.

THE LONG ROAD HOME

FRIDAY, SEPTEMBER 2   When a stream of low-flying helicopters woke Robyn at dawn, she had no idea that her next sleep would be thirty-six hours away. What she did know was that hope couldn't change her situation. The water was not going down. No one was coming to take her and Day to a safe place. She was stuck with scant supplies, dependent on two boys in a stolen boat to deliver food and water. Her apartment—normally pristine and orderly—was miserably hot, damp, and filthy. A week's worth of wet clothes lay strewn by the front door exactly where she'd shed them. The floors were coated with a sheen of toxic muck she'd tracked in, despite her best efforts to clean her feet.

Robyn had gone down the rabbit hole and found herself in a world where security was just a memory. Outside her four walls, she had no influence or control—the Mad Hatter was in charge. But inside those walls, she saw changes she could make to improve her situation. She gathered some cleaning supplies and began to scrub the floors. By noon, she had almost finished sterilizing the front rooms when she heard Bobby call out from the street. They talked for a few minutes before she asked a favor. She wanted him to find some bird food—her landlords had run out of seed for their parakeets. The veteran burst out laughing, but promised to do what he could before he waded away to finish his rounds.

Robyn worked on her house the rest of the afternoon. Late in the day, she was mopping the kitchen when she heard Bobby calling again. The words "bird food" were the only ones she could make out, so she raced to the front porch. Bobby stood chest deep in the water before her house, grinning in triumph although his hands were empty. Then something snagged Robyn's eye. A burst of bright orange rounded the corner at the end of the street. Confused, she asked Bobby what was going on, but by the time the words were out of her mouth, two boats with Coast Guard markings had motored into view. Bobby had led the rescue teams to her house. For the second time in Robyn's ordeal, tears streamed down her face.

As the boats approached, she stood paralyzed by disbelief. One of the boats stopped in front of her gate, as casually as a cab. The two crewmen wore fire department uniforms and bright life vests. "Come on," one called. "We're taking you and your pets."

Startled into action, she asked for a few minutes to gather her things. Then she alerted Hal and Charlie, insisting that they come along. In her apartment, she quickly kenneled Day, changed into some fresh clothes, and grabbed a handful of clean underwear, her camera, two journals, and a dictionary. She was ready to go.

The firemen didn't want her to get into the water, so they eased the boat in through the gate until it bumped against the submerged steps to her porch. Robyn handed Day across, then with one hand gripping the porch railing and the other the hand of a fireman, she stepped onto the bow. Once aboard, the firemen helped her into a fluorescent life jacket. Hal and Charlie boarded next, bringing only their dog. Their cat had escaped on the rooftop days before, and they'd released the birds earlier in the afternoon, hoping they'd fend for themselves. The ever-adaptable Boots settled down at their feet at once, eager for another adventure. As the boat began to move towards Bienville Street, Robyn waved to Bobby and took his picture. The vet stood in the water and waved back. He wasn't going to leave his post as long as anyone in his neighborhood remained.

The boat floated through the flooded streets, the firemen on the lookout for other stranded survivors. A few blocks away, the stench that had surrounded Robyn's house grew more powerful, intensifying until it stung her nostrils. Looking ahead, she saw what appeared to be bundles of clothes that had been carried by the current and pushed into a cluster at the end of a street. Before she could register exactly what she was seeing, Charlie said, "There's those dead people." Robyn lowered her camera and turned away in revulsion.

To distract herself, she talked to her rescuers, who were members of the Phoenix fire department. They were part of a rescue team called Arizona Task Force One. The two men handled the boat with an expertise she wouldn't have expected from desert dwellers. When they reached Canal Street several blocks over, the name of the street took on a new meaning. Boats filled with people moved up and down the lanes, making it seem like some surrealistic Venetian waterway.

Robyn's boat didn't pick up anyone else and eventually made its way to the intersection of Metairie Road and Interstate 10—about two miles from her house. There the elevated freeway rose well above the floodwaters, but the ramps leading upward now serviced boats instead of cars. At the top of the overpass, the Mid-City neighbors gathered, several of them holding dogs or cats. They waited to board a collection of vehicles that included two large cargo trucks and a tour bus. Robyn roamed through the crowd, her camera capturing exhaustion, confusion, and relief on the faces of survivors and rescuers alike. In two of the shots she framed, enormous plumes of smoke rose in the distance, streaming into the twilight behind the silhouettes of weary firefighters.

Originally, the task force had anticipated transporting sixty evacuees. By the time they left at dark, over a hundred people and a variety of pets were in their charge. People piled into the backs of the covered trucks, but Robyn was lucky enough to be assigned a seat on the bus. Members of the rescue team clustered around the driver in the front and she sat directly behind them, Day's carrier on her lap.

Robyn and the others hadn't been told exactly where they were going, but she hoped it'd be some Red Cross station where a nice nurse would meet her, offering a hot meal, a shower, and a clean cot. She'd be able to use a telephone, let her family know she was safe, and find out about her father.

She listened closely to the firemen in front of her. After a while, she understood that they'd been given little or no instruction and seemed to be at a loss as to where to take the survivors they'd rescued. The general consensus was to drive west, but the direct route was blocked by the water. They were forced to head back on the interstate into the heart of the city and work their way out on back roads. As they drove slowly down the deserted freeway, they passed throngs of stranded people standing on the side of the road. For at least a mile, Robyn watched the faces of families huddled together, waiting with resignation. Some looked longingly at her bus as it passed. She noticed a few official cars scattered through the crowds at long intervals, but there were no signs of food stations or transportation.

They passed the Superdome and had connected with a back road going west, when Robyn first heard the New Orleans airport mentioned as a drop-off point. Apparently, it'd been set up as a National Guard camp and a clearinghouse for refugees. She knew from the radio that conditions there were abysmal, yet it was fifteen miles closer to Baton Rouge. At least she was moving in the right direction.

By the time the convoy arrived at the airport, a thick darkness enveloped the city, unrelieved by any electric lights. As they turned onto the access road, the headlights of the bus illuminated two armed guards barring the way. Both were in uniform, although Robyn couldn't make out the markings. One of guards cradled a large rifle in his arms.

A member of her rescue team got off the bus and approached the guards, engaging them in conversation, gesturing towards the convoy. Robyn couldn't hear the negotiations outside, but suddenly the short-wave radio by her driver crackled. She clearly heard a horrifying command as it pierced the quiet of the bus.

"You have ten minutes to vacate the premises or we're going to open fire on you and your refugees."

Incredulous, Robyn looked at the other passengers behind her. Several of them had also heard the threat and their eyes met with expressions of bewilderment and horror. The firemen on board remained calm and did not comment. Then the door to the bus opened and the liaison rejoined his group. All he said was, "OK, fellas, pull out." No other words were spoken. The convoy reversed its direction and headed back into no-man's land.

According to other witnesses, Robyn's account of the event and the wording of the threat is precise. Although the firemen never knew for certain who issued that terrible warning, one of the team later said, "It was total anarchy—anarchy that existed for days. I remember what one policeman told me. He said that we might be standing on American soil, but it wasn't America anymore."

One of the fireman walked down the aisles, handing out the only comfort he could offer—Snickers candy bars. He apologized over and over, wishing that his team could do more.

"The thing I'll take with me the rest of my life," he said later, "is the way those individuals were so stoic and thankful. They knew we didn't have any other options, and they were thanking us for trying to help. There we were, the fire department from one of the largest cities in the country, and we didn't have more resources to offer them."

Robyn listened as the firemen tried to come up with a new plan of action. The radio communication between the convoy vehicles buzzed with questions and ideas. Her heart squeezed as they turned back towards the city. They began to backtrack on Airline Highway, the old main artery between Baton Rouge and New Orleans that runs parallel to the interstate. After traveling a few miles, they pulled into the parking lot of an abandoned strip shopping center. Across the street, a National Guard unit was setting up an encampment on a football field.

Everyone got out of the vehicles, stretching their legs while their fate was decided. Robyn took the opportunity to slip behind the deserted stores and use the bathroom on the ground. When she returned, she and her fellow passengers were loaded onto another bus for reasons that were never made clear. As it pulled back onto the highway, the word quickly spread among the survivors that their new destination was the refugee camp at the interchange of Causeway Boulevard and Interstate 10.

To those who'd been listening to radio reports, this news evoked anxiety that bordered on panic. The horrors of the Causeway camp had already become legendary throughout the city. While the bus headed towards the Causeway, Robyn checked her cell phone and was surprised to find it still held a small charge. Even though she hadn't been able to get a signal since before the storm, she punched in her sister's number.

She was shocked as the call went through and Andrea's partner answered. Jeb was excited to learn that Robyn was alive and in good hands. In the frantic few moments they had before her phone cut off, she assured Jeb that she'd call back shortly when she could tell him more. Then, staring at the dead phone in her hand, she realized she hadn't even had time to ask about her father.

When Robyn got off the bus at the Causeway camp, she found she'd been transported from purgatory straight into the heart of hell. The camp had originally been set up as a triage center for the critically ill, but by the time Robyn arrived on Friday night, most accounts estimate that it had swollen to between five thousand and seven thousand want-to-be evacuees. Beneath the New Orleans overpass huddled the largest homeless colony in modern U.S. history.

Masses of people stood or squatted on ground that was covered by a thick layer of garbage. Some used pieces of cardboard for seats or bedding. The only cots she saw were being used for critically ill patients, many of them elderly and unconscious. They lay in rows, without even a tent overhead to shelter them.

Helicopters roared in and out of the camp without respite. The thrashing of their blades hurled a blizzard of trash through the air and the engine noise assaulted the ears of the weary crowds. Large generators added to the cacophony. The machines powered enormous work lights that glared down on the camp, adding to the surreal vision of despair.

Robyn followed the other people from her bus to the back of a nearby truck where they were each handed a plastic spoon, a can of ravioli, a snack bar, and a juice drink. She spotted Hal and Charlie in the crowd and worked her way through to them. Her landlords had heard that soon other buses would be arriving to take them to Houston, but as Robyn began talking to the people around her, she understood that no one was going anywhere soon. Some of those she approached had been in the camp for three or four days already. She heard that only three buses had arrived that day. No one could tell her who was in charge or where to ask for more information. Apparently, the authorities were as baffled as the civilians.

Someone pointed out a generator where people lined up for the chance to charge their cell phones. Robyn left Day in the care of her landlords and stood for almost two hours before she was able to plug in her phone. While she waited, she struck up conversations with those around her. Everyone was in the same sinking boat—nobody wanted to stay, but no one could get out. Those with family on the outside had been told no civilians were allowed anywhere near the city. All anyone could do was to wait for official transportation that hadn't materialized.

When Robyn was finally able to plug in her phone and call her sister, Andrea had been waiting and answered immediately. First, she reassured Robyn that their father had survived without injury. Then she wanted to know where Robyn could be picked up. Robyn didn't know what to tell her. The only thing she knew for sure was that she was not going to stay in the camp. She told Andrea that she would walk west along the interstate. If her sister drove east, eventually they'd run into each other. They agreed to the threadbare plan and disconnected.

Robyn rejoined her landlords, who had more bad news— the Guard was coming around to take people's pets. Robyn wasn't about to give up Day, and it seemed clear that if she was going to leave, the time had come. She struck out for the camp perimeter. When she reached the edge of the camp, a policeman stopped her at the barricades.

"You don't want to go out there," he warned. Robyn explained that her sister was planning to meet her on the interstate. The policeman told her that civilians weren't being allowed past LaPlace, twenty miles away. Robyn was undaunted and shouldered the cat carrier. If she had to walk twenty miles, she might as well get started. Again, the policeman tried to stop her.

"You're going to get away from these lights and you won't be able to see your hand in front of your face," he said. "It's not safe out there, but I can't hold you."

The policeman hadn't been exaggerating. Once Robyn left the boundaries of the camp, the darkness became impenetrable. She treaded carefully, feeling her way along through the littered streets. The cat carrier and the bag with her few chosen possessions grew heavier by the moment. Eventually, she turned back and could see only a faint glow from the camp behind her. Suddenly, a beam of light pierced the darkness and came to rest on her, blinding her with its glare. Robyn froze in terror, unable to move in any direction.

Then a compassionate woman's voice came out of the night.

"It's OK, darling."

Robyn sighed with relief. She followed the beam of light to its source and found herself in a small camp of refugees. They told her that they'd also found conditions under the Causeway unbearable and had escaped earlier in the evening. There were seven or eight adults and three children gathered at the side of the road. One toddler slept on the ground, another wandered between the adults, and a small baby rested in its mother's arms. When they offered Robyn food, she politely refused. "I've got some almonds," she said, not wanting to take what scant supplies they might have. They urged her to stay with them for the night, but Robyn declined. The fright had convinced her of the danger of walking alone. She left the group and returned to the camp's circle of lights, thinking that if she were persistent, she could find some sort of transportation.

When she arrived back at the camp, she approached several people before she understood that there was no hope of getting any ride out. Giving up Day or sleeping in such a place were both out of the question. Just past midnight, she made a decision to leave again, determined that she wouldn't be so easily frightened this time around. As she neared the barricades, she spotted a familiar face. A gentle-faced man with glasses was walking in the same direction, leading two dogs on leashes. One of the dogs was a Weimaraner and looked as if it might provide some protection.

"Hey, weren't you on my bus?" Robyn asked. "Where are you going?"

The man hadn't been on Robyn's bus, but he'd been in the same convoy, riding in the back of a cargo truck. He introduced himself as Michael Homan, a professor of Bible at Xavier University. He was fleeing the camp in hopes of keeping his dogs. Later he would write, "I could not have ever told my children that I gave up the dogs to save myself."

His story was much the same as Robyn's—he'd been trapped in his Mid-City house until he'd been picked up by boat and brought to the Causeway. In the hours that Robyn had stood in line to make a call, Michael had explored the camp. His own written account describes what he witnessed:

> I saw murdered bodies and elderly people who had died because they had been left in the sun with no water for such a long time . . . I saw many people with Down's syndrome, and casts, catheters, wheel chairs, all sorts of stuff . . . Total disorder reigned on the ground inside the camp. I was glad I had my dogs with me, as that place was anything but safe. People inside the camp told me that they had been there three days. They were sitting outside without food and water in near 100-degree heat just waiting for buses . . . I've traveled quite a bit, and I have never seen the despair and tragedy that I saw at this refugee camp. It was the saddest thing I have ever seen in my life. I am still so upset that there were not hundreds of buses immediately sent to get these people to shelters . . .

The two new friends cast their lots together and resolved to head for LaPlace. As they were leaving, they were approached by a man Robyn had spoken with earlier. His name was Carlos and he asked if he could join them. Robyn and Michael accepted him into their makeshift tribe, and, about one o'clock in the morning, the three began a journey that would last through the night. Robyn had spent much of her life working in the movie business and she tried to visualize how the group would look on film. No writer could have invented a stranger cast of characters: a skinny white woman atheist, a kindly professor of religion, an African American oil rig worker, a black cat in a kennel, a Weimaraner, and a small, white fluffy dog.

SATURDAY, SEPTEMBER 3   They trudged through the night, headed southwest. Carlos said he knew a shortcut to Airline Highway, so they walked through dark neighborhoods that had been abandoned. Although Robyn is physically strong, it didn't take long for her to tire. She'd been exhausted when they'd left the camp, and the four-year-old sandals she wore had not been made for long treks through mud. She turned down repeated offers from the men to carry her cat—Day was her responsibility and her burden alone. She moved the carrier clockwise around her fatigued body: first she carried it on her right hip, then moved it to her right shoulder, up to the top of her head, down to her left shoulder, and finally to her left hip. By the time the carrier had made the circuit, she had to stop. She insisted that the men go on without her, but they refused. Exhausted as well, they all took a long break before continuing on together.

As they walked through one neighborhood, they spotted a house with a candle burning on the front steps. Robyn called out a tentative, nonthreatening "Hello?" Through the thick stew of the night heat, in the utter quiet of a ghost town, they all heard the distinctive sound of a shotgun being cocked. They picked up their pace and walked faster.

Finally, fortune favored the persistent. They came across a shopping cart that had been abandoned on the side of the road. With relief, Robyn loaded it with her bag and cat carrier. Pushing the rickety cart over the trash-strewn streets in the dark wasn't easy, but it allowed the trio to move faster. A mile or so later, Robyn struck the jackpot. She found a new Sam's Club cart in good condition and promptly upgraded.

Even in the dark, Carlos's sense of direction never failed. About 4:30 in the morning, they spotted Airline Highway ahead. Smatterings of light promised electricity, and the group walked faster. When they reached

Airline, Robyn found that they'd arrived back at the shopping center where she'd switched buses hours before. She took the opportunity to go to the bathroom behind the buildings in the same place she'd used earlier. Across the street, a sentry at the National Guard encampment watched them without comment. They didn't bother asking him for help.

Still headed in the direction of LaPlace, they walked west along the highway. All of them were reaching the end of their endurance, and Michael's feet were bloody, yet it seemed reaching LaPlace was their only option. In the predawn light, they checked out commercial buildings they passed, looking for an outside outlet where Robyn could charge her phone. While they no longer had hopes of Andrea being able to meet them on the interstate, Robyn wanted to let her sister know their situation.

The group decided if they split up, they'd find a working outlet faster. They were approaching a large intersection and Robyn veered off alone towards a Goodyear station set back from the corner. The broken windows tattled on the looters who had been there before her. Scoping out the territory, she noticed a man across the street at a bus stop. Although he seemed preoccupied with trying to fix a bicycle, her street-wise intuition picked up a weird vibe. She wondered if he might be a lookout for looters who might still be inside. She approached the building cautiously and tested the outside outlets. None of them worked.

She pushed her cart up to the intersection, where the three had agreed to meet. Michael had arrived before her, and she was surprised to find him engaged in conversation with the bicycle man. She shot her friend a questioning look. Michael defended his new acquaintance and explained that the man was just one more stranded soul trying to get out of town, but Robyn wasn't convinced. The trio left the bicycle man behind and continued together down the side street to check out another group of commercial buildings nearby.

They had no better luck on the side street and decided to return to Airline. At the intersection where they'd rendezvoused earlier, they'd all noticed a service station on the corner. Lights from the coolers inside had beckoned them with the promise of electricity, but they'd written it off as too risky. A large branch had crashed through the door, and looters had broken even more glass to gain entrance.

Frustrated, Robyn suggested entering the service station. There'd been no sign of anyone inside, and the electricity was obviously working. She'd go in alone and make her call, which would only take a few minutes. The group stood in a parking lot next to the station, the men trying to convince Robyn to abandon the plan, but she'd already made up her mind. Finally, she flagged down a passing police car and asked the driver what she should do. His answer wasn't encouraging.

"If there's looters in there, they'll shoot you," the policeman said bluntly, and then he peeled away to take care of more urgent matters.

Under a gloomy predawn light, the trio considered the policeman's warning. Other official vehicles passed them with lights flashing, but no one stopped. Then a black sedan began to circle them slowly, as if sizing up the ragtag group. The third time the car drove past, Robyn pointed at the driver, issuing a challenge.

"What do you think you're doing? Are you a cop or what?" she shouted. The driver answered with a sheepish "yes" and then drove away.

Despite the risk, Robyn was still determined to enter the station. Both men tried to change her mind, but she was bone-tired and willing to take even a foolhardy gamble for any chance to talk to her sister. Another marked police car passed, and Robyn motioned for him to stop. She told him of her plan to enter the store and asked that he circle the block while she was inside. He agreed to help and turned the corner.

Robyn took a deep breath, left her companions, and pushed her shopping cart up to the door. She walked up to the doorway and called out a questioning "hello," hoping no one would answer. Then she waited for five minutes, listening for any slight sounds of activity inside. The cop who had promised to circle the block never returned. If she went in, it'd have to be without police protection.

Robyn finally worked up the nerve to enter the store and ducked through the broken glass door. Stepping behind the counter, she wasted no time searching for an electrical outlet. She found one immediately, but noticed that a door to the back office was cracked. Light shone through the opening. Hoping that no one was hidden in the back, she plugged in her phone and made the call to her sister. Her heart beat a staccato rhythm as she willed Andrea to answer.

Andrea was ecstatic to hear her sister's voice, but the two spoke with urgency, aware that the connection could be broken at any moment. Andrea told Robyn that after her call from the Causeway, she'd realized the impossibility of trying to get into New Orleans with a newborn. She'd considered who would have the best chance of success and then called their uncle Jerry in north Mississippi. He'd managed to get to the coast to help his brother just days before. When Andrea had explained the situation to her uncle, the retired military officer volunteered without hesitation. He set out from his home immediately, only stopping to pick up his son-in-law for "backup." Shortly after midnight, the two men hit the road for the five-hour drive to New Orleans.

Andrea told Robyn that their uncle should already be in or near the city. However, the only directions Andrea had been able to give him before he'd left were a vague "she'll be somewhere near I-10." He'd be waiting for a call from Andrea with Robyn's exact location.

While Robyn knew she was on Airline Highway, she didn't know the name of the intersecting street. She was contemplating going outside to look at the street sign when suddenly her heart leapt. Someone was trying to enter the door to the station. She recognized the intruder as the bicycle man. Rage flattened her fear and she shouted at the man with great authority.

"Don't you dare come in here!" she commanded. "Right now, you go to the corner, then come back and tell me the name on that street sign!"

Astonished, the man sullenly obeyed. He called in the name of the street to Robyn and then quickly disappeared. She relayed the street name to Andrea and disconnected. Before she joined her friends back on the street, she checked the candy counter, hoping to find some Snickers bars. Sadly, the looters had also had a sweet tooth. All that remained was an empty box.

Outside, she excitedly told her friends about their impending rescue. Both men were skeptical and expressed doubts that her uncle would be able to get past the roadblocks. Robyn just smiled. Then they worried that Jerry would take his niece, but leave them behind. Under the circumstances, who would give two complete strangers and two dogs a ride?

"You don't know my uncle," she declared. "He won't leave you here. In fact, not only will he take you with us, he'll buy you breakfast."

Robyn's faith in her uncle was justified. By the time Jerry reached the first barricade outside of Hammond, Louisiana, it was about 3 o'clock Saturday morning. He boldly swung his SUV into the line for ambulances. When the guard approached his window, Jerry held up his ID badge, knowing that on close inspection, he could be turned away.

"I have a niece in there," he said simply. The guard's eyes met his own for a long moment. Then the guard said, "Be safe," and waved him though.

Jerry talked his way through two more blockades before he reached New Orleans about dawn. He and Steve roamed the city, asking policemen for directions to various shelters. They searched the camps for Robyn in vain. Jerry's cell phone wasn't getting a signal, so he had no way of contacting the outside world. Finally, he drove to the highest point of the interstate he could find. From the top of the airport exit, he was able to get a call through to his daughter at home who'd been keeping in touch with Andrea. The reception was terrible, but the convoluted chain of communication worked. Jerry was able to make out the words "Airline Highway" and "tire store."

Airline Highway is a very long road. Jerry drove up and down its length, looking at every tire store before they spotted Robyn about 9:30 in the morning. She stood in the parking lot of the Spur station with two men. Once Jerry had his arms around his niece, he found it difficult to let go, but his sense of humor reigned. With his first words, he teased her.

"Well, you're only seven miles from where you're supposed to be," he said.

She laughed through her tears and asked how her dad was.

"He's OK," Jerry told her. "I was there on Wednesday and he's doing just fine."

Robyn introduced him to Michael and Carlos and smiled when—without comment or question—her uncle began making space for them in his SUV. The men had helped his niece and he wasn't about to leave the heroes behind. The group wasted no time heading out of the city. At first, Robyn tried to persuade Jerry to take her to her father's house in Bay St. Louis, but he refused. He'd already seen the devastated conditions on the coast and realized that Robyn needed a safe and comfortable place to recover. Andrea's house in Baton Rouge had electricity, running water, and a clean bed waiting.

They stopped in Hammond for breakfast at a Waffle House. The bedraggled group found seats, and Robyn ordered scrambled eggs, grits, home fries, wheat toast, and a waffle. The skinny white woman devoured all the food placed on the counter in front of her, weeping the whole time she ate. Other diners in the restaurant regarded her with curiosity. Finally she tried explaining her tears to the stranger who sat to one side.

"I just got out of New Orleans," she said.

The man just nodded, not comprehending all the terror that simple statement implied.

The group finished their breakfasts and rose for the final leg of their long journey. Robyn wiped her eyes with a rough paper napkin and headed for the door. On her way out, she saw Jerry at the register, paying the bill for them all.

EPILOGUE—JULY 2006   Jerry did more than treat Carlos and Michael to breakfast. After dropping Robyn off in the care of Andrea in Baton Rouge, he drove the two men another two hundred miles to the Jackson, Mississippi, airport. Carlos had escaped New Orleans with "only the clothes on his back" and had no money with him. Jerry purchased him an airline ticket to Washington, D.C., where family awaited.

Michael had phoned ahead to his wife and children. They'd been staying a few hours away in Hattiesburg where they'd gone before the storm. When he arrived at the airport, the family joyfully reunited, dogs and all.

In June, nine months after their ordeal, Michael Homan came to Bay St. Louis for another reunion—this one with Robyn at her father's house. He brought his family with him, and, while the kids swam in the pool, he talked a little about his experience. He's an honorable and a sensitive man. The pain and suffering he witnessed will clearly stay with him for the rest of his life. Yet he's struggling to channel his anguish into positive paths.

Michael and his wife could take their children and move to some part of the country not marked by this enormous tragedy, yet for now they've chosen to remain in New Orleans. They hope that their children will grow into stronger and more compassionate human beings by learning that the world is very different from the way it appears on television sitcoms. Their eleven-year-old daughter made a movie about Katrina and New Orleans.

That day they spent in Bay St. Louis, we all gathered around the computer screen and watched it with awe. It shows that even the very young are capable of great awareness.

The Arizona Task Force One is credited with saving more than four hundred lives, yet the frustrations they faced on Friday were just beginning. Later, in a move that Phoenix mayor Phil Gordon characterized as "crazy" and "shameful," FEMA suspended the Arizona rescue team because they had brought along four armed police officers for protection as they worked.

Robyn titled one of the photos she took of the firemen "My Heroes." Ten months later, she was finally able to track down some of the men who saved her and wept with gratitude while they spoke. They promised to send her an official fire department shirt and hat.

Hal and Charlie had to give up Boots that night at the camp, but they were reunited a few weeks later. Their cat also eventually made its way home. They never saw the parakeets again. The two men plan to remain in New Orleans and renovate their house.

The people at the Causeway camp began to be evacuated in earnest on Saturday. By Sunday, the camp was empty. Today, it's just another major interchange. Driving past, you'd never dream that the median had served as a temporary resting place for the bodies of those who died there.

Robyn's tears in the Waffle House were the first of many. On the morning after she arrived in Baton Rouge, Andrea took her to McDonald's so Robyn could fulfill her dream of having an Oreo McFlurry. She cried in the drive-through. Shortly later, she wept in the middle of an Old Navy store, while Andrea shopped to buy her sister some clothes. For the next month, tears would overtake her whenever she entered a restaurant or a store. Like many Katrina survivors who suffered the deprivations of the aftermath, she was staggered by the everyday opulence and order that most Americans take for granted.

Robyn is still haunted by dreams of rising water and of people trapped in attics. But almost a year later, she's hard at work and focused on the future.

"It could have been much worse," she says. "I could have been responsible for children instead of a cat. And if I'd been able to leave my house earlier like I wanted, I would have wound up at the Convention Center or the Superdome. In the big picture, I'm one of the luckiest ones."

PART FIVE

Storm Journal

THE SHAPE OF DESPAIR

While Robyn struggled for survival in a city submerged, those same first days of Katrina's aftermath found those of us on the coast facing a different set of challenges. In these next two chapters, I've drawn from my journal notes and interviews to detail a week of life among the ruins.

WEDNESDAY EVENING, AUGUST 31 Three nights after the storm, Jan and I sat alone on my candlelit porch. The eerie, unrelenting darkness hid the desolation from our sight, but we could sense the enormity of the destruction that surrounded us. It stretched out in every direction, just beyond the tiny halo of our candle. I could imagine the heartache from countless losses gathering strength in those fields of debris, beginning to take on the shape of despair. I saw it as some powerful and malicious creature out there in the dark—watching us and licking its lips, waiting for the right moment to pounce.

Jan and I talked softly that night, our companionship keeping the hopelessness at bay—at least for the moment. Yet we wondered aloud why no one had come to the aid of our town. We didn't know that while we spoke, a letter was speeding around the country, forwarded again and again across the Internet. It reached people who'd never even heard of Bay

St. Louis, yet were moved to action by the simple words of Lucy Keenan and Drew Bruch.

Lucy and I had been the best of friends for fifteen years. Earlier Wednesday morning, when I'd finally gotten through to her on the phone, she'd asked for a list of supplies the community needed. She and her husband, Drew, were devising a rescue mission. I didn't take her seriously. The couple lived in Washington, D.C., over a thousand miles away. Lucy was completing her doctoral program in psychology and was slated to start an internship in New Jersey the following week. The newlyweds were also scheduled to close on a new house before the weekend and were packing for the move. Under the circumstances, I couldn't see how they'd be able to help.

I should have known better than to underestimate Lucy. Wednesday night, she and Drew sent out an e-mail plea to a long list of friends. Here's an excerpt:

Hi, we are Lucy Keenan and Andrew Bruch.

Our dear friend Ellis Anderson, a resident of Bay St. Louis, Mississippi, has contacted us with an urgent appeal for help . . . Bay St. Louis is one of the communities hardest hit by Katrina and has received no outside help (i.e., NO Red Cross, NO National Guard, nothing). This is a small community without resources. Those homes that are still standing are lacking roofs and more storms are coming. Neighbors are helping neighbors, but they need support (roofing supplies, food, water, toiletries, etc.) They need YOUR help. Drew and I are driving a truck down from DC and filling it with the supplies that they need. This is an urgent request. Please act ASAP . . .

Thanks so much,
Lucy and Drew

PS. Many of you may not know me and Drew personally, so this is who we are: Drew is a document translator (French and German) and I am in the final year of my doctorate in psychology at George Washington University. My family house was in Pass Christian (just over what used to be the Bay Bridge from BSL). I'm sure the house is match sticks . . .
We know how to get into the community and we know exactly what they need. All we need is your support.

THURSDAY MORNING, SEPTEMBER 1   Rip van Winkle wouldn't have been able to sleep through the thunder of helicopters swarming overhead at dawn. For Jan and me, they were more effective than any alarm clock. Peering out my windows, I noticed that many of this morning's airborne caravan had military markings. Was the National Guard finally beginning to arrive? We had no way of knowing for sure, but we rose with the feeling that our town had become a battleground. During the next few days, the constant barrage of surreal images and events would reinforce the sense that we were living in a combat zone.

Jan left to salvage what she could from her shattered house, while I started out on my morning bike trek to the bridge—still the only place where most cell phones had a shot of getting through. I pedaled through once-familiar streets, now transformed into scenes from a nightmare. The blistering sun had dried up much of the mud, so at least the going was easier. Surprisingly, most of the main routes had already been cleared for at least one lane of traffic. The crews from Georgia Power swarmed like ants, single-mindedly forging their way through our town with chain saws.

I'd only ridden a few blocks when the chain came off my bicycle wheel. The early morning sun glared down, determined to roast me. Not a leaf was left on any tree to provide shade. My only option seemed to be to lug the bike back to the house in the crushing heat. This small defeat tipped the fragile balance of my emotional scale. Suddenly, I was ready to scream with frustration.

Then a neighborhood boy riding past on his own bike stopped beside me. I recognized him as my neighbor Gabriel. He's about twelve years old, has red hair and a winning grin—which seems appropriate for someone named after an archangel. Within minutes, we were joined by two men, both of whom offered to lend a hand. When the team had finished repairing my bike, I rode away—momentarily revived by the realization that at least some things in my town hadn't changed.

When I finally arrived at the bridge, a call to Lucy was the only one that went through. She chided me for not having a list of supplies ready, then rattled off details about rental trucks and gift cards until my cell battery ran low. I was suffering from input overload, still not able to imagine how she'd pull off a rescue operation. Just to placate her, I promised to write up an official list and call back when my phone was recharged.

The Carron home, one of the few left standing on Citizen Street in the quarter mile between my house and the beach. My friend Phil's house once stood just a few doors away. Photograph by Joe Tomasovsky.

Afterward, I detoured slightly on my way home—I hoped to find news of my friend Phil. On the afternoon of the storm, my neighbors and I had watched as firemen searched the remains of his demolished house, believing that he might be trapped inside. While Phil hadn't been discovered buried beneath the debris, I still didn't know if he was safe.

Although I ran into several neighbors, no one had word about Phil. Then, a block from where his house had stood, I ran into a grim reminder of his possible fate. A group of uniformed men moved slowly across the fields of rubble. They wore safety gear that looked as if it would have been appropriate for a radiation spill. Some held the leads of dogs that nosed suspiciously over the splintered mounds of debris. I paused to talk to one of the team and learned they'd been sent from Virginia. The dogs were specially trained to hunt for decomposing bodies. Before the end of the week, the battered remains of five victims would be found in my immediate neighborhood.

THURSDAY AFTERNOON   Once home, I shifted gears again and spent the rest of the afternoon trying to bring some semblance of order to my house. When I'd bought and renovated the historic school a few years earlier, I'd created two separate apartments. Before the storm, the dogs and I had lived on one side. The other half had provided me with some income as a rental. Joe suggested that if I could make at least one room of the house comfortable, it'd provide a peaceful haven for shell-shocked friends.

I started in the kitchen on my side, where the ceiling had caved in and a putrid film covered the floor. I didn't need a trained dog to alert me to the fact that something had died in the room—even though I'd emptied the fridge, it still gave off toxic fumes. Pulling it out from the wall, I found the decaying body of a mouse. I guessed that it had crawled beneath to hide during the storm and been electrocuted. Retching, I disposed of it in a plastic bag and moved on. My kitchen was obviously not the right room to tackle first.

And neither was my living area. I stood and surveyed the sad wooden ceiling, already beginning to mold and warp. Katrina had torn away sheets of tin across the entire roof, but on my half of the house even the wood supports beneath had been ripped out by the winds. Jimmie and Hugh had been able to cover only a small part of the enormous opening with a few sheets of salvaged tin. The next rain would still pour directly onto my ceiling.

While the roof over the rental side had also been compromised, it'd provide more protection. And although the apartment living room looked as though it'd been ransacked and then sprayed down with a fire hose, it seemed the least daunting project. As I worked, several people stopped in. Friend or casual acquaintance, we embraced, thrilled to find each other alive. We swapped names of others we knew to have survived and sighed with relief with each revelation. The box of tissues on my front porch table became a hot commodity. Most of my visitors had lost homes and possessions, and, although many tears flowed, no one complained. That day, to have escaped with our lives seemed miracle enough.

Later in the afternoon, Hugh came by and invited me for a ride up to the main highway. He was willing to risk using a little of his precious tank of gas for a chance to get a few supplies. According to rumor, a National Guard unit had arrived and was giving out ice and food. As we talked on my porch, a short convoy of canvas-backed trucks, jeeps, and Humvees drove past, confirming the rumor. We watched the stern-faced men, many outfitted with desert camouflage uniforms and rifles. For me, the show of lethal weapons made their presence an unsettling sight as well as a welcome one.

Hugh and I threw a few empty coolers into the back of his car and struck out. A few blocks from my house, we paused by a street party in full swing. Neighbors had set up several grills and were barbecuing the last of the meat from their useless freezers. A man built like a fullback broke away from the gathering and ran over to the car.

Ronald Reed is a local handyman and had worked for both Hugh and me in the past. He was pleased to see us and launched into a story describing how he'd pulled his elderly neighbor from her house during the surge. Ronald doesn't swim, so he'd slung "Miss Scotty" onto his back and bulldozed his way through neck-high rapids to higher ground. We didn't doubt a word of the extraordinary tale—his strength is legendary. Before we drove on, Ronald asked if I needed help at my house the next day. I accepted his offer gratefully.

When Hugh and I reached Waveland, I realized I hadn't begun to grasp the scope of the devastation. The two towns of Waveland and Bay St. Louis are nestled side by side on the westernmost part of the Mississippi coast. The bay itself wraps around behind the towns, so they're actually situated on a peninsula. When a thirty-five-foot wall of water had charged in from the Gulf, it had surprised everyone by attacking from *behind* with equal ferocity. Most of the entire peninsula had been flooded.

Highway 90 is the main thoroughfare that runs through the two towns. It parallels the coast a few miles inland before it crosses the bay to the east. Now, only several pilings of that massive bridge remained. That was my cell phone hot spot and I'd seen the damage there. But it never occurred to me that the highway had been inundated in the very heart of the towns, miles from any shoreline. Hugh and I paused to survey the main intersection of highways 90 and 603. A hotel on the corner had traditionally served as an evacuation spot for elderly residents during storms. The bottom floor had been gutted by the tidal surge.

Across the street, the Kmart parking lot was crammed to capacity. People who lived in low-lying areas always took the precaution of moving their vehicles to that "high ground" before a storm. Now colorful heaps of smashed cars made it look like a demolition derby dump. The familiar Kmart sign still hung forlornly above the entrance to the gutted store. Hugh told me that the water had risen to the bottom of the big "K."

The National Guard distribution site had been set up in the parking lot of another shopping center near the intersection. Hugh parked his car on the highway, and we trudged across burning pavement towards a grouping of military trucks. Throngs of grimy disheveled people stood in line. They waited patiently under a merciless sun, most wearing exhausted expressions of resignation.

Other survivors explained the system to us. There were two lines, one for food and the other for ice. The food queue was relatively short, and we quickly reached the head of the line. Two young soldiers stood in the back of a canvas-covered truck and handed down packets of food. I stared at mine curiously. I'd never seen an MRE before. I learned that the letters stood for "meals ready to eat," and they were standard food for troops in combat zones. When I saw that the bland tan wrapping of mine was labeled "Shrimp Creole," I had to laugh. The classic New Orleans dish had become a military staple.

The line for ice was much longer, so Hugh and I traded off standing in line on the simmering asphalt. While Hugh took his turn, I waited nearby under the eaves of a shattered shoe store. A young man standing in the shade next to me apparently had the same arrangement with a friend, and we struck up a conversation. He'd heard the shoe store behind us had been looted. I didn't want to believe it, but the smashed glass and empty shelves seemed to confirm the story. It was another reminder that opportunists live everywhere—our coast just seemed to have fewer of them.

The man told me he was from Long Beach, a coastal town about fifteen miles to the east, then explained how he'd weathered the storm in his own house, three miles inland. After the surge had retreated, thrashing fish had festooned the chain-link fence of his yard. Saltwater fish.

Then he pointed to his friend in line. The unkempt middle-aged man wore flip-flops and stained shorts, his dirty hair matted against his forehead. "That's the richest man in Hancock County," my new companion remarked. "He lost everything in the storm—his business and his house." The richest man seemed calm considering the circumstances and completely at ease as he chatted with Hugh. The Great Equalizer had reduced even millionaires to waiting in line for a bag of free ice.

THURSDAY EVENING   On the way home, Hugh detoured to the ruins of the bridge so we could try our cell phones again. When I got through to Drew, I reeled off my long list of supplies. It was an odd assortment of items: chain saws and toothbrushes, baby wipes and batteries, diapers and flashlights, camp stoves and tampons, nonperishable food items, squeegees and shovels for mucking out houses. Blue tarps to cover roofs that had peeled away in the winds. And mosquito repellant. Lots of it.

Drew told me that their e-mail plea had already raised almost twenty thousand dollars with the help of my friend Peter Kramer. Peter lives in the small town of Washington, Virginia, and is a world-class craftsman of fine furniture. He'd orchestrated a deal with some major retailers so that donors could contribute online via credit card. I began to believe the trio of can-do friends might just pull it off.

I also managed to get a call out to my cousin Bo, an attorney in Nashville. We're about the same age and had been close when we were children. Bo had taught me how to ride a bike and had picked me off the pavement several times. Now, forty-odd years later, I was asking him for help again, knowing he wouldn't hesitate. When I heard his voice, I didn't waste time with pleasantries.

"Bo," I said. "It's worse than you could ever imagine. I need you down here now. It's really, really bad." I tried to sound calm and businesslike, but ended up crying.

"I'll leave tonight," he promised.

Before the battery died, I got another call through to Andrea. She mentioned that her partner, Jeb, would be coming to Bay St. Louis the next day, but that good news was overshadowed by the bad. She still hadn't heard from her sister, Robyn.

On the way home, Hugh tried to counteract my brooding with an account of an earlier expedition. He'd struck out early for Waveland to check on the house of his best friends. When he'd run out of cleared road, he'd parked his car and begun the treacherous trek into no-man's land. Even though he knew the route well, it was difficult to tell exactly where he was—street signs no longer existed and all landmarks had been reduced to rubble. The area "had the aura of a killing field."

Hugh was carefully working his way through the wasteland of fallen trees and crushed houses when he spotted three men approaching from the opposite direction. One carried a large camera, another held sound equipment, and the third, he said, "was dressed in wilderness gear—you know, with stuff out of an L.L. Bean catalogue. He was a skinny young guy, with short white hair. He looked sort of familiar, but I couldn't place him."

When the men grew near, they didn't introduce themselves, but it was obvious that they were a news team. They stopped and tried to engage a very reluctant Hugh in conversation.

"But it was like being at a funeral—our whole town was gone," he said. "My mourning was a very private thing and the camera was intrusive."

The railroad tracks where this image was taken are over a third of a mile from the beach in Waveland. Photograph by Joe Tomasovsky.

The men persisted, and, finally, the L.L. Bean man asked Hugh if he had anything he wanted to tell America.

"Well, yeah—OK—I got something to say," Hugh replied heatedly. The newsmen sensed a dam ready to break and eagerly readied themselves for a flood of emotion. The cameraman focused his enormous lens and the soundman extended the microphone. Hugh looked directly into the camera.

"Where the fuck is President Bush?" he demanded, shaking with intensity. "My main mission in life now is trying to find water each day. I got fifteen people living next door to me and they need help! Where is it?"

The reporter exchanged glances with his companions, who lowered both camera and mike.

"We probably won't use *that* one," the newsman said. "But everyone's asking the same question."

Hugh wasn't surprised. Then he asked, "By the way, who are you?"

"I'm Anderson Cooper," the man answered.

"Who?" Hugh repeated. He doesn't watch much television.

"I'm with CNN," Cooper patiently explained. "National news."

Hugh shrugged, wished them luck, and said good-bye. He continued on towards his friends' house, but soon gave up the mission. Even if he could find their lot, it was obvious by looking at the rest of the neighborhood that nothing would be standing. Besides, he needed to go find more water.

THURSDAY NIGHT   Back at the house, Hugh and I were joined by Jan and Michael, who's an old dog-walking buddy. Michael had made it back into the Bay from his mother's house in Meridian. He was trying to secure what was left of his own home and asked if he could camp out on my porch for a few days. He's a quiet-spoken, steady man, and I was delighted that he'd be joining us. Both he and Jan were filthy, having spent the day slogging through the foul-smelling mud inside their houses. We all cleaned up with water from my bathtub reservoir before Joe served another hot meal he'd cooked on his camp stove.

While we ate on my porch in candlelight, Jan related a story from her grueling day. She'd been digging through the slime and silt inside her savaged house and came across three silver treasures—her daughter's baby cup and a pair of candlesticks that had been wedding day gifts. Jan had cleaned the items the best she could and laid them in the open trunk of her car parked on the street. She returned inside and went back to work. Hours later, she remembered the exposed silver in the trunk and raced back to her car in a panic. She'd noticed a number of people wandering down the street, many of them strangers. Jan was certain the silver would be gone, stolen by looters.

The silver items were just where she'd left them. Beside them in the trunk were a bottle of bleach, a container of baby wipes, toilet paper, paper towels, and a bag of potato chips. "I thought they were taking things," Jan said. "But they were *leaving* them."

FRIDAY MORNING, SEPTEMBER 2   I didn't sleep well and rose at dawn with nightmares still clouding my vision. My spirits were bolstered by the arrival of Andrea's partner, Jeb. He'd driven in from Baton Rouge and delivered all sorts of supplies. As we emptied his truck of groceries, Jeb filled us in on his newborn son. Both Joe and Jeb had been in the delivery room when Andrea gave birth just weeks before. Joe had photographed the entry of his first grandchild into the world. While he seemed pleased to hear of his grandson's progress, I understood that his mind was fastened to the fact that one of his own children was still missing. With each day that passed, Robyn's chances of survival grew smaller. Reports were estimating over ten thousand dead in New Orleans.

Jeb stayed to help for several hours and, before he left, gave me a ride to the downed bridge to try my cell again. The service was still barely functioning, even at the "hot spot." While I was able to get out a few calls, the entire process was extraordinarily frustrating. People stood beneath the broiling sun and punched in number after number, hoping just one might get through before the battery died.

I carried around a long list of numbers given to me by friends. All over the country, people were wondering if their family and loved ones on the coast had survived. Generally, if one person on the outside could be contacted, they would act as a "switchboard" to alert more of a survivor's network. For instance, later I'd find out that my childhood friend Nan had called my parents, learned that I was indeed alive, and posted the information at various sites on the Internet.

Jeb promised to make several calls for me when he got back to Baton Rouge. He dropped me off at my place, and I started working with Ronald to clean the house. The refrigerator in my kitchen still reeked, attracting hoards of flies. Ronald single-handedly moved the refrigerator out to my back deck, where he began to bleach it out. In the process, he found two more mice casualties rotting inside.

The stench from the refrigerator permeated the house, so I stepped out onto the front porch for a breeze. I was surprised to find the smell even stronger outside. Puzzled, I looked up the street and saw the bloating body of a large dog lying by the side of the road. Another dog anxiously paced around the corpse. I thought I recognized them as two of the strays I'd seen wandering the street on the afternoon of the storm, but I wasn't certain. Both were German shepherd mixes. The dead one had obviously been killed days before and I'd never even noticed.

Grabbing some dry dog food, I walked down my steps to the street. The rank odor rising from the carcass made me glad I hadn't eaten breakfast. Calling softly, I approached the dog guarding the body. It was an adolescent—gaunt and stressed—perhaps keeping a deathwatch over its mother. The pup raised its hackles as I grew near, backing off and growling. I poured some food onto the ground nearby and then retreated to watch. The dog must have been starving, yet it sniffed at the food and walked away, back to the remains of its companion.

FRIDAY EVENING   That evening, Hugh and I biked together to the bridge. Georgia Power had finished the task of clearing most of the fallen trees and major debris from the roads, but the crews now worked on lines, determined not to stop until the last light had faded. The streets of the town may as well have been dirt roads—they were all covered with a thick layer of dried mud. Several military vehicles passed us at a fast clip, whipping up tornados of thick dust. I held my T-shirt over my face, but the silt was so fine it filtered through effortlessly. Soon, the inside of my mouth felt as if it contained enough sediment to sprout seeds.

Hugh and I paused often to wash out our mouths with water we'd brought. He shook his head. "All the chemicals that have been dumped in the bay for decades—that's what we're breathing now. It's all over us, too." He wiped his shirt across his sweaty forehead and showed me the black cloth. "We need to get off the main roads."

Once we made it to the bridge, I was able to connect with my cousin Bo again. He answered from his home in Nashville and explained why he'd been delayed.

"Honey," he said, "I know I promised I'd come right away, but before I left late Thursday night, I called the highway patrol to find out which roads were open. They told me they weren't letting anybody in. Period. It's the same story every time I call back."

Fury ratcheted my voice up an octave. "That's an absolute lie!" I screeched. "Some of my neighbors made it back in, from all directions. They say there aren't any roadblocks. There's a curfew after dark, that's all. Why are they lying? They're keeping out people who could help!"

"I don't know," Bo answered. "Look, I'm putting together stuff here to bring. I've been in touch with your friend Lucy. We're working together now and planning to meet at your house. You just hang in there, baby. I'll be there on Sunday."

My next call got through to Lucy, and I caught her helping to load the truck. Bo had passed on the information about roads being closed, but she was confident that blockades or checkpoints wouldn't be an issue.

"It's taken lots longer than we thought," she said, "but we'll be there as soon as we can. Maybe tomorrow night, maybe Sunday. We got lots of the supplies on your list, but we're planning to stop and pick up more on the way. Is there anything else you want?"

While I named some other items, Lucy told me later that I seemed fixated on obtaining a pair of size twelve work boots—I mentioned them several times. Ronald had lost all of his shoes and clothes in the storm and had only tattered shorts, a T-shirt, and a single pair of flimsy flip-flops. Neither Joe nor Hugh had anything that would fit him. "And bring some very, very big shorts and clothes for him, too," I added. "But don't forget the boots. It's too dangerous here to be walking around in flip-flops."

Then she gave me an odd heads-up. "There's some reporters who have gotten involved, from a D.C. newspaper. It's kind of weird, but they're tagging along, taking lots of pictures." Lucy proved how well she knew me by adding one last note. "I'm pretty sure they're going to want photos of you. I'll try to call when we're getting close and remind you to comb your hair."

By the time Hugh and I biked home, I was coughing severely. The bitter grit in my mouth refused to wash away, even after I brushed my teeth several times. Hugh wasn't feeling well either, but for a different reason. He showed me an ugly wound on his arm that was beginning to fester. He suspected it was some sort of spider bite. We rinsed off the paste of grime, and I gave Hugh some antibiotic ointment to stave off infection.

Michael and Ronald soon joined us for another of Joe's hot meals. That night, he'd prepared a feast from some of the groceries Jeb had brought. The small group was already eating when Jan appeared. Although she'd already had dinner, she joined us. We pressed her for the story of her day, but she waited politely until we finished the meal before she began her tale. Later, we'd understand why.

That morning, Jan had been working on her house and was hailed by her neighbor, Bob. He told her he'd found a body just a few lots away. Jan had then used some of her precious remaining gas to report the victim. She drove from one emergency operations site to another, yet no one wanted take the responsibility for retrieving the corpse. She was sent from place to place, at each asking the same awful question: "Where do I report a body on my street?"

Back at her house, she'd watched as a team finally came to pick up the victim. They were carrying out the body when they stopped to ask Jan if she could identify the woman. Jan suspected it might be one of her disabled neighbors, but just by looking at the arm of the corpse, she was able to say, "It's not her." A uniformed man tucked the limb back beneath the plastic and carted the body away.

SATURDAY MORNING, SEPTEMBER 3   I'd gone to bed bone-tired and woke up exhausted. My threadbare sleep had been interrupted throughout the night by violent fits of coughing. I was undeniably sick.

I skipped the morning bike ride to the bridge and sat down on the back deck to wash dishes. It was a messy task. I used rainwater I'd caught earlier in the week, liberally adding bleach. Joe trudged up my back stairs, and I could tell by the look on his face that he wasn't bringing good news. He'd heard from a neighbor that the National Guard was forcing everyone remaining in town to evacuate. My mouth dropped open in shock at this announcement.

"We'll have to leave," Joe said. "They'll make us. My truck still starts and I think I can get it out of the driveway now, so gather up what you want to take. They say another storm is out there and if it hits while we're gone . . ."

He didn't have to finish the sentence. In their vulnerable states, neither house would have a prayer of weathering another hurricane. While we wondered if the rumor was true, we decided it'd be best to prepare for the worst. After Joe left, I moved through my home like a sleepwalker. *Say good-bye*, I told myself. *You'll probably never see any of this again.*

My artwork collection was still stashed in the center walk-in closet, the most protected place in the house. It had the best chance of survival, so I concentrated on other possessions. Finally, I settled on taking my computer, my violin and guitar, and my grandmother's music box. There wouldn't be room for the family photos. Ronald helped me cover the piano with the same tarp that had saved it during Katrina. I placed my photo albums on the bench and then we wrapped the plastic sheeting with yards of duct tape. When we were finished, I walked over to Joe's and found him in his flooded and roofless garage. He was tossing out a lifetime's collection of antique photography magazines, books, and camera equipment, all ruined beyond redemption.

"I'm ready," I said, and listed the items I planned to take.

Joe looked thoughtful. "I'm not sure all that will fit," he told me. "If we have to leave, I'm going to try to get Cleo back into her cage and bring her with us. I'd like to release her someplace where the trees still have leaves. Between her cage and the two dogs, space is going to be tight."

I went back to my house, grabbed the computer discs I'd made before the storm, and bid farewell to my computer and my violin. I placed the few items I planned to take by the open door. From my vantage point, I could see across my porch and out to the street beyond. The pup still kept watch over the broken body, not understanding the meaning of futility.

SATURDAY AFTERNOON   The children who lived next door ran into my yard, shaking me from my morbid contemplation. Imani is about twelve, and she carried a box of chalk in her hand. Her younger brother, Omari, followed her up the steps to my porch, breathless with excitement. They pointed down onto Citizen Street, where they'd drawn a large hopscotch board on the pavement.

"Check it out!" Imani said. "Isn't it cool?" When I asked where they'd been for the storm, they double-teamed me, alternating lines as they told their story.

"We went to my grandma's house in Waveland cause we thought it'd be safer." "But the water came up there and into the house." "Daddy put me on his shoulders cause it came way up on him and you know how tall he is!" "It was really scary!" "Mom says we should have stayed here instead, our house didn't get as much water." "We might move to Atlanta for school." "There's so many flies!" "Can we play with Jack and Frieda now?"

Joe joined me on the porch while I watched the children tousle with the dogs amid the debris in my yard. We waved to their parents, who looked on from their own porch. Then Joe wrinkled his nose.

"You know, somebody's going to have to bury that dog," he said, pointing across the street. "They're already talking about cholera on the radio and that body's just a breeding ground for disease. It puts those kids at risk."

I sighed. I couldn't imagine how we'd be able to dig a hole big enough for a ninety-pound German shepherd, much less get the rotting carcass into the grave. We were discussing possible methods of burial when I spotted a small convoy of military vehicles coming up the street. On impulse, I ran to the street and flagged them down. I can't remember exactly what I said, but pointing at the bloating corpse and using the words "disease" and "children" seemed to make an impression. An older man in charge promised to take care of the matter immediately. Before he drove away, I asked about the rumored evacuation. To my relief, he assured me that no such plan was being considered.

Shortly later, I watched as a backhoe and refuse truck pulled up in front of my house. The young dog backed off in the face of such intimidating machinery. It looked on as the body of its mother was scraped off the roadside and unceremoniously dumped into the back of the truck. Both vehicles drove away, leaving only a cloud of dust and a very bad smell.

The pup tried following the truck at first and then returned to the dark spot on the pavement where its mother had lain. It sniffed the ground, circling in agitation. I decided to take down more food and water and try to coax it into my house. The dog eyed me with suspicion, and my soft crooning did not soothe it. It crawled beneath a wrecked car and glared at me. Finally, I left my offerings and walked away. Back on my porch, I watched it lap up some of the water and then lope off in the direction the trash truck had taken. I tried calling again, but it didn't turn back and eventually vanished from sight. I never saw the dog again.

SATURDAY EVENING   The two-mile ride to the bridge seemed like a marathon. I gagged on the dust, coughs tearing at my chest. I didn't understand how a virus could possibly survive in my body—the sweat pouring from me as I rode should have flushed it out.

The cell service was beginning to improve—my call to Andrea went through immediately. When she answered, the tone of her voice told me the good news before she finished a sentence. Robyn was safe at her house in Baton Rouge. Her cat had escaped as well, and they were both catching up on sleep. Andrea told me that Jeb was planning to bring Robyn over in the morning so she could see Joe.

I made a few more quick calls, but I couldn't wait to tell Joe the news. On the way home, I flew through the streets, powered by adrenaline and good cheer, my first burst of happiness since before the storm. When I arrived at Joe's house, I bounded into his yard shouting with glee. His reaction was typically understated.

"I knew she could take care of herself," Joe said simply. Then he smiled for the first time in many days.

We cooked dinner in the new camp kitchen Ronald and I had set up at my house and enjoyed a celebratory meal. Everyone congratulated Joe and we broke open another bottle of wine in honor of Robyn's rescue. Robyn, Jeb, Lucy, Drew, and Bo would all be arriving tomorrow, bringing an infusion of hope. The blanket of despair lifted for a moment, allowing us to take a breath.

Hugh sported an enormous bandage on his arm and we persuaded him to tell his grisly tale. That morning, he'd visited an emergency clinic set up by the National Guard to have the suspect bite checked out. Hugh described the MASH unit as operating with extreme efficiency. Despite a large number of patients, he'd only waited about fifteen minutes before being seen by a doctor. The physician diagnosed the wound as a brown recluse spider bite and told Hugh that if it wasn't properly attended to, he could lose his arm.

"The doctor said that he was going to clean it out and that it would sting a little," Hugh said. "He insisted that I wouldn't need anything for the pain, but when I saw him pull out this long, skinny knife, I told him I definitely wanted something. The doctor called out over his shoulder—*Hey, nurse, give this man a bullet to bite on!* He thought that was pretty funny.

"A nurse in cowboy boots came over, and, although she didn't bring me a bullet, she held my other hand while the doctor operated. He took that skinny knife and sliced down into my arm, digging around until he pulled out this long hard core of pus. After that, he took a needle and jabbed it deep in the hole, shooting me up with antibiotics. I'm thinking—*sting* a little bit?!! I should have taken him up on the bullet offer!

"That whole team was just awesome," Hugh continued. "They functioned seamlessly, with high spirits and a great sense of humor. And I'm here to tell you—it didn't hurt nearly as much as it might have after hearing I might lose my whole arm. All things considered, it turned out OK."

Later, Hugh said his good-byes all around. In the morning, he would head for his family's summer camp cottage in Louisiana for a respite. He promised to keep in touch by phone, yet it was hard to watch him drive away, not knowing when we'd meet again. Jan, Michael, and Ronald spread out around my house to sleep. I worried that my coughing would wake them—the complete silence allowed every slight sound to echo through the house. Sweat made the sheets cling to me like Saran wrap. I wasn't sure if I had a fever or if the night was just extraordinarily hot. And whether I closed my eyes or opened them, I saw only a vision of a most bewildered dog. It trotted down a dusty road, following a once-familiar scent, now tainted by decay.

TRAIL OF TEARS

SUNDAY, SEPTEMBER 4   I leaned over the porch railing and watched the reunion below in my driveway. Robyn and her father embraced and didn't part for a long while. Joe's T-shirt was drenched with sweat, covered with grime. Robyn didn't seem to mind. They stood in my yard, surrounded by piles of mangled roofing tin and broken branches, yet the wreckage faded in the face of their joy. I couldn't see their eyes because mine were full of tears. It was Sunday morning, less than twenty-four hours after Robyn's uncle had rescued her from New Orleans. Only a week before, I'd been finishing last-minute storm preparations, imagining that the hurricane would cause some minor inconvenience at worst. Instead, the world had upended.

Later, Robyn trudged up the steps and we found a quiet corner to talk alone for a few moments. The house had taken on the appearance of a gypsy camp. People passing by were drawn by the signs of activity and leapt from cars to embrace neighbors in the yard. My porch swing was rarely empty. It had become a favorite shady place for friends to share stories of survival. Like weary vagabonds, some stashed bundles of personal belongings in odd corners of my house for temporary safekeeping.

I offered Robyn a cold bottle of water from the cooler. "I knew Dad wasn't dead," she said. "I was sure I'd feel it if he were gone."

"He never lost faith in you either," I told her. We only had time to exchange a few more words before Joe came in, telling Robyn it was time to go. Jeb was taking her back to the relative comfort of her sister's house in Baton Rouge. As I watched Robyn's slender frame descend the steps, I wondered how that seeming fragility could embody such strength. What little she'd told of her New Orleans ordeal had caused my stomach to roil.

I took a few moments to wash down a dose of the antibiotics Jeb had delivered, then turned back to the task at hand, which had taken on absurd importance. With a lunatic's obsession, I was constructing a sculpture in honor of Lucy's impending arrival. Whenever my friend had visited in the past, she'd always enjoyed checking out my latest art acquisition. Now my house was barren of any art. I'd stripped the walls and shelves during storm preparations the week before and all paintings, pottery, and sculpture remained packed in my closets. Although my home was in havoc, I was determined that when Lucy arrived, she'd find some shred of my former life intact.

I taped a pastel drawing over the face of my useless television set. Then, after stringing four or five equally inoperative remotes together, I nailed the cluster on the wall above the television, like a strange catch of electronic fish. I fanned the remotes across the wall, fastening each in place when I was pleased with the result. The drawing covering the TV depicted a small sailboat resting on a tranquil tropical beach, with palms swaying in a gentle sunset breeze. I hoped Lucy would appreciate the irony. To view my new "sculpture," one would have to pass the broken boat resting amid debris at the bottom of my steps.

A few hours later, I heard a rumble of arrival when a large truck pulled into my yard, and I flew down the steps to welcome my friends. Two other cars in the convoy had also parked and passengers began to get out, but I ignored them and made straight for the truck. Lucy leapt out of the cab. She bound her arms around me as if I'd been raised from the dead, and I clung to her neck like I was receiving a transfusion of life.

A young man wreathed with camera gear pointed an enormous lens in our direction. While we embraced, weeping and laughing, the shutter clicked madly as he moved around us. Lucy pulled away from me enough to whisper apologies for the intrusion.

"It's the reporters I told you about," she said softly. "It's kind of annoying, but they mean well. But look at you! Even though I warned you they were coming, you still didn't comb your hair." We both laughed and hugged tighter.

I shared more embraces with Lucy's husband, Drew, then greeted the rest of the convoy party. Lucy introduced the photographer, Andrew Harnik, and his reporter colleague, Kristine Antonelli. They'd been assigned by the Washington, D.C., *Examiner* to cover the extraordinary trek to deliver supplies. I guessed both journalists to be in their midtwenties. Their faces already wore a peculiar expression of shock, one that I'd see often in the months ahead. People from the "outside" who had watched televised

Katrina coverage came to the coast assuming they already knew what the devastation would look like. Once surrounded by the actual carnage, the scope of it would never fail to overpower them.

I smiled to see Vic, whom I'd met for the first time just a few months before. He was the boyfriend of my cousin Kim, and the couple had recently visited me on the way home from a New Orleans vacation. After the storm, Vic and Bo had connected with Lucy, conspiring with her by phone to help with the rescue operation. Vic had driven from his home in the mountains of North Carolina, joining with Lucy and Drew en route to the coast. Bo had left Nashville and would be arriving later that night.

I led the group around Lionel's boat in the yard and handed out cold bottles of water from a cooler on my porch. My dogs and Lucy were old friends, and they gave her an enthused greeting. Frieda was Lucy's favorite, even though the terrier had devoured the extravagant cake I'd ordered for my friend's surprise thirtieth birthday party years before. Then Lucy wandered into my house and started crying again.

"Oh, my god," she gasped. "Your beautiful house!" Her tone left no doubt that its beauty was a thing of the past.

I pointed out my new art installation, but Lucy seemed focused on the radical changes. Personally, I thought the place looked pretty good—at least I'd cleaned up most of the mud from the floors. I tried to see it from her perspective. Small heaps of belongings lay everywhere, walls were streaked with grime, the beadboard ceiling was already beginning to warp and mold. Plywood covered the main windows, upholstered furniture was soggy, and overhead lighting fixtures had been shattered. I'd already forbidden the group use of the toilets and had shown them the plastic bucket latrine beneath the house.

I put my hand on her arm. "Lucy," I reminded her. "I'm lucky. I still have a house." And her tears welled again. She already knew from Internet satellite images that her family's handsome home in Pass Christian no longer existed.

At least Andrew seemed to like my TV art project and took several photographs. He was busy shooting more views of the house when I saw Joe walk up the steps. Joe pointed out that we needed to get the supplies distributed as soon as possible. Since none of us had considered this important aspect beforehand, we came up with a barebones plan to unload the goods into my driveway and yard. Concerned about my fever, the group assigned me the task of town crier. A few minutes later I drove away in Vic's jeep, calling friends from a cell phone as I steered. When I managed to get a call through, my message was jubilant. *Supplies have arrived! Come to my house right away! Spread the word!*

I first headed toward a makeshift emergency center that some intrepid neighbors had set up in the Old Town Elementary School. When I'd passed the school the day before, I'd noticed several military vehicles and clusters of National Guardsmen stationed outside. I imagined them coming to my house, loading up provisions, and bringing them back to the school, an easy distribution solution. The soldiers were still at their station when I arrived, so I approached a uniformed group leaning against a Humvee and quickly presented my proposal. Their faces remained impassive.

"We're here to prevent looting," said one, shrugging.

My incredulity almost made me shriek. The cavalry had finally arrived, but apparently they had orders not to do any work.

"We don't have a looting problem," I argued. "We have a food and water problem."

"We can't help you, ma'am. We have our orders." The soldier shifted his rifle.

I turned away, fuming, and sped off in the jeep, no destination in mind. Close to Highway 90, I screeched to a stop beside a shiny new truck parked on the side of the road. In the back, several men sat talking, dressed in identical spotless T-shirts. Since most locals were branded by mud, I pegged them for fresh members of a volunteer group.

"You're here to help, right?" I asked.

Several heads nodded in unison. I gave a short synopsis of the situation and finished with an offer to lead them to my house.

"We can't do anything without orders from our administrator," a spokesman for the group announced.

I pulled away, shaking my head. The storm had occurred just one week ago and bureaucracy was already fouling the lines. I drove aimlessly for a few blocks before I was struck with sudden inspiration. I changed directions and peeled away toward the Bay St. Louis fire department, steering the jeep around the road-warrior route choked with ruined cars, downed trees, and broken patches of pavement.

Three years before, the quick response of the department had saved my gallery when a fire threatened to reduce the historic cottage to ashes. I was certain those same heroes would come to the rescue again. At the station, I found Rusty, a fireman I recognized, and babbled out the details. Several of his companions gathered to listen. Their faces were drawn with fatigue, but they promised to be at my house in ten minutes with a trailer. They'd load up the supplies and drive around town to pass them out.

By the time I arrived back at my house, the yard had been transformed into a Walmart sidewalk sale. Neighbors picked through boxes of clothing, food, diapers, bedding, cleaning and camping supplies, and even toys. I saw one box that held a few dozen pairs of colorful children's sunglasses and knew they must have been an inspiration of Lucy's. She now wore a stylish paramilitary cap over her thick hair and hefted boxes from the truck with the rest of the crew. Ronald had taken a break and sat on the steps, grinning as he tried on a new pair of size twelve work boots. A few minutes later, Rusty and his team of fireman arrived on schedule and began loading the goods onto their trailer.

Kristine, the journalist, moved through the madness interviewing neighbors, while her colleague Andrew worked to photograph the distribution efforts. He paused to approach me and asked for a tour of the town before the daylight began to fade. I wasn't needed at my house for the moment, but part of me was reluctant to show the battered corpse of my community to an outsider. I felt protective of her memory and hated for any stranger to view her desecrated remains. Another part of me understood that most media had presented a tunnel vision perspective of Katrina, focusing solely on New Orleans. If the rest of the country knew of our plight, perhaps more people would be moved to help. I agreed to serve as his guide, and we drove slowly towards the beach.

As we approached the shoreline, we stopped where part of the road had been washed out. Two of my neighbors sifted through the remains of their house, and Andrew walked over to interview them. For the moment, I couldn't bear hearing another storm story, so I wandered over to the ruins of a brick house that had faced the beach on the opposite corner.

Beach Boulevard in Bay St. Louis, looking west toward Waveland. Photograph by Joe Tomasovsky.

Among the jumbled piles of bricks, an ebony grand piano lay on its side. The piano was surrounded by an odd assortment of knickknacks—little porcelain figurines, small mementos from trips abroad, candy dishes. It was one of the "shrines" that I had seen appearing around the town. As survivors found personal belongings of neighbors whose homes had been destroyed, they'd arrange the objects at the edge of the lot to await the return of their owner.

My eyes roamed across the debris field, searching for an item I could add to the shrine. I was beckoned by a wink of light and, looking closer, saw a piece of hand-blown glass peeking out from a heap of masonry. I gently pulled away the bricks to reveal a fanciful Venetian cake platter. Tendrils of delicate glass spun along the base, waltzing up the pedestal to pirouette around the edges of the plate. When I'd freed it from the rubble, I held it up to the light for inspection. Not one of the fragile flourishes appeared to have broken. Realizing that I'd uncovered a true miracle, I settled it into place by the piano as the centerpiece of the shrine.

When Andrew had completed his interview, we drove west along the torn beach road toward Waveland. The depth of the devastation increased as the elevation gradually dropped. A solid row of houses had once faced the beach, backed by pleasant neighborhoods. Now, not a wall stood within our field of vision.

We spotted a beaten telescope sitting by the side of the road, sadly drooping from its tripod. I knew it must mark the place where the house of good friends had stood. I'd spent fine evenings on the balcony of their raised house, peering through that same telescope at constellations rising above the dark Gulf. I asked Andrew if we could stop and do a quick search of the area in hopes of finding another cake platter miracle, some tiny thing to salvage for my friends. He gamely agreed and we trudged up the rise together, picking our way across the debris. As we explored, I tried to convey the kindly nature of our community to the photographer. I wanted him to understand that the ruin before us represented more than a loss of homes and possessions.

I pointed to a barren lot nearby and explained that just a few weeks before the storm, I'd met the retired woman who'd lived there. We'd introduced ourselves in a local salon after I confessed I'd dented her gleaming red Jaguar in the parking lot. Instead of berating me, she joked that it was becoming a habit—someone else had dented the same fender the last time she'd been in for a haircut. She told me not to worry. Under the circumstances, her generosity had seemed staggering to me, and I repeated the story to Andrew as an example of the Bay's bon vivant approach to life.

Andrew pointed up to something behind me. "You mean *that* Jaguar?" he asked. I spun and looked skyward. The mangled red car hung suspended in the top of a tall tree.

Evening was approaching by the time we arrived back at my house. Most of the supplies had been distributed and the remaining ones safely stowed. Andrew and Kristine bid farewell and left to pursue more stories. The remaining party cleaned up on the back deck, sluicing off the sweat and grime with one of the plastic bag sun-showers that Lucy had brought. I reveled in the luxury of other items they'd delivered. Battery lanterns made the kitchen seem almost cheery while we cooked a meal of pasta and garlic bread on the new propane camping stove.

After dark, the reunion of friends seemed complete when Dawn arrived with her boyfriend. Lucy, Dawn, and I had met in New Orleans over a decade before, our trio bonding tightly over shared defeats and celebrations. Inspired by my love of the Bay, Dawn had purchased a quaint cottage in Pass Christian three years before. She'd worked hard to remodel it and had created lush, rambling gardens in the yard. We knew from reports of the Pass that not much had survived—Dawn's house had probably been pulverized. She and her boyfriend, Joe, had driven in from Texas, hoping to salvage at least a few of her belongings the next day.

We were all exhausted, but before we turned in for the night, the three of us pulled on memories to dispel the horror around us. We laughed about the previous Mardi Gras, when we'd set off a lighthearted condiment battle at a New Orleans bar, shooting mustard and catsup across a table, covering costumed friends. We joked about a dinner at my home just months before, when we'd tried to barbecue on the back deck. When the coals stubbornly refused to light, Lucy had attacked them with my blow dryer, creating a fireball that had nearly torched my house.

The campout group that night included Lucy, Drew, Dawn and "her" Joe, Vic, Michael, and Ronald. Sleeping pallets lined the front porch. I sweltered for a bit in my loft bed, then moved to the battered leather sofa below, hoping that the open front door would catch a breeze. Jack settled on the floor, Frieda curled next to me on the couch. Once I reclined, coughs tore at my chest, permitting no sleep. I knew that I was interrupting everyone's desperately needed rest, but was helpless to control the fits. A few hours later, Lucy came into the hallway, sat on the edge of the sofa, and placed her palm on my forehead.

"You've got a really high fever," she said. "Are you OK?"

As an answer, I began crying. She held me closely to her, as if she were my mother, and the tenderness made me weep even harder. "Shhh," she murmured. "You're going to be fine." I didn't contradict her, but finally fell asleep while she stroked my uncombed hair.

It was still dark when another coughing fit woke me. As I struggled to subdue it, a large figure came into the hallway and reached down to me. My dogs stirred, yet didn't seem alarmed. I understood it was someone they both knew.

"It's Bo," said a gentle voice.

I struggled upright and clamped my arms around my cousin. I'd been surrounded by the best of friends, but for some instinctual reason, being held by a blood relative offered incredible comfort. A torrent of tears rushed out again and I heaved with relief.

"Ah, baby, don't cry," Bo whispered. "Here, look. I've brought you some presents."

The sense that I was dreaming grew when my cousin clicked on a flashlight to illuminate my gifts. He pulled a box of chocolates out of a plastic bag and offered me one, smiling. Like a greedy child who'd just gotten a shot at the doctor's office, I stopped crying and popped one into my mouth. The rich taste slid across my tongue, exotic and impossibly good. Then he reached into the bag again and drew out a small white teddy bear. Frieda sniffed at it suspiciously. Bo grinned as he held it out, but the stuffed animal reminded me of an innocence stolen by Katrina. I started sobbing again.

"Maybe we should just stick with the chocolates for now," Bo said, handing me another piece of candy.

We talked for a few minutes longer, then he kissed me on the head, said goodnight, and went out onto the porch with his sleeping bag. I curled back on the sofa, the taste of chocolate still in my mouth. I thought that surely I'd hit bottom and would begin to feel better the next day. Help had arrived, I was surrounded by loved ones, and the healing had begun. If I'd known the truth, sleep would have been impossible, but I drifted off at last, holding a white teddy bear and an elderly terrier in my arms.

MONDAY, SEPTEMBER 5   A flotilla of helicopters swooping overhead heralded the dawn, waking everyone in my new expanded household. While we shared camp coffee in the kitchen, Bo explained why he'd arrived so late. Driving through the night, he was south of Hattiesburg when he saw an inferno ahead of him in the darkness and slowed to a stop. Apparently a car loaded with cans of gasoline had exploded. Bo waited for over an hour for the road to reopen, frequently glancing back at the containers of gas he carried in his own SUV.

Lucy started off the day by playing nurse, tending to Ronald's two brown recluse spider bites. The day before, we'd convinced him to visit the National Guard medical tent, where they'd excised the festering wounds. The medics told him they'd seen many similar cases—apparently hundreds of the poisonous spiders had been flushed out of hiding by the surge. Ronald had been given instructions to clean the wounds, but since he'd been bitten on his backside, he had to ask for help. Lucy volunteered for the daunting job and Ronald bared his buttocks in the middle of my living room. Neither of them flinched as she swabbed at the open sores, cracking jokes as she worked. I couldn't watch the grisly procedure. The only thing that kept my arachnophobia from revving into high hysteria was the fact that Ronald didn't know if my house had been the location of the spider attacks.

It was still early morning when the group separated for the day's work. Lucy, Drew, Dawn, and her boyfriend, Joe, headed for Pass Christian to see if anything remained to salvage from Dawn's home or Lucy's father's house. Since the bridge between the Pass and the Bay had been destroyed, they planned to detour north and work their way down—a trip that would take most of the day.

Soon after they left, Jan stopped by to fill her car's tank with some of the gas the rescue crew had brought. She would drive back to her home in Pittsburgh, recuperate, and make plans for restoring her Bay cottage once things had settled down. While we'd been casual social friends before the storm, the catastrophe had made us sisters of survival. Jan laughed while showing off her travel outfit—she was dressed in her pajamas.

"It's the only clean thing I had left," she said.

Bo and Vic began to unload the remaining plywood from the rescue truck, stacking it beneath my house. My cousin was hefting up a heavy sheet of the wood when a stern voice came from behind, demanding to know what he was doing. Bo turned to face directly into the barrel of a rifle. A National Guardsman steadily aimed the lethal weapon at my cousin's head, while four other armed soldiers watched from an armored truck. Bo quickly explained the situation and then asked if the guardsmen would lend a hand. The soldiers declined and drove on.

The two men had finished unloading the truck by midmorning and moved on to tackle my roof. Their mission was to "dry in" my house to prevent additional water damage. They planned to stretch a series of tarps over the gaping holes, but since the storm had actually ripped out several of the underlying roof supports, they would first have to create a new framework, onto which they could nail the plastic.

To begin the work, Bo made a bold run up to the peak of my house, over thirty feet from the ground. If he'd lost his footing, his likelihood of survival would have been slender. Later, he'd tell me that that run was the scariest part of his whole Katrina experience. Once Bo was in position, Vic passed up the ladders that would allow the men some small purchase while they worked over the open expanse of my house. I climbed onto the lower kitchen roof and passed them boards, tools, tarps, sheets of tin, and bottles of cold water. From our vantage point, we could see Joe clambering across his own roof next door, nailing blue tarps in place.

The fiendish heat baked the bottom of my tennis shoes, and I wondered if the soles might melt. I took frequent breaks, but the men kept at their job from hell. I watched Bo dangle high above the ground, aware that the tragedy of Katrina could get much, much worse in just a heartbeat. At times, the sight of Bo and Vic risking their lives on my behalf was almost more than I could bear—saving the house at the expense of injury or death seemed foolhardy. When the panic overwhelmed me, I'd beg them to come down and forget about it, but they'd tease me for being a sissy and make light of their risk. By late afternoon, a small section of the roof had been tarped over, and we called it quits for the day.

The light was fading when Lucy's team returned from Pass Christian, utterly whipped and bearing a seemingly impossible report: Pass Christian looked worse than Bay St. Louis. Lucy had trouble even recognizing the place where her father's house had stood. Her salvaging efforts had offered pathetic returns. The group had retrieved a few pieces of family china, crystal, and silver—elegant dinnerware for a grand house that no longer existed.

Dawn's small pink cottage had been twisted and washed off the foundation. A neighboring house had slammed into it. By slithering underneath the wreckage she'd been rewarded with some photographs and a strand of pearls. Lucy told me privately that she'd seen a mattress hanging in the top of a tree at least twenty-five feet in the air. That compelling evidence of the storm's ferocity had made her want to vomit.

The four friends wanted to leave the Bay immediately, in order to beat the strict "after dark" curfew. Lucy's new internship in New Jersey had officially begun that same day and the couple had a twenty-hour drive before them. She hoped to start the job only two days late instead of three. Dawn and Joe were headed to Texas where Dawn's sister had offered temporary refuge. The group hurriedly gathered their personal effects, and I followed them down to the yard.

I hugged each of them good-bye, but had a hard time releasing Lucy. I'd never imagined a friend who would work so hard or take such risks on my behalf. While I longed to go back to the land of sanity with them, I wasn't ready to leave either my house or my town. Bo and the dogs stood by me as they drove away into the dusty twilight. I knew my friends couldn't see me, but I continued waving long after the vehicles had disappeared from view.

TUESDAY, SEPTEMBER 6   Only four of us convened for coffee the next morning—Bo, Vic, Ronald, and I. None of us had slept well—an orphaned dog had taken up residence across the street and howled pitifully most of the night.

The roof work on my house would continue, but it had advanced enough so that I wouldn't be much help. I was glad to be useless. While my antibiotics had appeared to be taking effect the day before, my fever had returned and my cough had deepened. The long run of sleepless nights and the heat were taking their toll on my last reserves of energy.

Bo and Vic had already climbed onto the roof when Joe came over to see if we needed anything from the real world. He was on his way to Baton Rouge, where he'd spend the night with his daughters and buy a cell phone, a new necessity in the post-Katrina world. I put in my request for an item

Lucy hadn't brought—cough syrup—and waved him off. As I stood in the drive, an SUV pulled up in front of my house, a grinning friend behind the wheel. A few days before, he'd stopped in to see if I needed anything "imported" from Pensacola, where he'd been heading. Joking, I'd asked for "a big bottle of really good tequila." He'd obviously taken me seriously—he reached into the back seat and handed me a heavy brown bag. "I hope you have some limes," he said, winking, and I laughed. Indeed, I did. Guessing that a well-stocked bar might come in handy, Lucy had brought me an entire sack of them.

Bo's cell phone was functioning more reliably than my own, so I spent most of the afternoon relieving the minds of family and friends. Bo's wife, Pam, offered to be my Internet go-between. I gave her my e-mail account information, and she spent the next few days working from their Nashville home, answering letters from my friends around the country. *She's fine,* Pam wrote, again and again, *she's fine, if a little frazzled and understandably worse for wear. My husband is with her in Bay St. Louis, drying in her roof.*

More friends stopped in throughout the day, many to say farewell for the time being. Those who no longer had homes were scattering across the country to regroup with the care of family and friends. Some who still had houses standing had secured them and were leaving until basic services were restored. It was futile to try to make repairs or clean up mud without electricity or running water. I felt as if Katrina had abruptly ended the lovely lawn party that had been our life in the Bay. The band had fled, tablecloths sailed, and the guests all dashed for cover, buffeted by gusts as they ran.

That evening, DeNeice and Mark Guest arrived and asked if they could stay for the night. The Waveland couple had evacuated before the storm and ventured back to view the slab that had been their home. Mark is a jazz guitarist, and, earlier in the year, I'd started working as vocalist for the trio he led. Just a few weeks before the storm, we'd debuted the act before a restaurant packed with enthusiastic friends, in a building that now lay shattered in the Gulf.

After we'd cooked and devoured dinner, I began dispensing margaritas to my friends, made with my Pensacola import, Lucy's limes, and ice provided by the National Guard. The old saw about alcohol rendering antibiotics ineffective didn't stop me from sampling one, and the drink worked at once to relax the clutch of tension in my chest. Bo and Vic visited with the Guests, the bizarre circumstances and the alcohol making them instant allies. Two more neighbors dropped by, drawn like moths to the bright lantern light flooding out from my house. After a few margaritas, these curfew violators forgot about the possibility of arrest that would await them when they headed for home.

As the evening grew late, I sat on the front porch with Mark, and we mourned the end of our musical collaboration. The Guests would have to relocate, probably to another state. I sipped my drink, noticing how the corona of light from my living room died abruptly in the front yard. Maybe my vision had been affected by the tequila or my fever, but the impenetrable darkness appeared to be moving, like a sinister fog pushed by a breeze. Not another light shone within eyeshot. Yet, when I turned my face toward the house, I could almost imagine that my life was normal again. Laughing friends sat around my dining table, and animated chatter filled the room.

"Dammit, I want it back," I said to Mark.

He knew I was talking about my life, all our lives. His only response was to hold up his glass to mine, in a toast to the friendship that still remained.

WEDNESDAY, SEPTEMBER 7   Later, when I interviewed those who slept over on the night of the margarita bash, the first thing they all mentioned was the howling dog across the street. Earlier in the day, I'd attempted to coax the black lab into my yard for safekeeping, yet the dog was so traumatized, it bolted when I approached. It had mournfully bayed the entire night, seeming to voice despair and loss for the entire town. None of my household had managed to get much sleep, despite the numbing effects of tequila.

Mark and DeNeice left for a more permanent refuge with friends in South Carolina, while Bo and Vic prepared themselves for their final day on the broiling roof. I excused myself from duty, pleading extreme exhaustion and sensory overload. I crossed the yard to Joe's empty house, where

I hoped to catch a nap without the racket of hammering overhead. As I walked, my face felt as if it were literally sagging, pulled downward by the weight of oppressive thoughts in my head.

I had just stretched out on Joe's sofa when I heard a banging on his door. I answered the knock and saw two men in Georgia Power uniforms standing on the porch. They were probably surprised at my bleary shell-shocked appearance, because they opened with an apology for bothering me. Yet their next statement startled me into full alertness: they had come to hook up Joe's electricity.

My mouth flew open. I'd assumed that restoring electrical service in the Bay would take months. Now, just nine days after the storm, these two men from Georgia were going to perform the staggering miracle of bringing light back into our lives.

In the past, I'd sought out primitive adventures by traveling to third world countries or camping in the wilderness. After a short time, I'd returned home to a lifestyle where luxuries like flushing toilets, refrigeration, and hot water were a given. But being deprived of these "basics" in my own house had rattled me to the core. Like most twenty-first-century Americans, I regarded electricity and running water as entitlements, not extravagances. Over the past week, I'd come to realize how spoiled I was, especially compared to older generations. Thoughts of my hardy Appalachian grandparents would stifle my complaints when I used the plastic bucket latrine—they were both over the age of fifty when they were able to install a toilet in their farmhouse.

I babbled my gratitude to the two workmen, adding my appreciation for all the Georgia Power crews. Later, I'd learn that our own Mississippi Power had teamed with sister utility companies throughout the South. Crews had been positioned close to the projected path of Katrina, ready to arrive as soon as the storm had passed. As the winds died, they charged into the stricken coast, clearing the streets of debris and fallen trees. Most local roads were open by the time government troops arrived. Within ten days, power was restored to any building capable of receiving it.

The men were completing the hookup when Joe arrived home from his visit to Andrea's house in Baton Rouge. Robyn had insisted on returning to Bay St. Louis with her father, although her sister's house had offered more creature comforts. Both Robyn and Joe seemed refreshed and rested, smiling when I gleefully pulled them into the house for the big surprise. I demonstrated the new wonders by flipping on the kitchen light switch and opening the door of the humming refrigerator. Their astonishment matched my own since large swaths of the South were still without power.

Joe began a thorough inspection of his central air conditioning unit, hoping that submersion in the surge hadn't ruined it. I walked back to my own house with the cough syrup he'd brought, thinking I might be exhausted enough to sleep for a bit, even with the sounds of construction overhead. I stuffed my ears with foam plugs and collapsed on the single dry mattress, but my total exhaustion seemed to repel the sleep I needed.

I finally gave up later in the afternoon when Bo and Vic came into the room, announcing that the roof was officially dried in. My cousin then took me aside and told me that he and Vic were leaving that night, before curfew. I shook my head, trying to process the information. Somehow, I hadn't even visualized a time when Bo would leave. I started crying again, as Joe came into the room. The two men exchanged looks that seemed to ask, *which of us is going to tell her?*

Joe got the short straw. "Bo's taking you with him," he said flatly. "We've talked it over and decided you have to get out of here. He's leaving in the next few hours and you need to get packed."

My head reeled and I flushed with anger. The possibility had never been discussed, at least with me. It occurred to me that they'd been planning this for days without my knowledge, and I drew myself up in fury.

"I am not leaving this house!" I declared.

Bo put his thick arm around my shoulder. "Ellis, you're sick and you need to see a real doctor. And you need someplace quiet where you can get some rest. Let Pam and me take care of you, at least for a few days. When you're feeling better, you can come back."

I shook off his arm, and expletives flew as I stomped my feet like a child throwing a tantrum. I demanded to know exactly *how* I'd be able to return. My car had been totaled in the surge.

Bo pointed out that I'd be able to buy a car in Nashville. The two men met my other frothing arguments with calm answers. The dogs could go with me. Joe would keep an eye on my home. There was a mass exodus of survivors, and my house wouldn't be needed as shelter, at least temporarily.

I felt myself weakening in the face of their stern determination, but gave it one last shot.

"I am *not* leaving!" I shouted.

Bo took me in his arms again and looked me in the eye. "Cuz," he said softly. "You're going with me if I have to hogtie you and put you in my car. Just give it up now and start getting your stuff together. We need to leave before dark."

Still furious, I stomped into the next room, kicking aside any object in my path. Joe followed me and serenely began to pack up my computer, neatly coiling the cords. "You'll need this," he said. "Grab all the backup disks you made, while I load it into the car. I'll take down your guitar and violin, too."

I started crying again, knowing that Joe's packing list included the most important things I'd need to start a new life. If another storm blew in while I was gone, my house probably wouldn't make it. I packed my family photo albums in a plastic crate, then trudged up the steps to my loft. By the bed were two treasures that had belonged to my grandmother. One was a small brass music box. When I was a child visiting her mountain farm, it had played nightly while she'd comb out her long black hair and place her hairpins inside. Now it held a tiny porcelain doll with articulated legs and arms. It'd been my grandmother's girlhood favorite.

When I picked up the music box, the motion set off the wind-up mechanism and a few bars of that familiar melody floated in the air. I wept harder and reached for my wooden memory box, stuffed with keepsakes that traced my life from childhood to womanhood. It contained things like dried bugs, hair ribbons, concert ticket stubs, and a love letter from a French boyfriend whose name I'd forgotten.

As I placed the boxes in the crate with the photo albums, a lamp on my desk suddenly lit up. I ran out onto the porch and saw a Georgia Power truck parked by the power pole in front of my house. A lineman in an extended cherry picker bucket tinkered with the transformer. With a few more deft motions, he apparently restored electricity on the entire block. Neighbors magically appeared out of their houses to witness our first major community triumph since the storm. I cheered and my neighbors cheered and the work crews grinned, waving off our accolades as if to say, *hey, we're just doing our job.*

When Bo's car was packed, I took a last look around my battered home. Knowing that I might never see it again, I thanked it for being strong and kissed the doorframe in farewell. I locked the door, using my key for the first time since the storm. In the driveway, I handed it to Joe with instructions for him to give it to anyone needing a place to stay.

By this time, I couldn't stop the tears. I clung to Joe's neck, but he gently pushed me away and guided me into the front seat of Bo's car. Jack and Frieda were wedged in the back with my instruments and the computer. The box with my family treasures was tucked behind my seat. Bo patted my knee and pulled out onto the road, followed by Vic, who would caravan with us to Nashville. I twisted to watch as both Joe and my home faded in a cloud of dust.

I cried with abandon as Bo slowly drove north. Even though I'd heard that the storm damage was not confined to the immediate coast, knowledge couldn't compete with visuals. For mile after mile, the obscene wreckage flowed ceaselessly past the car windows. Hundreds of overturned cars, twisted trees, and shattered houses competed for my attention. Hopelessness fed the heaving fury of my sobs; the further we drove, the harder I cried. Bo reached over and took my hand, tearing up himself.

"Baby, it'll be OK," he said.

"No, it won't!" I sobbed. "Look at this! It just doesn't end! How will we ever, ever recover?"

A few moments later, the car jarred as the tires hit a crater in the pavement. My cousin and I clearly heard the strains of the music box as it chimed in response from the back seat. The lilting, cheerful tune reminded me of our grandmother's strength and love, instantly filling me with hope. Her spirit seemed to embrace me, quieting my tears, at least for the moment. I knew Bo must have felt her there with us as well, because his eyes met my own and he squeezed my hand hard.

"Just remember that you're not alone," he said.

Bo may have been referring to the imperishable bonds of family love, but in the years ahead I'd come to find a larger truth in my cousin's simple statement.

BOOK TWO

UNDER SIEGE

An ancient oak and a cheerful mural used to greet coast visitors at the intersection of Beach Boulevard and Washington Street. Photograph by Joe Tomasovsky.

PART SIX

Storm Journal

SEEKING THE REMAINS

Jean Larroux: "My sister Hayden compares Bay St. Louis to Whoville from the Dr. Seuss story of the Grinch who stole Christmas. When the Grinch comes down and steals all the gifts, he doesn't understand why the people are still singing on Christmas morning. That's us. All the stuff is gone, but we understand what we still have."

SUNDAY, SEPTEMBER 18, 2005   Three hours north of Bay St. Louis, I began seeing signs of damage along the interstate. As I drove back toward the coast, I passed groves of downed trees, exit ramps without signage, and billboards that had careened to earth like paper kites. Eleven days before, it'd been dark when Bo and I had passed through this same stretch on our way to Tennessee, so I hadn't witnessed this extended path of Katrina. She had thrashed her way inland further than I could have imagined.

As the devastation reeled past the windshield, I recalled the days I'd just spent in the "outside world." That heavyhearted evening we'd left the Bay, Bo had driven for about two hours before he'd been beckoned off the interstate in Hattiesburg by the lights of a chain restaurant. We found the manager locking the doors for the night. They had just reopened that afternoon and the crew was exhausted, but Bo persuaded them to let us in. We ordered from a pared-down paper menu and gobbled hot burgers and greasy fries from paper plates. Afterward in the ladies' room, I laughed hysterically as I flushed the toilet again and again, exhilarated with the novelty. When I finally exited the stall, I encountered another patron, staring at me wide-eyed. I tried to explain, *I'm from the coast and I've been peeing in a plastic bucket for ten days,* but she fled the room. She must have said something to the manager, because he gave us our meals on the house.

Arriving in Nashville around dawn, we'd slept for a few hours before Bo drove me to his family doctor's office. There I received a chest x-ray, a hepatitis vaccination (just in case), another shot of antibiotics, and two prescriptions for oral ones. The generous physician gave Bo a vaccination as well and refused to charge us.

Over the next week, I moved through the vibrant city like a befuddled actor who'd wandered onto the wrong movie set. I didn't seem to belong in this country where extravagance was a presumption. To others, I may have looked normal, but I felt branded by my experience. My odd behavior at times certainly didn't help me blend in. In a drugstore where I'd gone to buy a toothbrush, I wandered the aisles for almost an hour, mesmerized by the lavish selection of utterly inessential merchandise lining the shelves. Clerks watched with suspicion as I handled dozens of incomprehensible items like glittery hair mousse and costume jewelry for pets.

At Bo's, I had access to television, yet I found it impossible to watch. Katrina seemed to be treated as a passing news event—one that provided expensive advertising slots to sponsors pushing consumer consumption. The world around me moved on, mostly unmindful of the suffering on the coast. Once while eating with friends in a popular Nashville pancake house, my voice rose in a rant about the sense of betrayal my community had felt in those first days after the storm. I realized I'd used the "f" word several times only when a man in the adjacent booth lifted his head in irritation. He peered at me as if I was a lunatic. My face flamed when I recognized him as one of my favorite musicians, Lyle Lovett. *Sorry, Lyle,* I longed to say, *I'm not quite myself.* I did not ask him for an autograph.

I spent several days shopping for a used car—unsuccessfully, since the selection across the South had already been depleted by the thousands of coast refugees desperate for transportation. Bo ended up making me a great deal on the red Suburu SUV he'd used to rescue me. I happily accepted since I'd already developed a sentimental attachment to the sturdy road warrior.

Ten days later, when I was healed enough to head home, I considered leaving my dearest possessions at Bo's for safekeeping. Yet when it came time to pack, I wanted the things I valued most with me, despite the risk. I headed southward with the dogs nestled in the back with my computer, instruments, and the crate that held my grandmother's music box. Its chimes were silent on this day, although Bo and I had heard the melody play unprompted several times during our nighttime trek to Nashville. *It must have run down finally,* I reasoned, although it had not been wound in years.

For my trip back to the Bay, I'd dressed in a light cotton skirt covered with a brilliant poppy print. I imagined greeting Joe and my other friends with a healed body and a positive attitude. But as I neared the coast, my assurance faltered as I passed reminders of the pain ahead. I cranked up a peppy CD on the car stereo, belting out tunes along with the singer to bolster my courage.

Long before I left the interstate, I entered the world of brown. Tens of thousands of pines were dying from the salty surge, and the needles had turned to rust. Any tree with a leaf had been stripped clean. Even weeds and grass had withered from the assault of the storm. In the middle of a burning summer afternoon, I drove through a barren landscape that had been overtaken by an unnatural winter. I turned up the stereo volume and sang harder as my stomach twisted.

I left the freeway and headed south on Highway 603. It was still lined with the wreckage of a thousand cars—apparently none had been cleared away in my absence. A car dealership I passed made the ultimate statement in waste. Katrina had tossed the gleaming rows of new automobiles with the ease of a salad and left them strewn across the large lot in heaps.

My car's air conditioning system couldn't filter out the clouds of dust rising from the highway, so I stopped singing to cover my face with a tissue. The dust didn't seem to bother the dogs. They already associated the new fetid smell with home and stood peering out the windows, tails wagging. At the major intersection of Highway 90, only a few shattered traffic lights swung from tangled wires. A military man directed traffic with a rifle slung over his shoulder. I waited until he waved me through, took a deep breath, and crossed over onto the two-lane road that ran toward the beach. I seemed to be entering a cemetery. The familiar route that had once seemed so welcoming was shorn of landmarks. The upbeat music on the car stereo suddenly annoyed me and I turned it off.

A few blocks from my house, I spotted a wiry older man bicycling toward me. I recognized him as a friend who had always seemed the personification of optimism. It seemed a good omen that he'd be the first person I saw on my return, and I stopped the car, jumping out to hug him. The sweat and dust had made a paste on his face, but a smile shone behind his grizzled white beard. True to form, he seemed cheerful enough at first. Then his face grew somber.

"My best friend died in the storm," Bill said. "They found him drowned in his attic, wearing a life jacket."

The poor man didn't have an axe, I thought, and even though I hadn't known the man, my stomach lurched at the thought of such a lonely, desperate end. My friend Phil came to mind; I remembered searching for him after the storm. When we'd finally connected by phone, I'd wept with relief at hearing his voice. Bill had suffered the same anguish over his own friend, only to learn of a heartrending death. When Bill saw the effect that the story had on me, he quickly changed tacks. "You look great!" he said. "My, that's a lovely skirt you have on."

I was overcome with embarrassment, suddenly feeling like I'd worn a party dress to a funeral. We swapped cell phone numbers, agreed to stay in touch, and I drove on.

My heart sang out as I pulled into my driveway, despite the morose, deserted look of my home. Plywood over the windows, the beached boat at the foot of the steps, the mangled oaks in the yard—none of that seemed to matter—my house was still standing. Once inside, I sighed first with relief and then again in frustration. I'd have a hard time making a list of priorities; everything I laid eyes on shouted for immediate attention.

Anxious to see Joe and Robyn, I crossed the yard and knocked on his door. We'd managed a few phone calls during my time away, but the unreliable cell service had made it difficult to stay in touch. The day I'd left, both he and Robyn had seemed refreshed by the break in Baton Rouge. Now, my eyes widened when I saw Joe. He'd lost at least ten pounds, and, most disturbing of all, the expression on his face lacked any vitality.

I swallowed my shock and hugged him. "It's so good to see you!" I chirped. "Where's Robyn?"

He murmured something about her trying to nap in the front room. He told me that both of them had been plagued with nightmares and hadn't slept much since I'd left. I tried chattering for a few more minutes, then invited them over for dinner later and headed back to my own house.

Passing through the gate between our yards, my new poppy print skirt snagged and tore. I felt the tears begin to well, but stopped them with a wrench of determination. Things could be much, much worse. I was one of the lucky ones. I still had a home, an empty one that would be needed.

SEPTEMBER 19—THANKSGIVING, 2005   My house didn't stay empty for long. Over the next year, it became a revolving commune that my friends jokingly dubbed "Ellis's Restaurant," after the old Arlo Guthrie song. The first full-time residents to move in were the Fitzpatricks. The last week in September, Kevin, Kimberly, and their nine-year-old daughter, Hannah, trudged over to Joe's house for dinner one evening. I didn't know them well, but they'd been invited by another neighbor and were welcomed by all. Water service in our area had just been restored, so we were also able to offer them the unexpected bonus of hot showers.

During the meal, Hannah astonished Robyn and me by matter-of-factly describing her harrowing storm experience. The family had taken refuge in a building owned by a friend, a substantial industrial structure that was located on high ground and had never flooded. When the water invaded, Hannah perched in the attic with her grandfather and watched as her mother below struggled in neck-high water to save nearly a dozen of their dogs and cats, some floating in their carriers. The rising torrent knocked over containers of chemicals and gasoline, and the fumes threatened to asphyxiate the Fitzpatricks. Fighting the wind and water pressure, Kevin forced open a door for ventilation and for over an hour held it ajar. The surge rose to his shoulders and gusts buffeted his exposed head. Hannah breathlessly described her father's encounter with a log that had floated near, one that had become a life raft for a toad. As the log approached, Kevin saw that the toad was not the only passenger—dozens of frantic brown spiders seethed over the wood and the hapless amphibian. He reached out with his foot and pushed it away from the door.

Then Hannah calmly explained that several miles away, their beloved horse had died with more than a dozen others when the stable collapsed. The child was obviously moved by her experience, but her sturdy spirit refused to be subdued. Robyn and I exchanged glances as she spoke, understanding that we were in the presence of a remarkable being.

Hannah went on to detail her family's current living conditions. They had pitched two tents on their empty lot nearby. Her mom, Kimberly, would rise at dawn, wash and dress in the debris-filled surroundings, and then commute for over an hour to her job as a hospital financial analyst. Her father spent most mornings filling out paperwork, making phone calls, and handling the bureaucratic grind required to reassemble their lives. In the afternoons, Kevin would sort through the rubble on their lot, trying to salvage a few tools from his architectural practice. Hannah was supposed to start school the following week, and although she seemed excited about the prospect, she wondered how she'd do homework assignments in the tent.

The Fitzpatricks moved in the next day, occupying "my side" of the house. I shifted my headquarters into the building's large center hallway that contained my office, loft bedroom, and a lavatory. The apartment on the other side of the house became the "migratory" side, accommodating workers, volunteers, reporters, and friends—anyone who needed temporary housing. People often chipped in for house expenses, which helped me out financially, but my biggest boon came from the ceaseless camaraderie. The support of my new extended family kept me from wallowing in the terrible pit of depression that gaped before me.

Hannah became my lighthearted life ring. Most afternoons, she would come home from school, sail through her homework, then help me cook the evening communal meal—often we fed over a dozen people. We served a lot of Mexican food—it was relatively easy, inexpensive, and popular. Hannah proudly took on the title of Cheese-Grater Queen. We

Kimberly and Hannah Fitzpatrick, dressed for the first Halloween after Katrina. Since trick-or-treating door-to-door would have been impossible, several costume events were held on the coast so children could still celebrate.

both became proficient fly murderers. Houseflies had been scarce in Bay St. Louis before the storm, but now swarms of them had descended on the town. Kimberly delighted me once with the gift of an electric swatter shaped like a little tennis racket. Her daughter and I became instant pros, competing for the highest number of the pests we could electrocute.

Fiesta Fridays at my house officially began in October, when I ran into Rickey, the owner of the popular Waveland restaurant of the same name. The restaurant had been destroyed, but the chef's eyes lit up when I invited him over for Mexican food the following evening. He showed up after dark, bearing several enormous trays of enchiladas, enough food for fifty. When my eyes bugged out, Rickey shrugged. He remembered the large house parties I'd sometimes hosted before the storm and had assumed that I'd have dozens of people to feed. That evening, only the basic household crew had shown up.

Horrified that the delectable creations might go to waste, I jumped into my car, tearing across treacherous unlit streets. I screeched to a halt wherever I saw lighted windows or people sitting on porches and shouted, *Rickey cooked Mexican food! There's plenty for everyone! Come to my house, right now!* Within an hour, my home was filled with neighbors who had been fans of the chef, and they devoured every morsel Rickey had cooked.

That evening set a precedent, and the Friday night gatherings at my house became a tradition. For a few hours each week, we were able to shut out the awful reality that awaited us the next morning. The musicians among us played guitars, the tipsy, tattered crowd would sing along, and people forgot about the ten o'clock curfew. Usually, it would be well past midnight when people began to drift home to tents, ravaged houses, or cramped travel trailers.

Even in the early days of aftermath, the community instinctually sought out the fellowship that seemed to facilitate healing. Second Saturday Artwalk, the Bay's long-standing art and music festival, evolved from being a monthly regional attraction to a weekly mental health staple. Katrina didn't even cause a blip in the schedule. On Saturday, September 10—just two weeks after the storm—a small group of survivors gathered in the ruins of Old Town to ensure the unbroken track record of the event. I was recuperating in Nashville when I received a call from Vicki Niolet. She knew I'd left town, but told me that they were celebrating Second Saturday. When she explained that they'd wanted me to be a part of it—even if just over the phone—I wept tears of appreciation for their remarkable pluck.

For the following Second Saturday in October, shop owners Jenise McCartle and Mark Currier performed the Herculean feat of repairing their Old Town store and hosting a grand reopening for their artists' cooperative. The grateful reactions of residents that evening convinced the couple to hold the event on a weekly basis for the next several months. Each Saturday, the festival offered a touchstone of togetherness, a chance to wash off the mud and reunite with friends on an island of normalcy. And

A post-Katrina Second Saturday event in Old Town. Jenise McCartle, who pushed to revive the event after the storm, is second from left (in the black dress). My friend Julie Nelson, who lost her home in Waveland, is on the far right.

the orderly corner of Main Street and Toulme did provide the illusion that our placid town still existed—as long as one didn't walk the two blocks to the beach.

Enormous drifts of rubble lined most streets of the town. Vast fields heaped with debris remained untouched for months, feeding the feeling that we'd been forgotten—except by the companies who offered disaster tours. Large buses would creep through the town, and behind smoked glass windows we could see faces appraising our sad state of ruin. Nicholson Avenue had once been shaded by a magnificent oak canopy, making it the pride of Waveland. Now it offered scenes of spectacular destruction and quickly became a favorite route for the grisly tours. Residents in the neighborhood finally erected a large sign, neatly lettered by hand. The message to those "tourists" was simple:

SIGHTSEERS

This rubble represents
Our lives, our hopes and our dreams.

Please stay out of our way.

Katrina Survivors

The stagnant cleanup efforts seemed a symptom of an ailing federal administration, one overwhelmed by the stupendous breadth of the disaster. An alphabet soup of government agencies lumbered along and burdened our overwhelmed local officials—many of whom had lost their own homes—with reams of paperwork and complicated regulations. The pain and chaos that were exacerbated by bureaucratic blunders are perhaps illustrated best by "The Tale of a Mother Twice Lost."

As Katrina had moved toward the coast, Teri Lucas pled with her elderly parents to evacuate, but they adamantly refused. Gloria and Lukey Benigno had a track record of survival—they had made it safely through Camille in their Cedar Point home built by Gloria's father. Gloria insisted that Katrina couldn't be stronger than Camille, so Teri and her husband, Charlie, resigned themselves to staying in their own home next door in case her parents needed help. During the height of the storm, the surge rose so quickly that it was impossible to cross the seething flood between the two houses. Gloria's last words to her daughter came over the phone as water began charging into both homes. It was an apology. "I was wrong," Gloria told Teri. "This storm is much worse than Camille." Then their connection was cut.

As the muddy torrent rapidly climbed the walls of their house, Teri and Charlie realized they might be pushed to the ceiling and drown. Holding hands, they dove towards their living room floor and swam through the submerged doors leading to the porch, where they'd be able to punch through the screen if the water continued to rise. For over an hour, they struggled to stay afloat. Teri's life was saved by a wall ornament—she clutched a decorative life ring that read "Born to Sail."

When the surge finally began to retreat, she and Charlie created a makeshift raft from the debris and poled it next door to the Benignos'. Clambering inside, they first saw the body of Lukey, floating face down in the kitchen. Frantic, Teri floundered through the ruins of the house, screaming to Charlie, "I can't find Mama!" Long minutes passed before they realized that Gloria's body was actually next to Lukey's.

Charlie grabbed Teri by the shoulders and helped her outside. Then he carried out the bodies of his in-laws, placed them on the raft, and managed to steer it back to their own house. He tenderly laid the bodies in the garage, and Teri brought out a chenille bedspread to cover them. Later in the afternoon when the winds began to subside, the couple hiked over a mile to Highway 90 and reported the deaths to a police officer. He promised to send help as soon as possible. Around noon the next day, Teri sat crying in the front yard when an emergency team arrived. She and Charlie watched as the men photographed, tagged, and then carried away the bodies of her parents.

Later in the week, Teri's sister Aleana arrived from Seattle, accompanied by other family members and a team of relief workers. Aleana began making funeral arrangements for their parents, but had trouble locating their remains. Apparently the generators at the local funeral home had failed, so the bodies of all recovered victims had been transferred away from the coast. Aleana's detective work eventually discovered that a federal agency called DMORT—Disaster Mortuary Operational Response Team—had stepped in and transferred the bodies back to the coast again, to an emergency morgue at the Gulfport airport.

Teri was later interviewed at length by DMORT, filling out long forms with detailed medical and physical information about her parents. The officials swabbed her mouth to obtain a DNA sample. Finally, twenty-eight days after the storm, the bodies of the Benignos were released. Teri was able to visually identify her father's body, but was not encouraged to view the remains of her mother—extreme deterioration had taken place. She asked that her parents be cremated, but a last-minute intuition made Charlie issue an order not to mix the ashes of the couple.

Services were held for the Benignos on October 2, giving the family some small comfort at last. By the second week of November, Teri felt strong enough to return to her job as a surgical nurse. A few days later, she received a call while working, asking that she come immediately to the funeral home. There, Teri and Charlie listened dumbstruck as a pathologist explained that there'd been a mix-up. The couple had not been given Gloria's body, but the remains of a stranger.

The next day, Charlie grimly returned the erroneous urn of the stranger. Teri was finally given possession of her own mother's ashes the week after Thanksgiving. There was no charge for the new urn. She placed it next to her father's at the foot of her bed.

"They're staying right here for now," Teri said, over three years later. "I don't want to lose my mother again."

Teri and Charlie continued to live in their home while it underwent repairs. The wreckage of Gloria and Lukey's house next door confronted them daily, a forlorn reminder of the wrenching loss. When the demolition crew finally arrived in the spring of 2006 to tear down the crumbling Benigno house, the foreman driving the bulldozer began to weep.

"This is the worst I've seen," the man said to Teri. "Can I give you a hug before we begin?"

Teri embraced the man and put forth her own eleventh-hour entreaty. She asked to keep the front door of the house built by her grandfather. Charlie removed the door with the help of the demolition team. Then the couple sat in lawn chairs to watch as Teri's childhood home became an empty lot.

When Teri spared the door to her parents' house, she saved a piece of wood saturated with snippets of happy memories. Many Katrina survivors could have understood her odd request. In the months after the storm—before serious cleanup began in the spring—residents could often be spotted climbing over the sprawling hills of debris, seeking remains from their past. I was chief among them.

My noble dog Jack on one of our debris-salvaging expeditions.

If I'd been in any other American city, someone probably would have urged me to seek psychiatric help. I might have been confined to some safe haven with light green walls, group therapy sessions, and camouflaged bars on the windows. But no one in Bay St. Louis paid any mind at all, because most of us were mad in some fashion. Unnoticed, I explored the flayed new world around me.

While I routinely worked on house repairs for most of the day, by midafternoon I'd be in expedition mode. I'd whistle for Jack, and the dog would run beside my bicycle as I bumped over the pitted streets. I chose debris fields close to the former homes of friends and scaled the precarious piles searching for some treasure I might return, especially some work of art. I sought two special "holy grails"—an exquisite portrait of a friend and a painting by a master impressionist.

The jumble of chaos never failed to fascinate me. Refrigerator doors twisted with ancient shutters, dolls, dancing shoes, broken pottery, and shattered light fixtures. When I spotted a corner of canvas beneath a roof beam or washing machine, I worked with the careful intent of an archeologist to release it. Apparently, bad art was more durable. The only paintings I ever discovered had probably been created in amateur art classes. I found an astonishing number of compositions featuring one-dimensional vases of flowers or crudely rendered New Orleans streetcars. I placed these finds at the nearest "shrine."

I frequently came across architectural prizes, but mostly while driving through town on some errand. As damaged historic houses were gutted, one-hundred-year-old cypress doors or windows would be removed and hauled to the curb by naïve workers. They often watched with wonder as I loaded the "trash" into the back of my wagon and drove away with my load extending out the back. I simply couldn't bear to see more of our town's past hauled to pits and bulldozed into the earth.

The space beneath my raised house soon resembled a junkyard. Stacks of doors and windows joined the jumbled boxes of my personal debris. When I'd cleaned out my wrecked studio, I'd hauled back anything that might be saved. Those crates sat beside the soggy boxes of belongings that had been flooded in my storeroom during the storm. I aggressively ignored them all, while weekly adding historic salvage to the fetid clutter.

The upstairs portion of my home presented a better face. The commune managed some semblance of order, despite the number of people staying there. As Thanksgiving approached, I considered hosting my annual "Orphans' Potluck," a tradition I'd begun years before. The Fitzpatricks planned to spend the holiday with family out of state, but my open-ended list of guests still included over twenty people.

A friend in Alabama had donated generously toward the dinner expenses, so a few days before the holiday, Joe and I drove thirty miles to Slidell, Louisiana, and stuffed a cart at a big box grocery. Tired of eating from paper and plastic, I resolved to create a fine dining experience and also purchased dozens of glasses, goblets, and cups at a chain store sale.

On Thanksgiving Day, friends and family members crowded into the kitchen. The few who had facilities to cook brought their own specialties.

We had pushed aside the furniture in the large living area on the migratory side of the house and set up several tables. The finished result resembled a summer-camp dining room decorated with garage sale finds, but it offered a token of elegance. Before we ate, someone suggested a prayer, and I was tagged with the duty. I cannot recall my words, but suppose it was much like those being offered at other tables along the coast, one of gratitude for those we loved and humble thanks for being alive.

Before we settled into the meal, Robyn stood and read a letter to her uncle Jerry. He and his wife had driven down from their central Mississippi home for the occasion. The words Robyn read were simple but eloquent, thanking Jerry for rescuing her from New Orleans. Hunger was forgotten as tears welled in every eye.

I tried to follow by reading a letter from our Alabama benefactor, but only made it through the first few lines before I broke down. I passed it on to my young cousin Carolyn, who was living with me for the month to help restore my house. Her steady, clear voice never faltered as she read. The letter did not express pity for our losses. Instead, it acknowledged our community's courage. My favorite lines were these:

This is a letter of gratitude to you . . . by example, you are offering others a doorway to learn . . . You have helped us remember who we really are to one another and what we can be.

When the guests had all departed, I sat alone on the front porch swing, sipping a glass of wine and contemplating that bittersweet Thanksgiving. I thought about the essay I'd written the day before and had e-mailed to dozens of friends around the country. It had seemed important to tell them that even in this beaten place, the people of Bay St. Louis would still celebrate the holiday, giving thanks for the simple blessing of being.

"THE BLESSING OF BEING" LETTER TO FRIENDS   *In the real world it's the end of November, but in south Mississippi, it looks like spring. Confused flowers bloom out of season and shrubs are festooned with fresh*

shoots. Trees are covered with new leaves the color of March, that translucent, sparkling green that speaks of promise and warmth.

But it's not warm. I stand in my yard bundled in jacket and gloves, surveying the swollen buds and new growth. There's the eerie sensation that I have somehow stepped into a parallel universe where time and place have been skewed or the world has somehow tilted slightly on its axis. Yet the laws of seasons have not changed. This false spring is an act of desperation.

Katrina stripped each plant and every tree completely. After the storm three months ago, it seemed as if a nuclear winter had settled in. Trees that never lose their leaves loomed like skeletons over their fallen comrades, mangled limbs torn and twisted. Even those coastal sentinels we love so well, the magnificent live oaks that have graced our neighborhoods for generations, stood barren and battered.

Before the storm, I'd never seen a live oak without leaves. I used to delight in explaining the process to astonished northerners. A freeze won't bother a live oak, I'd tell them smugly. They only lose their leaves in the spring, when the emerging leaves force the old ones off. It happens very quickly, so while they're not evergreens, they might as well be. And I'd always say this with a little pride, as if they were pets that didn't shed.

Katrina was no respecter of persons or plants. Without prejudice, this "Great Equalizer" took whatever we had. The oaks, the magnolias, the pecans, the camellias—all stood naked in the aftermath. Flowers flattened by the gales withered in the relentless sun of September. I found that wearing red outside was a bad idea. Dozens of starving hummingbirds that had somehow survived would dive bomb any bright color, hoping for a drop of nectar.

Like the trees, people on the coast have been stripped down to the bones. Homes and possessions—the things we always thought of as offering security and happiness—are damaged or gone. Most of us have lost family or loved ones, some killed by the storm, some forced by circumstance to leave the community. If you live here, something very, very bad happened to you and to everyone you know.

We'll celebrate Thanksgiving anyway, because, despite the tricks of nature, logic tells us that it's really November and time for the holiday. Yet like everything else here, Thanksgiving will be different this year. Tradition will take a sharp turn. Those of us remaining will visit with family and friends and eat our turkey beneath blue-tarped roofs or in FEMA trailers, in tents or relief centers.

Many of our community will find themselves in unfamiliar places, surrounded by strangers. It would seem that on this day of counting blessings, there are more losses than blessings to count.

But we have new blessings, the most significant being the gift of insight, the blessing of being. Those things we thought offered security and happiness have been revealed as cheap charlatans. We bought into the idea that more was better, that money would solve our problems, that possessions would give us peace of mind. The losses brought with the winds of Katrina changed all that. It now appears that we'd been buying snake oil, believing it would cure the cancer of our souls.

Of course, everyone here mourns the loss of material goods (and universally, photos are the most grieved items). There's not a person who hasn't taken a tremendous financial beating. But most will tell you that the gift of life itself and the spirit of community have been revealed as the true treasures. The scales have fallen from our eyes, and we see with a new vision. Here on the coast, our Thanksgiving prayer will be that we can hold on to that vision while we struggle to rebuild.

It's OK to wear red now. The hummingbirds have either migrated or found enough false spring flowers to feed them. Most of the trees still standing have new growth, despite the drought of the past three months. I'm seeing signs of hope in the people as well. Our roots run deep and are the source of our power as individuals and as a community. We can always grow new leaves.

FIVE POUNDS OF POTATOES

Jinx Vidrine: "I get so angry when people tell me it was just stuff we lost. It was not just stuff. There were things of the heart that were lost, things that were significant to my life. Like my sweet sixteen charm bracelet, pics from our adventure trips, my grandmother's rosary from her coffin . . . should I go on? My identity was stripped of the stories which no one else knew, the heritage which enwrapped me and gave me inner peace. Well, I will make myself cry . . ."

It was just a slip of paper, marked with pencil over fifty years before in a small midwestern town called Apple River. It didn't contain a message of importance, or a sweet sentiment. It was a grocery list, scrawled in haste by a busy farmer's wife. Yet of all the possessions that Katrina stole from my friend Julie, this scrap of paper was the hardest loss to bear.

She was folding laundry in my kitchen a few months after the storm. I had one of the few working washer/dryer combos in the county and my house often took on the appearance of a local laundromat. As she folded her boyfriend's work shirts, Julie spoke evenly of their freshly renovated cottage that Katrina had pulverized. The handmade cypress cabinets in their kitchen, the antiques and the books, the piano and her collection of music, her pottery studio—all gone forever.

Then Julie remembered the grocery list. Her face contorted as she told me of the little pad, part of her inheritance of heart. Most of the sheets were still blank, but one bore the handwriting of her mother.

"About halfway down the list," Julie told me, "she'd written 'five pounds of potatoes.' Then, in parentheses, she'd added 'if nice.' For me, that said it all—how she felt about her family, the care she put into something as simple as shopping for groceries. My mother wasn't buying potatoes for us if they weren't the best."

Julie dissolved into tears, and I smoothed a shirt in silence. Thirty years of friendship—yet I was clueless as to any words of comfort I might offer. The small collection of molecules that embodied the spirit of her mother lay at the bottom of the Gulf of Mexico, disintegrating more with each wave.

Every person has these touchstones, belongings without value to any thief, yet possessing the power to open doorways to other worlds. Fingering a small smooth stone can transport one back thirty years in time to the banks of a mountain river. Eyes resting for a moment on a painting can infuse a room with the scent of a Tuscan valley. Handling a letter of rejection can recall surmounted defeat. These are the tender things. These are the things of the heart.

The grocery list keeps good company. Millions of mementos were buried without ceremony in vast pits of debris or swallowed by the sea. I walk along the beach now and know that beneath the unruffled surface lie bones

Ruined family treasures were often tossed into trash piles as residents began to gut homes that remained standing.

and hair, wedding dresses and rings of gold. Flounder nibble at paper that once bore the images of prom nights and christenings and golden anniversaries. Crabs scuttle across splintered furniture that provoked squabbles among grandchildren. For decades to come, lines of fishermen will catch on torn bits of canvas, still bearing the brushstrokes of masters.

Even the landscape of the coast has been ravished of recollections. Historic houses that held generations of family memories have vanished, leaving only sets of steps that lead to nowhere. Massive oaks that easily bore the weight of climbing children have been toppled and hacked into pieces. Arbors and gazebos where lovers had whispered promises of devotion have been dismembered and bulldozed into trash heaps.

My friend Kat recalled the route she drove to work each morning before the storm. "I'd pass these visual triggers and a series of memories would erupt. Just seeing the arc of a particular tree branch would take me back to a picnic on the beach with my children when they were young. The drive was like a rosary of memories, and, strung together, they became a prayer. It was a rich part of living here."

In the months after the storm, the outside world bickered about blame and expenditures and disbursement of funds, but no actuary could calculate the emotional cost, no series of run-on digits convey the bereavement. Survivors struggled with grief, reaching for anchors that had washed out to sea. The methods of coping were diverse. Some who had evacuated and been told their homes were destroyed never came back. Others returned for a few days, gathering what little could be salvaged, then left to start life in an unbroken place. Still others mined the mud, seeking anything that the storm might have spared.

Many searchers were stunned to find that Katrina had a sense of irony. My jazz musician friend Mark Guest had taken his favorite guitars and evacuated before the storm. He and his wife, DeNeice, returned to find pieces of their Waveland house strewn haphazardly across the neighborhood. He says his first thought was one of relief. Through the years, the responsibility of the family heirlooms had become burdensome. He was especially delighted to be rid of his grandfather's banjo. As a guitarist, he detested the sound of the instrument, yet sentiment prevented him from giving it away. Then, climbing over the mounds of debris in his yard, he found that the banjo had settled unharmed against the trunk of a tree.

DeNeice was luckier and discovered a gift of gold: her mother's charm bracelet had been left by a neighbor on the remains of their back porch. Another friend returned a month after evacuating and found a portrait of his mother resting against his mailbox. An architect became an archeologist, spending hours each day in searing heat, excavating his lot. Each small item Kevin rescued was damaged beyond repair. Yet even in a mangled state, the salvaged things—his father's watch, his baby mug, a painting of his children—fulfilled their purpose. They grounded him, gave him the strength to face another day.

And we need the strength because although more than a year has passed, the losses continue, bringing a bitter after-bite of sorrow. A conversation is often interrupted when the speaker stops in midsentence, overtaken by the thought of yet another object stolen by the storm. One neighbor found a cherished antique that had somehow survived the destruction of his home. Looters stole it from his yard before it could be moved. There was the sad afternoon when I paused at my kitchen window to look out at a row of shrubs I'd planted years before. The surge had beaten and salted them, but daily I cheered their brave new growth. As I watched, heavy machinery removing debris from the curb ripped the last one from the ground.

Of course, the coast hasn't cornered the market on loss. Every person of age has experienced that sting at some point in life. Yet in this society, we're trained to ignore it. We banish those impolite reminders of death and destruction to the back rooms of our minds, barring the door with sitcoms and music and small daily dramas. We gather possessions and pile them high, hoping they'll barricade us against the danger that surrounds us. Sentimental symbols become amulets of protection, futile charms against change.

Here, Katrina dismantled those barricades, broke down the door, rampaged through the room. Like Kali, the Hindu goddess of destruction, she wore a necklace of bones and danced on the treasures of the past. She took comfort and left chaos. Those who experienced the storm no longer have the luxury of illusion. The charms that kept the fears at bay have been removed. Yet like Kali, one of Katrina's hands held a scythe, while another scattered seeds. Her cruel harvest created room for growth. Illumination was her gift.

As with many gifts, it carries a curse. Solomon wrote, "In much wisdom is much grief. He that increases knowledge, increases sorrow." On the wisdom side of things, we have learned that money can't purchase security or meaning. The sorrow part keeps us searching for connections to our past without the symbols that had served so well as guides.

Long seasons have passed since the storm. Kat is stringing together a new rosary, one knotted with the pearls of art and flowers and songs she composes for the bees she's now raising. Kevin's father's watch will never run again, but it keeps a different sort of time in the architect's office where Kevin designs hurricane-resistant houses. DeNeice wears her mother's charm bracelet on occasion—with a new appreciation for the word "charm." Mark is still saddled with his grandfather's banjo. It hangs on the wall of the music room in their new house in North Carolina. Their son has expressed an interest in the instrument, so Mark may finally be freed of his bluegrass burden.

Julie and Tommy have been living in a twenty-foot travel trailer since the storm. They're building a new house in the country, miles away from the coast. Another grocery pad will find a place in her kitchen, this one unmarked by her mother. She tells me she's made peace with that loss. Each time she makes a shopping list, five pounds of potatoes—if nice— will come to mind.

"Every single thing can disappear," she says. "But the memories remain."

THIS PROPERTY
IS CONDEMNED

"Call her what you want. Do with her what you will. But remember, This Property Is Condemned."

That's the risqué blurb from the poster promoting the 1966 movie starring Robert Redford and Natalie Wood. Yet the titillating hype, an all-star cast, and director Sydney Pollack didn't save the movie from being a dismal flop. Bay St. Louis didn't care. This Property Is Condemned had been filmed in the heart of Old Town, so it was our flop, our single moment in the glamorous spotlight of Hollywood.

Several buildings in town were featured in the film, but the architectural star was an old brick icehouse built in 1929 by one of the town's mayors. Although it was in sad shape, it had survived Katrina—only to face demolition by an owner who planned to build townhouses on the site. MSNBC covered the story on their Web site and some of the comments from readers floored me. One guy from L.A. wrote: "Who cares? Bulldoze the thing. That's progress. If you want a memory preserved, snap a photo and get over it."

—Notes from my journal, August 2006

I'd always poked fun at the theory that the anniversary of a traumatic event resurrects feelings of anxiety and depression. The skeptic in me scoffed at such psychobabble—after all, a date is just a number on a calendar. Yet as Katrina's first anniversary drew closer, I found myself growing edgy and ill-tempered. Sleep eluded me at night. An unsettling knot of dread grew within as August 29, 2006, implacably approached.

On Saturday, August 26, I pulled up a weather map on my computer and examined tropical storm Ernesto. The five-day cone showed it heading into the Gulf, on a bull's-eye path for Bay St. Louis. *That's a good sign,* I wrote in my journal. *Hurricanes never, ever hit where the five-day cone predicts. It's practically a good luck charm being chosen early on as a direct target.*

Despite my whistle in the dark, that ominous dotted line on the map meant that I might soon have to board up my windows, gather up my dogs, my photos, and my grandmother's music box and hit the road once again to drive north in a thicket of traffic. But as I began making a list of hurricane preparations, Scarlett O'Hara materialized in my head and stamped her foot. *Think about that tomorrow*, she advised. I grabbed my bike and headed to a town gathering at the Depot. Bay St. Louis was throwing a party to commemorate Katrina's anniversary.

Jack trotted alongside as I pedaled up the entrance to the old Depot. Whenever I see the building, a scene from the movie wavers before my eyes, young Robert Redford standing before the façade, jacket tossed over his shoulder. A lot of people in town remembered seeing him in person when Hollywood had descended into the Bay. The script had been inspired by a Tennessee Williams play about shattered illusions. In the wake of Camille and Katrina, both the theme and the name of the movie seemed prophetic.

The fanciful architecture of the Depot building must have delighted Sydney Pollack. Constructed in the 1920s, it appears to have been transported from an Arabian Nights story and magically settled into the spacious park. This evening, smoke from several grills spun out across the grounds, and the parking lot in front of the train station was filled with a mélange of generations and ethnic backgrounds. A rhythm and blues band rocked with a solid backbeat as couples danced. Dozens of children darted through the crowd, while others bounced on the mammoth branches of live oaks that

"Katrina woman" Vicki Niolet, cleaning out her studio at the Lumberyard Arts Center after the storm. Photograph by Joe Tomasovsky.

languidly dipped to graze the ground. Two young girls recognized Jack and ran to greet him. He pranced toward them, lured by the hot dogs in their hands. The children obliged him by sharing, and then he moved on to cruise the crowd, graciously accepting both pats and leftovers from his fan club.

With almost every step, I ran into someone I knew—friends, neighbors, or former customers from my art gallery. Several of the women wore pieces of jewelry I'd created in my past life. A few explained that although they'd lost most of their earthly possessions, they'd taken my jewelry with them when they'd evacuated for Katrina. As they talked, I was overcome by an emotional brew of sorrow, pity, and gratitude for being so honored. In awe, I inspected the jewelry I'd made just a few years before. The woman who

Bay St. Louis mayor Eddie Favre—in short pants, of course—at the shoofly oak on the grounds of the old city hall.

had created those pieces seemed a naïve stranger, and I longed to reach back in time and warn her about what was to come. But if I'd explained the package deal she would not have changed her course. The experience of the past year had brought me both pain and enrichment beyond measure.

The stories of saved jewelry were mixed in with those about insurance and FEMA trailers and the price of building materials. Katrina dominated every conversation. Even references to the past often began "before Katrina." It had become a bold, indelible mark on the timeline of our community. Vicki Niolet predicted that, far in the future, storm survivors would be very unpopular.

"I can see us now in the old folks' home," she said. "They'll warn each other when they see us coming up the hall. They'll say, *Run! Here come those Katrina women!*"

Near the trailers on the grounds that now housed the temporary city offices I spotted the mayor of Bay St. Louis, listening intently to a few constituents. Though Eddie Favre's wardrobe on this steamy night matched most of the crowd's, he'd made national news after the storm by swearing off long pants, lightheartedly vowing to wear only shorts until the city was restored. Residents now wondered if they'd live long enough to see him in slacks again. Many local governments like ours faced the seemingly insurmountable challenge of replacing offices, computers, lost records, school buildings, vehicles, and maintenance equipment. Roads and infrastructure lay in shambles and would take years to restore. Most of the coast's property tax base had been flattened or washed into the Gulf. Although state and federal grant funding would play a major role in rebuilding, a complex bureaucratic labyrinth impeded progress and sapped energy from overworked civil servants. Yet any interaction I had with my city officials or employees left me feeling proud. Many of them were trying to rebuild their own homes while juggling a triple workload and still managed to maintain a cordial attitude.

Jack had found his friend Kevan Guillory in the crowd, and I gave the Bay Town Inn hero a hug, always elated to see him. I mentioned the sad fate of the tree that had saved his life and those of Doug and Nikki. The barren skeleton still stood, but the oak would never bear leaves again. I guessed that drought had finished off the tree, but Kevan disagreed.

"You'd be dead, too, if I made love to you for three hours," he said.

My lingering anxiety evaporated before my laughter faded. Suddenly, I felt some protective, universal cog click into place and was left with a strange premonition of peace. I knew that Ernesto wouldn't harm us, and although the anniversary wouldn't be easy, we'd all be safe—at least for now. I told Kevan goodnight and rode home through the humid dusk, Jack loping serenely by my side.

My intuition about Ernesto proved to be accurate; by the morning of the anniversary, the storm was no longer a threat. I rose at 5 a.m., packed my camera and a cup of coffee, and headed out for a sunrise memorial service in Waveland. Frieda still snoozed soundly on the bed, but Jack would not be denied and followed me down to the car. As I drove down the broken beach road, the upper half of his body hung out the window, ears flying back with the wind.

Traveling the familiar route was disconcerting, even after a year of exposure. If I looked toward the water, everything appeared unchanged—the placid waves reflected the colors of the breaking light, squadrons of huge dragonflies patrolled the beach, solitary blue herons fished for a morning meal. But when I turned toward the shore, the landscape seemed foreign. Although a few new houses were under construction, not one of the old guard remained within sight of the road. Overgrown lots and pilings rising from empty slabs marked the places where homes had once stood. Gaunt, maimed trees lined the road. Many were limbless and their leaves grew directly from the trunks, making them look like bizarre telephone poles that had sprouted to life.

Arriving late for the service, I parked in a sandy lot and commanded Jack to stay in the car. I trudged toward the crowd that had gathered to face the beach and a gospel choir. Standing in the back, I saw that the singers were nearly outnumbered by the media representatives covering the event.

The choir members all wore the black of mourning and had assembled beside a tortured tree. Their sweet voices swelled with a song of praise and comfort as the sun rose behind them. I held on to my composure until a good friend came over and hugged me. That small kindness triggered the memories from that awful morning a year before. Suddenly, I was back in

Joe's house, counting the steps in terror as the surge relentlessly climbed higher. I wrenched my mind back to the present, but that didn't help. I visualized the tranquil plate of water in front of me rising up over thirty feet, dwarfing the assembly of puny humans and towering high enough to cover the tall tree beside the choir. Breathing deeply to subdue the panic, I gripped the arm of my friend.

When the service ended, the crowd was led across the beach road to the Gulf's edge. Volunteers handed out flowers, and, after a short invocation, the group tossed them into the water as symbols of surrender. As my flower floated gently out to sea with a raft of others, I still retained a sense of the vast, uncontrollable power that hid beneath the sea's smooth surface. I had seen the force that could lay waste to the best efforts of humans in the course of a morning. I scanned the solemn faces around me, drawing comfort from their serenity. These people of the coast understood the fragility and brevity of life, an awareness reinforced each time another storm approached. This toughened tribe possessed the knowledge that the most important things cannot be purchased, neither can they be stolen by any act of God. While I could choose a safer place to live, it'd be hard to find a better one.

The late August heat showed no respect for the early morning hour, so Jack and I were both panting by the time we got home. Planning a long anniversary tour of the town, I grabbed some bottles of water and swapped the car for my bicycle. I wheeled it from beneath my house, threading the narrow path between moldering boxes, scavenged millwork, and plastic crates filled with ruined belongings. The mess embarrassed me, but I'd become a master at avoidance. For months, while each "to do" list had been topped with the command "GO THROUGH BOXES," there had always been something better to do, like scrubbing toilets or getting a root canal.

Jack and I headed up Citizen Street toward the beach, passing the empty lot where Augusta's house had stood. She'd hoped to save it, but it was finally deemed irreparable and was demolished. For the time being, she was living with her son, Donald, and exploring options of rebuilding a cottage with the help of volunteers.

A few months ago, she'd stopped for a visit and found me beneath my house, making a rare effort to sift through the contents of my wilted rubbish. I explained that I couldn't just throw the boxes away—they might contain one unsullied sentimental treasure. Augusta smiled in sympathy and told me a story.

"The week before the storm," she said, "before Katrina had ever been thought of, I was lying in my bed, looking at all the things in my room. It struck me how much I'd loved all those objects, so I got up and went from article to article, thinking I had truly enjoyed them to the utmost. It was like I gave all those things up before the storm came and took them, so it didn't go hard on me at all."

She looked at me with eyes that seemed to carry the wisdom of a thousand years, and I fell into their depths. "That what's gone, is gone," she said. "Now, I'm looking to the future, I'm looking for what-else."

Past Augusta's lot, few houses remained. The major debris removal hadn't "ramped up" until early spring, and, although most of the lots had been cleared, some were still strewn with wrecked cars and wooden beams, chunks of roofing and walls. I was able to pass without the temptation to explore. My own salvage expeditions had become infrequent, my compulsion soothed by a strange find a few months before.

Jack and I were slogging through a muddy field that the U.S. Army Corps of Engineers had finally begun to clean. They'd already hauled away much of the debris, but off to the side, I spotted a large slab of wood they'd missed. The size of it alone attracted my attention—it was over six feet in length and thicker than my arm. I peered closely at the grain and realized that the rectangle was made from solid mahogany. Trying to lift it from the muck, I was shocked by the weight and couldn't begin to budge it.

The rain had started to fall again by the time I got home and rounded up Joe and Kevin Fitzpatrick. They rolled their eyes when I asked for their help and teased me about my salvage mania as we drove back to the site in Kevin's truck. The men followed me through the sloppy field, then hefted the block between them. The weight mired their feet in mud, and the rain pelted down as they carried their burden to the truck. Unloading the find back at the house, both men admired the wood and didn't seem to regret the drenching they'd taken to save it.

"Looks like maybe it was a mantelpiece," Joe said, and the next day I took out an ad in the Sea Coast Echo, the Bay St. Louis newspaper. Found in the vicinity of Ramaneda and Third Street. One mantel. Describe to claim.

The first day the ad ran, a woman called, hoping that it might be the one from her destroyed house. Her mantel had been ornate and made from cherry, yet when I described the simple block of mahogany, her voice still rose in excitement. She was certain it had been a neighbor's. Although the neighbors had passed away, she gave me the name of their son. I knew the man—he was the husband of Barbara Brodtmann, a friend and fellow artist.

Woody was thrilled when I called with the news. He'd found no other object from the ruins of his mother's house, and the mantel had been a much beloved feature of the home. When he came to retrieve it, he ran his hand over the fine wood, his marveling smile releasing a dark bird of bitterness that had nested in my heart. It took flight over the fields of ruin and never returned again.

I hung a left on Hancock Street, passing lots overgrown with an exotic variety of weeds I'd never seen before the storm. Katrina had recklessly sown

The Main Street United Methodist Church after the storm. Photograph by Joe Tomasovsky.

seed from bird feeders all over the neighborhood. The sunflowers nodding among the mystery gardens revealed that they'd been planted by the capricious storm. I pedaled on toward Old Town, where another anniversary service was slated for 9 a.m. at the foot of Main Street. There, I found a loose cluster of residents standing on a slab overlooking the beach. Their attention was fixed on CNN reporter Kathleen Koch, who faced a camera and spoke earnestly into a microphone. Koch had grown up in the Bay and had made her old friends proud by following the story of our town's plight with an insider's sensitivity.

One man towered over the small group that had braved the burning sun, and I recognized Rick Brooks, minister of the Main Street United Methodist Church. The church had become a national photographic celebrity after Katrina had desecrated the historic house of worship by shearing off the copper steeple and scornfully hurling it to the ground in front of the building. I asked the clergyman if any sort of official anniversary ceremony had been planned.

"Nine o'clock is the hour the surge came in last year, so they've asked all the churches in town to ring their bells then," Rick said, and then he smiled wryly. "I guess they forgot that none of us have any bells left to ring."

I surveyed the scene before me, my perspective widened by the many missing buildings. The railroad bridge had been rebuilt, but construction on the new highway bridge that crossed the bay had just begun in February. While several historic buildings nearby were undergoing restoration, others awaited demolition. I'd heard rumors of condo and casino complexes quietly competing for placement on this bluff. I tried to imagine a future where high-rises threw long shadows on the narrow streets and gaudy neon signs competed for attention. Long before I'd moved to town permanently, Bay residents had successfully battled the location of a casino where I now stood. I wondered if they still had the will or the energy to beat off another barrage.

Turning back into the town, I considered biking over to Cedar Point, the hard-hit neighborhood on the other side of Highway 90. A few weeks before, I'd driven through the area, and the stark scenes of desolation had flashed through my brain for days after, a macabre slide show that wouldn't end. Mimi's home of thirty years had been nestled there. Now the house was gone and so was Mimi. That hasty hug we'd shared the day she'd been rescued from the Bay had been our last. She lived her final days in a comfortable senior care home near family members in Arkansas. I'd heard she was an adored Katrina celebrity, so Vicki's prediction was wrong—at least in Mimi's case. Mimi and I had spoken on the phone in May, laughing about her wanting to wear lipstick and perfume even in the primitive poststorm circumstances. Five minutes after we ended the conversation, she called me back, to tell me one more time how much she appreciated our friendship. We never spoke again. Her son Jimmie had contacted me on June 12 with news of her death at age ninety-two.

Jack seemed game to go further, but thoughts of Mimi made me forgo the trip to the point and turn for home. I rode by containers of flowers, noble efforts at beautification created by struggling merchants. On

Beach Boulevard on the first anniversary of Katrina.

Second Street, I paused in front of a restored historic cottage, checking out the progress on a new coffeehouse that would soon open. Near the tracks, Kevan and Doug worked on another historic building, and I stopped to take their picture. We talked briefly about the difference a year can make. The glint in Kevan's eye made me suspect he was still thinking about his tree joke. His wink confirmed it, and I rode off, still smiling.

I meandered through the neighborhood en route to my house, stopping the bike occasionally to take a snapshot. I especially enjoyed photographing our homemade street signs. Some were hand-painted by residents who had grown tired of giving directions like "turn left at the collapsed house." Recently, the town had been gifted with a set of nifty new plastic ones, installed by an enterprising volunteer group.

Homemade signs helped residents and visitors navigate through streets shorn of landmarks. Many are still in place, years after Katrina.

FEMA travel trailers were almost as numerous as houses in the neighborhood, some decorated with strands of Christmas lights, flower boxes, or wind chimes. Friends who lived in them had once joked about the cramped quarters, but as the months passed, the laughs became rare. I knew one woman who had struggled for months with the decision to stay in the area or move on. One morning she awoke in her FEMA trailer to find that the sewage had backed up in the night, covering the floor. She started packing her bags. I thought of other friends who had left. Hugh had sold his house in the Bay and moved to his family home in Louisiana. My storm companion Jan was in the process of restoring her Bay house to either sell or rent and was shopping around the country for her next permanent residence.

While a number of visitors still filtered through my house, the major commune had disbanded. The Fitzpatricks had moved into a FEMA trailer earlier in the year. I still saw them often since Kevin had set up a temporary architecture office in the storeroom beneath my house. Hannah's grandfather dropped her off there after school, and the two of us would bicycle through the streets. Lately, we'd been going to the beach in the afternoons and playing a game we'd invented, Archaeology. We'd look for odd objects that Katrina had sucked into the Gulf and later regurgitated onto the shore, then make up stories about them. A ballet slipper would inspire a tale about a dancer who fell in love with the shy young clerk in the shoe store. A refrigerator handle might involve a Great Dane who secretly raided the freezer in the night, indulging his yearnings for ice cream.

Hannah and I also kept watch for a large alligator that had moved into a nearby canal emptying into the Gulf. Other neighbors had testified to its enormous size, and we worried that it might find an elderly terrier like Frieda a tasty morsel. Before we ever had a sighting, the authorities captured and removed the gator, causing our beach adventures to lose an intoxicating element of suspense.

I'd started playing another game, one I kept a secret from Hannah and other friends. I called it the Perfect Picture game. The goal was to find snapshot-sized scenes in my town that showed absolutely no sign of Katrina. The game had been especially challenging right after the storm. Broken limbs, torn streets, and mangled houses relentlessly assaulted the eyes. With the Perfect Picture game, I'd discovered I could turn off my peripheral vision and focus on one small area. By looking at something like a plot of flowers and mentally blocking out the wreckage behind it, for a few brief moments I could pretend that Bay St. Louis had not changed.

I kept count of Perfect Pictures, and, as the year progressed, the numbers rose. Eventually, I'd see several in a day, so I raised the bar and started looking for Full Screens. The new mission was to find a place in town where I could stand facing in one direction and find nothing in my immediate field of vision that reminded me of the storm. On this day of the first anniversary, I had yet to score with the Full Screen version.

Much later, I would understand why the game seemed so important to me. The miraculous gifts of the storm were those of the spirit. Each day,

One of my Citizen Street neighbors, Florence Young, was known for her well-tended gardens before the storm. Her house was destroyed by Katrina, but, while living in a FEMA trailer, she replanted her beds (with the help of volunteers from California), providing a bright spot amid the devastation. Photograph by Joe Tomasovsky.

survivors were bolstered by those around us who boldly faced off a tag team of troubles. Corps of volunteers invigorated the community, reviving us with dynamic generosity. Yet it was difficult to pair any *image* with those inspiring qualities.

Meanwhile, the losses of Katrina were imminently visible, branding the brain with panoramas of despair and pain. The theatre of our minds constantly replayed movies of rising water, broken bodies, and torn landscapes. A simple errand like driving to the post office required navigating ragged roads that passed beaten, still abandoned buildings, memorials to misfortune. Finding even a small visual balm—like a small garden planted by a neighbor—gave us the power to heal our dreams and restore our peace.

I wasn't much for landscaping, but was appreciative of my neighbors who had taken the time to brighten the surroundings. I guessed that Joe's vast yard might provide me with my first Full Screen. He'd planted dozens of young trees, shrubs, and ornamentals, creating a Zen island on Citizen Street. I found him playing in his yard with Susie, the puppy he'd rescued soon after the storm. The fifty-pound lab mix presented a formidable opponent as they tousled with a soccer ball. Susie had seemed to distract Joe from the loss of Cleo the squirrel. A few weeks after the storm, Cleo had chattered at Joe from her perch in a tree, then disappeared for good. We hoped that she was raising her babies somewhere in the town, teaching them to regard humans as clumsy creatures best avoided.

A year ago, I'd made the decision to ride out the storm in Joe's house, naïvely thinking it might be a bonding experience. I'd imagined a short adventure, rather like a camping trip, not a year-long expedition into the heart of darkness. The ordeal had drawn some coast couples closer, but for many others, Katrina had sloshed over the embers of romance, extinguishing even double-digit marriages. Joe and I were old friends whose courtship had budded just months before the storm. In the aftermath, we'd gradually fallen back into more familiar patterns of companionship and alliance. This morning, I wanted him to critique my morning's cache of photographs and asked if he was game for lunch. We agreed to go for sandwiches in an hour and I rounded the corner to my own house.

The three large oaks in the side yard were finally beginning to fill out—I'd ignored my water bill and left the hose running on them throughout the drought. Behind the oaks, the sight of my house itself was cheering—the Webb School seemed to exude playful kid energy, absorbed from the generations of children who had cavorted on the grounds and chattered in the classrooms. Most of the major reconstruction on the schoolhouse had been completed. And while the old gal needed serious cosmetic surgery, the bones beneath had been structurally reinforced with a conglomeration of brackets and braces and clips. The fortifications had been recently completed, and Webb School possessed new mettle. I felt confident that my house could coolly confront most storms even if they were blustering bullies.

The investment in my home had been emotional as well as financial. Like everyone else in Bay St. Louis, I'd had two choices—move elsewhere or commit to rebuilding. Those who chose to stay understood there'd be a high price to pay: years of inconvenience, inflated insurance rates, a precarious business environment, and the threat of more hurricanes. I didn't fault those who had moved on, and some days, frustration, fatigue, and fear made me long to follow them.

But intangible dividends were granted to those who remained. The people of Bay St. Louis had resolved to rebuild an entire city from the ground up—a seemingly insurmountable challenge. To be part of that community effort provided inconceivable exhilaration and satisfaction. For many, the allure of manicured lawns, unmarred vistas, and pristine buildings could not compete with the gifts of the spirit offered by this tattered town—one crushed, but hardly conquered.

PART SEVEN

Revelations

TAKE IT ALL

The trees had stood strong against gale-force winds for over twelve hours and had resisted the power of an unprecedented tidal surge. They survived the twelve-week drought that followed the salting of the earth by the storm. Seven months after the hurricane, in a valiant show of persistence, the branches began to bud, covering the limbs with the effervescent green of new spring growth. Millions of other trees had fallen in south Mississippi, but the tall trees growing on Citizen Street, not far from my house, were going to make it.

The patch of woods spread across a large marshy parcel bordering the lot where my neighbor Augusta's house had once stood. To my knowledge, no house had ever been built on the site. The lush thicket served the neighborhood well, providing shade, a wildlife refuge, and improved drainage.

*As I biked toward the beach one warm spring afternoon, I noticed a sign had recently been posted on the property. Painted on a rough piece of plywood and nailed to a tree trunk, it had apparently been left as a directive to the U.S. Army Corps of Engineers crews who were beginning to clear debris from lots across the city. The sign read: **Take it all.***

My face flamed with anger. I didn't know who owned the property, but they were clearly ignorant jerks. If they wanted to sell the land, barren lots would bring less money. Should they want to build there eventually, they'd have no shade and serious drainage problems. I tried to imagine what the block would look like denuded of the woods. It was a depressing vision, especially since we'd already lost so many other trees in the neighborhood.

I rode back to my house and returned to the lot with a fat black Magic Marker. No cars were coming, no witnesses walked the streets. I parked the bike, jumped across a ditch, and reached up to add an amendment to the sign. **"Take small trees only. Live oaks and magnolias are protected by law."** *I counted the large trees I could see—at least twenty sizeable ones soared above the under-growth, and I identified several live oaks and magnolias among them.*

A week later, I biked by and noticed that my amendment had been crossed out. Three more signs had been posted for emphasis. **Take it ALL,** *each one said.*

I called Augusta and we shared concerns. She was hoping to eventually rebuild her home on Citizen and had always loved the shade the woods had pro-vided. We thought that perhaps the city would be able to prevent the slaughter. A few nights later at the city council meeting, I mentioned my worries during the public forum. I was relieved to learn that the corps of engineers were not allowed to cut down any trees that weren't leaning at least 30 percent. Federal tax dollars were earmarked to take care of "leaners" and "hangers"—trees that presented threats to residents—not to clear property for future development. Augusta and I were reassured, and I took the black Magic Marker out of my bike basket. The owners of the property could demand anything they wished, but obviously they weren't going to get it.

A few weeks later, I biked down the street. Only two trees remained where the woods had been. The rest had been pushed over and hacked to pieces in the course of a single day. The wood wasn't even granted the dignity of being used in some way. The remains had been bulldozed into a pile near the street where the logs would be hauled to a hole in the ground, buried and left to rot.

As I stared in horror at the massacre, another neighbor driving by stopped to comment. I used several expletives to express my dismay, wondering how the corps could have gone against directives. My neighbor reasoned that a private contrac-tor may have been the culprit and reminded me that trying to assign blame now would be a waste of time. It'd take at least half a century to recover the loss.

Then, leaning out of his car window, he brought up an excellent point. "The property belongs to the owner," he said. "They have the right to do what they want with it."

In a flash, I saw that the fundamental issue went far beyond the slaughtered trees before me. The debate had been raging for centuries. Do personal freedoms and an individual's pursuit of profit have priority over the well-being of the community as a whole?

Our town had lost so much in the storm itself, yet we faced innumerable new threats. I'd seen damaged historic buildings, part of our town's legacy, torn down for the sake of convenience. I'd witnessed the invasion of thieves and con men who preyed on our desperation, thriving in the turmoil. I knew of short-sighted development schemes that proposed to fill wetlands, the very resource that would help protect us from future storm surges.

The Rolodex file in my head spun out of control, revealing an abundance of perils that I'd never considered. I understood at last that although the community had survived the ferocity of Katrina, the storm had unleashed forces that could finish us off for good. And with an extremely compromised immune system, Bay St. Louis was incredibly vulnerable to any virus that might attack, from within or without.

I bid farewell to my neighbor and pointed my bike towards home, suddenly feeling very, very tired.

—Notes from my journal, March 2006

While the coast thrashed in pain, Katrina's bloodletting attracted speculators and opportunists from afar. Disguised as sweet-talking do-gooders, some counterfeit contractors preyed on homeowners desperate to rebuild. They'd insist on a handsome deposit—often withdrawn from depleted life savings—and then disappear. Community chaos and fractured communications worked to the advantage of these vermin; sometimes they'd have the gall to scurry into an adjacent neighborhood and pull the same con.

Some stole from us outright, looting the last surviving keepsakes of survivors or pilfering building materials from construction sites. My friend Jan lived in Pittsburgh while she tried to oversee an extensive restoration of her Bay St. Louis house. She'd return to the Bay on occasion to check on the painstakingly slow progress. During one inspection, she discovered that thieves, in the span of a night, had totally stripped her house of the new copper plumbing. Completely dispirited, she posted a "For Sale" sign in front of the cottage.

In other cases, our resolve to persevere was undermined by carelessness or ignorance. Two weeks after the storm, a contractor for the state highway department bulldozed dozens of ancient oak trees from a median in Gulfport. Stan Tiner, executive editor of the Biloxi *Sun Herald*, blasted the carnage. He called the trees "living cultural connectors to our past" and wrote that their destruction was "insensitive and insulting to the people who live here."

He pointed to a disturbing trend. "None of that seems to matter to those, most notably developers, who represent a second wave of destruction and who are reducing South Mississippi's tree population at an unbelievable pace. They are bulldozing untold acreage, marching across the landscape like an army of carpenter ants clearing every piece of vegetation, as if on a mission."

That mission often seemed driven by a motive of profit. Razor teeth flashed behind earnest smiles as profiteers repeated phrases like "shot in the arm" and "clean slate." One California planning firm working with the city of Biloxi quit in 2006. According to the *Sun Herald*, the planners charged in their resignation letter that "city leaders are letting developers drive the rebuilding process and also are allowing the destruction of the community traditions."

Biloxi wasn't the only coastal area facing extraordinary developmental pressures. In more sparsely populated Hancock County, the onslaught had begun even before the storm.

A few miles west of Bay St. Louis lay Clermont Harbor, the home of my friend Lori Gordon. In Lori's neighborhood, raised fishing camps and simple homes lined the streets where generations of families had enjoyed a serene lifestyle in a place that seemed untouched by contemporary concerns. Kids and their parents walked to the beach, carrying fishing poles and folding chairs. Lori's studio perched above a majestic marsh, and the paintings that were birthed there often depicted the startling beauty that surrounded her.

Just a few months before Katrina, the county had rezoned eleven hundred acres nearby—mostly wetlands—threatening to change Clermont Harbor forever. More casinos would join the single one already established, and several high-rises were slated to begin construction. One proposed tower would loom over the marshes a mind-boggling forty-five stories. County officials hoped the area would build out with more than ten thousand high-rise condo units—rivaling the combined housing stock of Bay St. Louis and Waveland. They envisioned a "New Vegas," one that would create jobs and fatten tax coffers.

As a response to the rezoning, Lori and I founded a watchdog group called Coastal Community Watch in May 2005. The CCW mission was to "facilitate citizen participation in Hancock County developmental issues." Lori and some of her neighbors filed a legal appeal to the zoning decision, backed by CCW. Residents of nearby Waveland and Bay St. Louis joined the fray, donating thousands of dollars to help fund the appeal. Many had concerns like my own—wondering how our family-oriented lifestyle could withstand the pressures of a mega resort city nearby. When Katrina struck, over eight hundred members belonged to Coastal Community Watch. Most seemed to understand that development was inevitable and necessary, but hoped for projects sensitive to our heritage.

Katrina added a sad twist to the story. While the appeal was making its way through the legal system, every house in Clermont Harbor—including Lori's—was flattened. Yet the membership of Coastal Community Watch actually grew after the storm as many residents in the Bay and Waveland recognized a new threat: the annihilation of our community character.

The fact that thousands of houses and historic buildings had vanished overnight didn't seem to matter. Our unique identity had withstood both wind and water. And although thousands of people may have lost everything they owned, they didn't want to sacrifice the one thing that seemed to have survived—the invisible essence of their towns. "Preserving the character" became a community mantra.

In October 2005, at the request of Governor Haley Barbour, hundreds of the country's top architects and planners converged on the coast for an extraordinary renewal forum. They formed teams to focus on each coast city, then met with community leaders and residents to draw out a vision for the future. The final report for Bay St. Louis begins with a section titled "What We Heard You Say." Number one on the list reads: *Keep the small-town character, the architectural heritage and the natural beauty. Build on the arts character. Provide for growth without destroying what makes Bay St. Louis so liveable.*

FEMA's Long Term Recovery Plan for Hancock County states the same edict culled from community input: *Preserve the small-town character of Bay St. Louis and Waveland.*

Yet the directive didn't stop developers from tempting local leaders with dreams of instant recovery, numerous jobs, and new revenues to replace the tax base gutted by Katrina. A particularly alluring prospect was presented by the Paradise Properties Group, who claimed they were planning over $5 billion in projects in Hancock County.

One local architect wisecracked, "It's ironic that they chose the name of something they'd probably destroy."

The group boasted of plans for glitzy condo towers, casino complexes, and commercial retail centers along the Hancock coastline, including sites in Bay St. Louis and Waveland. Yet shortly after a FOX news broadcast featured these economic emancipators, a 2006 MSNBC report revealed some astonishing facts.

Donald and Richard Kern, two brothers who were key players in Paradise Properties, had been involved in an Internet stock scam that had fleeced millions from unsuspecting investors in the late nineties. A civil case brought against the Kern brothers by the Securities and Exchange Commission had resulted in a fine of nearly $10 million dollars—a debt they had yet to satisfy.

The extent to which the community may have been snookered was brought to light when MSNBC reporter Mike Stuckey asked Donald Kern about the projects the brothers had supposedly developed elsewhere: *Asked to name a single project, he replied, "Off the top of my head, I can't remember them right now."*

Paradise Properties Group scrambled to recover when local media outlets ran with the story, but although it assumed a lower profile, the corporation didn't dissolve. In January 2007, the *Sun Herald* reported on its plans to plunk a massive casino complex in Bay St. Louis on the city's main gateway. The rendering printed in the newspaper showed a sprawling scenario that included a convention center, casino, condos, and a hotel—

The first block of Main Street, one year after Katrina. The proposed casino in Old Town would have required the demolition of several surviving historic buildings.

although much of the proposed fifty-five-acre site contained federally designated wetlands.

Frazzled Bay residents were still trying to process this startling information when another group of developers stole the thunder. The new group unveiled a venture that called for the demolition of surviving historic buildings in a three-block area of Old Town, the city's sacred cow of culture. The $100 million concept proposed the building of a counterfeit historic complex that would contain a forty-thousand-square-foot "boutique" casino, a four-hundred-room hotel, and a parking garage.

Invited to speak before the city council, the developers faced a standing-room-only crowd in January 2007. People spilled out into the lobby, while I squeezed into a tiny space by one door, curious to see the reactions of my community.

While a few spoke in favor of the plan, the majority of citizens seemed staunchly opposed. Even downtown merchants, who would benefit from promises of subsidized rent in the new complex, expressed reservations. An Old Town property owner who probably stood to profit by the proposal called the idea a "mismatch and a cultural clash." The city motto—"A Place Apart"—was invoked by several others in pleas to preserve our city's character. A former city councilman predicted that "if you open up this can of worms . . . you're going to have worms all over town."

Less than two months later, the *Sea Coast Echo*, a local newspaper headquartered in Bay St. Louis, ran a full-page ad that appeared in two separate editions. The message was simple: *We, the undersigned, believe that locating a casino in Old Town Bay St. Louis (in the vicinity of Beach and Main Streets) would be a case of inappropriate placement.*

Beneath were the names of eighty-two citizens who had pitched in to pay for the ad. Many were prominent businesspeople in the community. The ministers of two Old Town churches had also signed on. The casino proposal evaporated like a shallow puddle on a sizzling summer street.

Meanwhile, illegal wetlands fills were beginning to occur at an alarming rate. Authorities learned about one when a Coastal Community Watch member getting a haircut heard about suspicious earth-moving activity from his barber.

Then, in the fall of 2007, a young woman appeared before the Bay St. Louis City Council, bringing photos of a massive wetlands fill adjacent to her property. Chrissy Schuengel had begun investigating when a mild rainstorm caused the yard of her newly built home to flood. She calmly stated her case before the council. Since apparently no permits for the developers' work had been filed—with either federal agencies or local authorities— Chrissy insisted on an immediate halt to the wetlands destruction. Her forthright manner and unwavering stance impressed me, and I couldn't resist comparing her to Joan of Arc.

Within a few weeks of the council meeting, two environmentalist friends of mine volunteered to fly over the property behind Chrissy's. They returned with a series of staggering images. The seven-hundred-acre site, which contained a large percentage of wetlands, had been riddled with roads. A huge swath of raw earth gaped where the pine forests had been razed. Canals cut through the property like wide ribbons. Chrissy sent the digital images and her meticulous documentation to the U. S. Army Corps of Engineers, the EPA, and Gulf Restoration Network, an active environmental group in the region. For months, the "Maid of the Bay" dogged both federal and local authorities, her persistence paying off in June of 2008, when the EPA finally decided to pursue a criminal investigation.

The laissez-faire attitude towards wetlands adopted by some developers seemed to be inspired by the theory that it was better to ask forgive-
ness than permission. It must have appeared to be an especially effective
tactic in a post-Katrina world where authorities—who had been overbur-
dened in the best of times—now carried a workload that bowed them to
the ground.

To exacerbate the situation, the corps of engineers announced in October 2006 that it proposed relaxing restrictions for filling of "low quality"
wetlands in six coastal Mississippi counties. The permitting process would
no longer require cumbersome public hearing or comments. It would also
increase the acreage that was eligible for "fast-tracking" from one to five.

Proponents claimed the move was necessary to rebuild needed housing. Opponents wondered why *any* new housing was being constructed on
wetlands prone to flooding, especially since the counties contained plenty
of higher elevation property.

"Five acres!" one insider exclaimed to me in alarm. She'd worked for
years in a state regulatory agency that had monitored wetlands fills. "That's
huge! We're talking a 500 percent increase overnight!"

National environmental groups jumped into the battle, foreseeing the
potential for other states to concoct reasons to pressure for an easing of
federal guidelines. The corps offices were inundated with over five thousand comments. In response, the corps added a few caveats to the regulations and trimmed the proposed five acres to three.

Two Gulfport community groups took issue with the ruling and filed a
lawsuit with the corps. The Mississippi Department of Marine Resources
shot back with a press release calling the suit "frivolous" and "damaging
to Coastal recovery." The release, dated August 30, 2007, quotes Governor Barbour: "This issuance of RGP-20 is one of several things that the
Mobile District Corps of Engineers has done at my request to acceler-
ate the recovery process following Hurricane Katrina. It's something we
asked the Corps of Engineers to do and we will vigorously defend it in
court. Mississippi applauds the Corps of Engineers for taking this inno-
vative action."

An environmental activist friend expressed amazement when he read
the release. "Even though it's not supposed to happen, local officials exert

influence on the corps all the time," he said. "But it usually happens very quietly. To my knowledge, this is the first time a governor has actually *bragged* about it."

The "frivolous" lawsuit didn't go away and was still ongoing as of July 2009. Coast attorney Robert Wiygul called the whole thing "silly" and said that the new streamlined permitting process hadn't been used once since it had been put into place.

Wiygul noted, "The fact is, that facilitating building on wetlands has nothing to do with affordable housing, expediting recovery or anything else except making money for developers. Insurance costs and the overall economy are the issue."

By late 2007, the insurance crisis and the stumbling national economy began to stall grandiose projects along the entire Mississippi coast. Steel skeletons of condo, retail, and casino complexes stood as new monuments to thwarted ambitions. While developers foundered for lack of investors, Bay St. Louis residents used the unexpected breathing space to consider what the future might look like.

Hundreds of Bay residents met repeatedly over a two-year period to give input on a new comprehensive plan, one that would guide development of the city for the next twenty-five years. In spring of 2009, the city council unanimously adopted the plan, laden with references to "preserving the character." During one series of public meetings, the *Sea Coast Echo* ran a story with a bold headline blazoned across the front page: "Residents: 'No More Casinos or High-Rises.'"

During the tedious process, a few people appeared to jockey for zoning changes that would impact the value of their own land holdings. Yet few really seemed to blame them for trying to manipulate public policy for personal profit. Once, after listening to me fume about someone I'd pegged as a self-serving schemer, a regal community leader gave me a mild rebuke. Her face had aged to reflect her character—kind, perceptive, and sincere.

"That poor man," she drawled in authentic pity. "And he came from such a fine family. It's so sad, you should feel sorry for him. Everybody knows that all he cares about now is money."

"All he cares about now is money." The observation offered the ultimate in disdain, but also a lesson in compassion. Poverty of the soul—not a lack of

The indestructible Augusta, in front of her old house in early spring 2006, shortly before it was demolished.

wealth—made one an object of pity in Bay St. Louis. Once again, I experienced the thrill of realizing that I lived in a most extraordinary place.

Augusta reinforced that feeling during a visit one afternoon to tour her new house. It'd been built over the past few years with the help of family members and volunteers. During the process, she hadn't had time to pay much attention to the comprehensive plan or the threat to the wetlands or the possibility of high-rise towers in the town. What little free time she'd had, she'd spent fishing from local piers. "Your mind just relaxes. You can't think about your problems when you're casting a line."

First we looked over her vegetable garden in the backyard, where dozens of ripening fruits clustered on towering tomato plants. Inside, she led me from room to room, while I marveled at the artful way she'd decorated. Augusta's green thumb had been working magic inside as well as out— philodendrons escaped from baskets that dotted the cottage, tendrils creeping across shiny floors and climbing the corners of her living room.

As the visit ended, the eighty-one-year-old matriarch stood in front of her new home and gazed at the overgrown field next door. A weathered "For Sale" sign, posted shortly after the woods had been cleared, hung forlornly from a pole near the street. Yet volunteer trees had already sprung up and were shooting skyward at an astounding rate. Some were already taller than my head.

"It won't take too long for those trees to be giving me some shade," Augusta said, smiling. And I understood then that absolutely no one had the power to take it all, at least not in Bay St. Louis.

GRAPES OR GIANTS

Most of the people here are demoralized, with no money and no time. They work regular jobs, then come "home" to face the endless task of trying to put their lives back together. I have yet to see a government worker gut a house, put up new drywall, or clean out someone's refrigerator. If it weren't for the volunteers, we would have just folded like a cheap umbrella in a downpour.

"I was cleaning up around the house one day a week after the storm and heard a knock at my door," Hugh remembered. "I found this effervescent guy standing on my porch. He was about twenty-five years old, had a Bible in one hand and a chain saw in the other. He asked if he could cut down the trees that were leaning on my house.

"I looked up and down the street and saw groups of his people working in that damned heat to clear the trees. None of them preached or required that you listen to them. They were all happy, running chain saws for Jesus."

—Notes from my journal, October 2005

On the afternoon of Christmas Eve, I headed towards the old Bay St. Louis Depot, driving on streets lined with head-high banks of debris. In the four months since the storm, a free medical clinic had been operating from the ground floor of the historic building. Generations of travelers had trooped through the tiled lobby, but now the lofty room was crammed with cardboard boxes and plastic storage containers spilling out crutches, bandages, and bottles of antiseptic. The old ticket office had been transformed into a pharmacy packed with rows of medications. Tan room dividers created tiny cubicles to give patients a modicum of privacy during examinations.

That afternoon, the usual crowds had thinned to just a few patients, and the sick friend I'd brought was seen almost immediately. Dr. Currier ("Call me Carol") was part of a volunteer team from the Virginia hospital sponsoring the clinic. While she was serving her volunteer stint, Carol stayed in a travel trailer parked in the Depot lot. Hotels weren't an option.

After she'd tended to my friend and given her free antibiotics for the bronchitis, we talked for a few minutes. Carol didn't appear to mind that she was spending the holidays away from home in a town full of strangers. In fact, she seemed downright jolly. I invited her to a gathering at my home the next day, but she already had a full dance card, telling me she'd pop over if she had the time.

Driving the few blocks back to my house, I guessed that about half of the houses in my neighborhood—at least the ones still standing—were occupied. Many of the residents who remained had decorated with a vengeance, their myriad strands of Christmas lights making a bright statement of survival. *We're still here*, they seemed to say. *And damn it, we're going to celebrate.*

My own house joined the luminous lineup with blue and white lights twinkling across the front veranda. The week before, a cadre of volunteers from a college in Georgia had been headquartered with me, and they'd pitched in to help decorate. After days of hard duty slogging through mud to help families repair their houses, they'd scattered for their own homes for the holidays. I found myself missing the survivalist sorority scene with its nonstop giggles.

But the next day would hardly be dreary. Friends were coming by for Christmas dinner and would share champagne donated by an Alabama woman they'd never met. Across the coast, children would receive toys to replace their possessions lost in the storm, gifts from more strangers across the county. Any hungry resident could gather at churches or food tents for

Lunchtime at one of the free camp kitchens that volunteers set up in town to feed survivors. Many operated for months, understanding that residents had little energy left to prepare nourishing meals. Photograph by Joe Tomasovsky.

fellowship and a fine meal. Our beaten little town glowed with beacons of generosity that had begun to shine months before the holiday season.

The mud hadn't even dried on the broken streets when volunteers in unprecedented numbers began streaming to the coast. Dozens of organizations and churches set up food tents and distribution points for clothes, groceries, and basic necessities like diapers and toilet paper. Hundreds of people who didn't belong to any official group also headed south, wanting to help in some way. Representing every swatch of society's quilt, the only common denominator among them all was an irresistible impulse to help. Even other countries opened their hearts. Qatar—a tiny speck on a middle-eastern map—set up a special fund and funneled millions into Gulf Coast education, medical care, and housing assistance.

In the chaos, convention gave way to efficiency, and sometimes odd alliances were formed. In Waveland, a group of free-spirited hippie kids in tie-dye teamed up with evangelical Christians from Texas, forming a peculiar partnership. Their Rainbow Kitchen became a favorite community gathering spot during mealtimes. The colorful encampment made up of painted school buses and tents provided a vivid and welcome counterpoint to the grays and browns of devastation.

On the coast after Katrina, every life with a loss seemed touched in some tender way by a kindness extended, frequently offered by complete strangers. My friends and neighbors often wondered at the magical motivation behind the generosity. Had the collective pain of our community telegraphed some sort of clairvoyant communiqués across the country?

The more spiritual of the volunteers sometimes spoke of a calling. While some credited that beckoning to God, others said they'd heard an inner voice. To those who had experienced the pull, the message seemed to be the same: *Rearrange your life and go there to help,* the calling demanded. *It seems crazy, but don't be afraid.*

The first time I saw Jean Larroux speak before the city council, it was obvious he'd heard that call. A weary cluster of citizens, some still in clothes spattered with mud from the day's work, sat on molded plastic chairs in the trailer where the weekly meetings were now held. City officials had dealt with residents' issues and a long line of representatives from agencies with acronyms like FEMA, MEMA, and COE. Then during the public forum, a young bearded man stood, his personal power shining through the exhaustion in the room like a roman candle in a cavern.

He introduced himself as Jean Larroux, using the French pronunciation, *Jzhawn Larooo.* For me, it brought to mind the swashbuckling pirates who had made their headquarters on the coast in centuries past. He even looked a little like a buccaneer.

Most of the locals seemed to know him, and I understood why as he talked of growing up in the Bay. Now a pastor, Jean announced the intentions of beginning a new ministry in town, one with the focus of healing and recovery. He said it would be named Lagniappe, and everyone smiled. It's a French word often used as slang on the coast and it means "something extra," like the thirteenth donut in a baker's dozen.

Later, I'd learn that Jean had been led back to his hometown by a series of events that began in August, as he watched TV in his Memphis living room. News coverage showed Katrina gaining strength and advancing toward Bay St. Louis. He placed frantic and frequent phone calls to his mother, who still lived in the Bay, finally persuading her to head north in a last-minute evacuation. His aunt and uncle, Gloria and Lukey Benigno,

made the fatal decision to stay in their Bay St. Louis home, which had survived Camille with no serious effects.

Jean, a popular pastor on the staff of a Memphis church with over three
thousand members, began relief plans even while Katrina still blasted the
coast. Working the phone on Monday, he contacted families he knew and,
within six hours, had secured enough donated emergency supplies to fill
a truck. He rallied a team made up of his father, his sister, Hayden, and
several friends. The group ignored official warnings that no one would be
permitted into the disaster zone, and three days after the storm, the small
caravan set out for Bay St. Louis. His cousin Aleana, daughter of the Benignos, was also a member of the expedition. She had flown into Memphis
from her home in Seattle when she'd received the stunning news that her
parents, Gloria and Lukey, had perished in the surge.

The team ferried the load of food and medical supplies past roadblocks,
detours, and debris-filled landscapes, not stopping until they reached the
ruins of the Benigno home at dark. There they found Aleana's sister Teri in
her house next door, trying to shovel out mud by the light of a candle.

For over a week, Jean and his team camped out in tents they pitched
in the driveway that once led to Teri's home. Jean remembers that period
as the "hell days." The group spent long days searching for missing people
and dispensing supplies and medications to survivors. The heat was so
intense that the team hooked up a room air conditioning unit to a generator in the driveway and took turns standing in front of the cool air. Jean's
sister, Hayden, a registered nurse, often administered intravenous fluids
to offset dehydration among volunteers and survivors alike. In one photo
taken at the campsite, the grinding fatigue is palpable. It shows Jean and a
friend sitting in lawn chairs, the tubes of IV drips running into their arms.
Both men are holding drinks and smoking cigarettes.

Jean remembers pickup trucks driving past him with bodies in the back.
He recalls a young man who said he'd helped the National Guard retrieve
the remains of fourteen victims. One joyous moment occurred when Teri's
wedding ring, lost while she struggled through the surge, was unearthed
from the mountains of mud shoveled out of her house. The group dissolved into laughter and tears before saying a prayer of thanksgiving.

"Pastors are supposed to be able to put suffering and tragedy in neat little file folders," Jean said. "But there was no way I could categorize those experiences."

Exhausted and debilitated from working in the brutal heat, the team finally drove back to Memphis to regroup and gather more supplies. When Jean arrived at his suburban home with his father, both men found it difficult to go inside. It was evening, and lights glowed from the windows. Jean could see his children in the family room, watching TV in a very perfect world. Jean's father is a Vietnam veteran, and, for the first time, his son related to a soldier's conflicted anguish in making the abrupt transition from tragedy to normalcy. The two men stood in the driveway and cried.

Jean said, "The only ones who could have understood were south of I-10."

Jean spent the next few months shuttling back and forth between Memphis and the Bay. When in Memphis, he observed himself feeling "anxious and burdened," only finding relief when he returned to the devastation on the coast. During this period, a passage from the book of Nehemiah began to nag at him. In the second chapter, Nehemiah bemoans the fate of fallen Jerusalem, his home. The prophet pleads, *"Send me to the land where my fathers are buried, that I might rebuild it."*

Another pivotal scripture struck the unsuspecting minister one evening at a Bay St. Louis campfire devotional, when he opened his Bible at random and began reading from Psalms. *"I waited patiently for the Lord, he turned to me and heard my cry. He lifted me up out of the slimy pit and the mud and the mire and he set my feet upon a rock, making my steps secure. He put a new song in my heart."*

"I started crying, because I understood then that I had to come home," said Jean. "It was truer than anything I've ever known in my life."

Unfortunately, Jean's wife, Kim, didn't have a simultaneous epiphany. In September, when he first approached her with the idea of moving to the disaster zone with their three young children, her initial response was adamant.

"Hell, no!" Kim said.

"At first, I thought that was my 'out' with God," Jean said. "He obviously wasn't calling her. And he wouldn't call one of us without the other."

Jean Larroux (in white hat on right) participating in a volunteer house-building effort in Bay St. Louis.

Then in the first week of October, Jean and Kim attended a conference, sitting in the front row of a thousand-member audience. The Scottish minister teaching that morning read from the book of Numbers, relating a story of scouts sent into the Promised Land before the tribes of Israel entered en masse. Ten of the twelve scouts returned to the encampment with tales of ferocious giants waiting to slaughter them all. They begged Moses to give up the invasion plan. But two of the scouts carried enormous clusters of grapes and testified to the land's great bounty.

Although the preacher was unaware of the dilemma facing the couple, he paused at this point in the story and seemed to look directly at Jean and Kim. He asked, "What do you see when God is calling you? Grapes or giants?"

A few days later, Kim approached Jean and told him that they'd have to go. At first the minister teased his wife and pretended not to understand.

"Where?" he asked.

She named Bay St. Louis. Jean reminded his wife of the comfortable life they'd be leaving, the suburban house, their family and friends, the children's schools.

Kim shrugged. "Grapes," she said, "or giants?"

Jean resigned from his Memphis ministry in October of 2006 and moved to Bay St. Louis in December. Kim and the children joined him in June when the school year ended. Over the next three years, the new church with the quirky name provided housing and meals for over thirteen thousand volunteers and acted as a community conduit for more than $4 million in donations.

"There are days when Kim and I ask ourselves *what have we done?*" mused Jean. "There are other sweet moments of divine clarity.

"Obeying a calling like that is not pious," he continued. "It's self preservation. I've read the book of Jonah and know what happens if you don't go. I figured that I was either gonna drive down I-55 or be vomited onto the beach at Waveland by a big fish."

Like Jean, Wendy McDonald also grew up in Bay St. Louis, where her family name is synonymous with real estate and hardware. For more than a hundred years, McDonald's Hardware store has anchored the small Old Town commercial district. Portraits of the original founders hang on the wall of the rambling building, their stern eyes overseeing sales ranging from lightbulbs to lumber. While I knew several McDonalds, I first met Wendy after Katrina. The petite woman had volunteered to work for the city, taking on a job no one had imagined would ever be needed.

That need first became apparent just a few weeks after the storm. Before the city managed to obtain some trailers for office space, the council met nightly in the train depot. One of the few municipal buildings to escape destruction, the upstairs space had become an emergency center of operations crammed with desks and chairs, boxes, charts and file cabinets. Officials and citizens would sit wherever they could find space, perched on flimsy chairs or on the edges of cluttered desks. Hands over hearts, they'd recite the Pledge of Allegiance facing a flag propped in one corner of the room.

One evening, a local restaurant owner standing in the back pointed out that a county in Maryland had sent representatives with donations, yet no Bay St. Louis official had time to meet with them.

The mayor sighed and explained that under other circumstances, he'd love to cook them a big gumbo dinner, but between the skeleton staff and the enormous task of trying to restore basic services, no one had even an hour to spare.

A few weeks later, Wendy McDonald resolved the city's problem by offering to "help fill the gaps." She and another former Bay resident, Rory MacDowell, formed a coalition called Hancock County Citizens in Action. Their mission was to coordinate information and resources among the local governments. To help reveal the true plight of the Mississippi coast, Wendy began to act as a liaison for Bay St. Louis and Waveland, giving "disaster tours" for visiting reporters, photographers, and officials.

The skills Wendy had acquired in three decades as educator and administrator served her well in the new job. In 2005, Wendy was enrolled in a Ph.D. program at the University of Texas and worked as dean of a college in Houston. But her ties to "her true home" were strong, and she often visited her parents, son, and many family members still living in the Bay.

When Katrina barreled toward the coast in August, Wendy's son evacuated to McComb, Mississippi, a few hours north of the coast. Her parents, C.C. and Eve McDonald, elected to leave their own home in the lower elevation Cedar Point area of town and ride the storm out in the home of a family member who had fled. The house was located on the Bay's bluff, but sat perilously close to the beach. Monday morning, as she watched news of the storm from her home in Houston, luck allowed Wendy a brief cell phone connection with her parents. Wendy had to strain to hear the voice of her eighty-two-year-old father over the noise of the wind.

"It sounds terrible," Wendy said. "You should have left."

C.C. ignored her rebuke, and, before the connection was lost, he calmly described the hole the storm had torn in the roof.

Relentlessly, Wendy scoured the television and Internet, hoping for some mention of Bay St. Louis. Her first burst of hope came with the

report of an eighty-year-old couple in the Bay who had survived by floating on a mattress during the surge.

"I thought, oh God, I hope that's them," she said. "That's something Dad
would have thought of."

Her son, Ryan, worked his way back down to the coast on Wednesday.
As he approached Bay St. Louis and saw the scale of the devastation, he
grew fearful that he would have to call his mother to report finding the
bodies of his grandparents. Instead, he walked up the small lane to the
house and found C.C. McDonald dipping water out of a neighbor's swimming pool. He greeted his grandson casually, as if nothing were out of the
ordinary.

Wendy contacted two cousins who also lived in Texas, and the men
agreed to trek with her to the Bay. She rounded up a generator, water, batteries, and a gas can, and the trio headed east on Thursday, reaching the
Bay on Friday.

Wendy was relieved to find her parents in relatively good health and
spirits. However, their home had been lifted up by the surge, twisted and
then set back down at a bizarre angle. Amazingly, no windows had been
broken in the mayhem. Delicate glasses in the china cabinet were still sitting upright on the shelves, filled with a vile concoction of mud and water
that reminded Wendy of little poison cocktails.

During that first trip, she stayed for a single day, working with her
father to salvage belongings from the house. When she returned to Houston, she established a new routine, working at the college during the week
and then making a fourteen-hour round-trip drive back to the Bay each
weekend. For every expedition to the coast, she filled her car with supplies for the shelters, focusing on kitchen equipment like cookers, pots
and pans, and propane tanks.

Soon, Wendy realized that the seven-hour drive between her two worlds
crossed more than a stretch of interstate. Spanning the enormous rift that
severed normalcy and calamity became increasingly difficult for her. When
she was in Houston, conversations seemed inane to her.

"I found I didn't care what was happening to the rest of the world," she
remembered. "Bay St. Louis was all that mattered."

In October, Wendy asked for and received permission from the college to take a three-month leave of absence. Soon after, working as a city liaison for Citizens in Action, she hosted a disaster recovery team from Habitat for Humanity. They pressed her to accept a job with the organization, coordinating the fledgling Habitat efforts in the Bay-Waveland area. Wendy accepted, with the stipulation that the position would be temporary since she planned to eventually return to her job in Houston.

Wendy extended her sabbatical from her deanship as Habitat's first house in Hancock County began construction in March 2006. The month of May found her on the porch of a Bay St. Louis cottage, talking on a cell phone with her supervisor in Houston, who demanded to know if Wendy was going to resume her job at the college. At first, Wendy reaffirmed her intentions to be back at work in the beginning of June. Then her supervisor asked what she'd do if another hurricane were to threaten the coast.

Wendy paused, imagining herself at her desk in Houston, hearing news that another hurricane was headed for the Bay. When she realized that she'd return to her "true home like a shot," Wendy resigned without hesitation.

During the next three years, she managed a team that built seventy-five homes in the Bay-Waveland area. Her belief that "skills appear as needed when a person follows their calling" became a self-fulfilling prophecy. The well-oiled Habitat machine assembled volunteer crews from across the country, sometimes completing a new house from foundation to furnishings in just a week.

"It's like being a new mother," she explained. "You don't see where the energy will come from, how you could possibly bear and then care for a baby. Then suddenly, you're a pack mule and you find yourself carrying around a fifty-pound child. You grow into the role."

A chance to "grow into the role" was an unexpected dividend for the thousands of teenagers and college students who poured into the disaster zone from other parts of the country. For most of them, the closest brush they'd had with true hardship and loss was the screen of a television, so their experience on the coast made a profound impact.

A group of young volunteers work to clear debris from a lot at the corner of Washington Street and Beach Boulevard.

I'd bike around town with my camera and photograph them at work. The images show kids shoveling debris out of mud in an empty lot that had been a home, or unloading young saplings in a tree giveaway. Young women who had never held a hammer struggle to pound nails into the frame of a new home. Teenaged boys proficient at high-tech computer games proudly perch on rooftops after hauling up several tons of shingles.

One afternoon as I picked my way across the debris field of a former school, I spotted a young man running. Obviously an accomplished athlete, he paused to stretch against a lone surviving basketball hoop. He waved as I approached and offered a greeting. Although he looked familiar, I couldn't place him. Since he wore the open smile common to most volunteers, I asked about his background and what had brought him to Bay St. Louis.

He'd grown up in Pass Christian, the town just across the bay, and had been educated at Coast Episcopal School. He pointed to the remains of a ruined building nearby, remembering classes he'd attended there. Now a Dartmouth graduate, he'd decided to spend time volunteering at St. Rose de Lima Catholic Church in the Bay before launching his career. When I asked about his home in the Pass, he explained that his parents had retired to Montana before the storm, but had maintained their house on the coast. It had been destroyed by the storm.

The mention of Montana jolted me, and I suddenly remembered that I'd met him in my art gallery before the storm. His mother had been a favorite among the artists I'd represented.

"You're Beau Saccoccia!" I realized. After explaining our connection and inquiring after his parents, I asked Beau how he'd decided to volunteer at St. Rose.

A few months before, in December 2005, Beau had visited his childhood home in Pass Christian, where most of the town's buildings had been scoured from the earth. While only two feet of surge had flushed through the Saccoccia home, the house had folded in on itself from the force of the storm. Beau walked through the yard littered with their belongings, occasionally stopping to pick up a muddy baseball card from his boyhood collection.

The family's piano on the ground floor had somehow survived the trauma in good condition. Beau corralled a few friends, and the young men knocked out a wall of the battered house, managing to haul out the monster baby grand. He donated the piano to Al Acker, the legendary choir director for St. Rose, the church he'd attended as a boy.

During that visit, some college friends volunteering on the coast introduced Beau to a secular organization in Biloxi called Hands On USA. This "accidental" community of volunteers had formed spontaneously in the storm's aftermath. The recovery program attracted a wide range of people—from retired house painters to truck drivers to college students. Beau joined the group and found fulfillment working alongside others, handing out water, food, and blankets to people in need.

Although he hadn't attended a service at St. Rose since he'd been in high school, one Sunday he found himself inexplicably drawn to a morning mass. The congregation embodied the essence of diversity. Established in 1926, it had originally provided a place of worship and a school for members of the African American Catholic community. In typical Bay St. Louis style, the church gently integrated itself over the decades. Father Sebastian, the diminutive priest who heads up the congregation, originally hails from India. His lilting accent presides over services renowned for their straightforward lessons and a dazzling gospel choir.

Each mass at St. Rose begins with a traditional salutation, when members turn to hug or shake hands with their neighbors, saying, "You're at the right place, at the right time." The ritual took on new meaning for Beau that morning as he watched the faces surrounding him filled with both celebration and grief. Then a reader in the pulpit greeted visitors to St. Rose, adding, "If you're here after a separation of months or even years, welcome home."

"*Welcome home*," Beau said. "That really got to me. There have been few things in my life that have felt as forward and clear."

The next day, he packed up his tent in Biloxi and set it up beneath an oak tree behind St. Rose, dedicating himself full time to their recovery efforts.

During the next two and a half years after our chance schoolyard meeting, I'd often see Beau working around town on behalf of the church. He began to coordinate efforts between St. Rose and other organizations, like Hands On, VISTA, AmeriCorps, and Lagniappe. The groups found they could maximize efficiency by sharing housing, meals, building materials, and supplies for distribution. Over three thousand volunteers funneled through St. Rose during that time, helping the local team undertake projects like home builds and educational programs.

Beau's initiative didn't go unnoticed. When President George W. Bush visited Biloxi in April of 2006, he was one of a handful of volunteers selected to have a meeting with the statesman.

Beau recalled, "The president somehow knew I was from Mississippi and asked me what I thought of the recovery. I gave some bland answer about how it was probably going to take fifteen years to recover. The president thought that was a good point, but suggested that a smart man like me should consider starting a construction company.

"Of course, he was right, but it seemed to miss the point of what we were doing as volunteers."

By the time Beau finally left the coast in quest of a career, the true point of volunteerism had been driven home.

"It's the necessity of community," he said. "And it's not found very often in our culture now."

The experience also left Beau with a question. "I want to know how we as a country can connect to that communal feeling without needing a disaster to precipitate it. It's something I'm still exploring."

Growing up on the Mississippi coast left connections that worked like tenacious tendrils of belonging in the hearts of people like Jean, Wendy, and Beau. Yet thousands of people who had never stepped foot in the state were also compelled to rearrange their lives in order to help complete strangers.

Maureen Gatto—or Mo, as she's known to her Mississippi friends— never knew Bay St. Louis existed before the storm. Yet she took a two-year hiatus from a successful career as an attorney to volunteer as a coordinator for one of the largest recovery programs on the coast.

My favorite photograph of Mo was taken on Easter Sunday, 2008. Mo's wearing a Scooby-Doo outfit. She was acting as grand marshall of the town's annual pet parade that benefits the animal shelter. A tangle of leashes encircle her as children and adults try to hang on to dogs dressed as chili peppers or ballerinas. It was a steamy day and Mo must have been suffocating beneath the fake fur, but a very genuine smile beams out from her goofy dog costume. When I took the picture, it was difficult to remember Bay St. Louis without that smile.

But Mo had first visited Mississippi just two years before, in April 2006. She had signed on for a one-week volunteer stint with twenty-seven other Pennsylvania lawyers in a trip to help retrieve documents from the damaged county courthouse. When they arrived, the courthouse was deemed too dangerous, so the attorneys were diverted to cleaning muck out of houses instead.

After one strenuous workday, Mo sat in a folding chair outside the volunteers' sleeping quarters, surrounded by absolute darkness and swarms of bloodthirsty mosquitoes. In a split-second decision, the attorney made an inner commitment to return to Mississippi and completely immerse herself in the recovery efforts. To accomplish that goal, she understood that she would have to upend her structured life in Pennsylvania and move full time to the Gulf Coast.

Back in her own home, Mo waited for two weeks, hoping that the strong feelings would subside. When the desire didn't fade, she began the complex process of putting her life in order to allow for a two-year commitment. She also began wondering how she would break the news to her husband.

One Sunday afternoon, sitting on the porch of her house with her husband, Dennis McKenna, she dropped the bombshell.

"Honey," she said. "I'm moving to Mississippi for two years."

After recovering from his initial shock, Dennis committed to supporting her by "keeping the home fires burning" in her absence. The two collaborated on a schedule that would allow them to visit regularly during the summer and on holidays.

Soon after, while attending a Pennsylvania social gathering, Mo had a serendipitous encounter with businessman Bill Eastburn. Eastburn was a cofounder of the Bucks-Mont Katrina Relief Project, which had sponsored Mo's original volunteer trip to Mississippi. When she explained her intent to move to the Gulf Coast, he stared as if she'd "fallen from the sky." Eastburn and the project's board quickly signed Mo on as the on-site coordinator for the program in the summer of 2006.

By that time, Bucks-Mont was already a well-known name in Bay St. Louis recovery circles. The project was the brainchild of Eastburn and two other influential businessmen from Bucks and Montgomery counties, near Philadelphia. Soon after Katrina, the men had flown toward New Orleans, wanting to "help in a big way." When their plane was unexpectedly rerouted to Stennis International Airport in Hancock County, they were shocked to find the area in ruins—understanding only then how the calamity in Mississippi had been underreported. After meetings with local officials, the Pennsylvania team changed their plans, shaken by the enormity of needs in Hancock County. They partnered with the Salvation Army and officially began the Bucks-Mont Katrina Relief Project, which soon captured the wholesale support of their Pennsylvania community.

The day she arrived in Bay St. Louis on behalf of the project, Mo was invited to a small, informal art opening at the makeshift offices of the chamber of commerce. She introduced herself to director Tish Williams, who carved out a place for Mo in the overcrowded office on the spot, dragging in a metal desk chair and a pop-up table for furnishings.

From that small space, Mo often worked hundred-hour weeks as the Bucks-Mont "on-the-ground" representative. Her directive was to find the greatest unfulfilled needs and bridge the gaps. She organized housing builds, coordinated volunteers, and oversaw dozens of projects—like acquiring uniforms for a basketball team. She made connections with other relief groups and often worked closely with Jean, Wendy, and Beau.

Months passed before Mo finally had time to lift her head and look above the high hedge of problems. She discovered that the allure of the Mississippi coast went beyond the battered landscape. As she wove herself into the community fabric, she sensed a warmth and charm that resonated with feelings she'd forgotten in her demanding "real world" existence. Though she had "good days and bad days," her initial strong feelings of connection remained consistent.

Like Beau, she was also attracted to services at St. Rose, although Mo didn't consider herself religious and hadn't attended mass in twenty-five years. In the church she discovered people who were blind to race, age, gender, and income—a community that seemed to embody her vision of a perfect world. And while Mo eventually grew used to southern hospitality, she found amusement in the surprised reactions of "rookie" volunteers who were new to the phenomenon.

"They'd be helping someone who was living in a trailer over two years after the storm, but was still full of southern charm," she said. "These survivors would hold their heads high and cook meals for the volunteers in their tiny trailer kitchens, offering the food with joy and embraces. The rookies would always be blown away."

I interviewed Mo as her two-year commitment drew to a close in the summer of 2008. The Bucks-Mont project had collected almost $3 million

Mo Gatto in her role of grand marshall of the annual "Paws on Parade" that benefits local animal rescue efforts.

in donations and in-kind services. They had helped build a child development center and launched plans for a new food pantry and animal shelter. Mo was making arrangements to return to her Pennsylvania life—to her husband, her legal career, and a home that had become a "bachelor's pad." She laughed as she talked about plans to realphabetize her spice rack.

"I was one of few people who could rearrange my life for two years to volunteer," she said. "Many others would have loved to have been in my shoes."

Mo may have been headed back north, but she was taking along the dream of retirement in Bay St. Louis. The powerful coastal connections she still felt were obvious when she spoke her next words: she used the present tense rather than the past. "I feel so lucky to be a part of it all."

THREE STORMS

Mississippi attorney general Jim Hood, testifying before Congress, 2007: "I'm here to tell you that there were three storms that have occurred . . . One was Katrina itself, the other was the failure of the insurance industry to pay what it owed, and now we're facing incredible escalation in costs to reinsure . . . This is the third storm . . ."

THE SECOND STORM   *"The insurance companies have raped the people in this community!" declared Dr. Wesley McFarland, and a roar of resounding agreement rose from the audience. Many of the five hundred coast residents packed into the Bay St. Louis auditorium for the town hall meeting had been patients of the popular physician. McFarland had room to be riled—he'd had to sue his insurer for settlement on his destroyed home. The elderly doctor described an attempted mediation episode when insurance representatives said they'd investigated his slab three times and had even taken pictures of it from an airplane. "Well, gee whiz, that's awful interesting," he told them. "I didn't have a slab."*

McFarland was part of a local panel of businessmen and homeowners assembled by Congressman Gene Taylor in August 2007 as an attempt to convince a visiting congressional delegation of the desperate need for federal insurance reform. Thirteen lawmakers, including Speaker of the House Nancy Pelosi, listened attentively from their tiered podium, waving paper fans against the close August heat.

The fervor of the audience reminded me of tent revivals I'd attended as a child. Applauding frequently, we hung on to every word, as Taylor conducted the proceedings with dignity and passion. He'd suffered the same losses as the rest of us, yet without hesitation, he'd taken up the weighty gauntlet of insurance issues on our behalf. In the two years since Katrina, the plainspoken congressman had never minced words and we loved him for it. In a 2006 CNN interview, he pronounced, "There ought to be a national registry of child molesters and insurance company executives because I hold them in the same very low esteem."

—Notes from my journal, August 2007

This sign asks neighbors a bitter question.

After "the first storm" left over 133,000 Mississippi homes either destroyed outright or massively damaged, hand-painted plywood signs cropped up along the coast, scrawled with scornful messages. One sign in the Bay accused two national insurers of being the "Axis of Evil." Another asserted, "Mediation is a hoax!" Another in front of a damaged Waveland house asked an insurance company, "Where are you?," then gave it a verbal kick to the shins, calling it a "Bad Faith Operator." Perhaps the most poignant statement was a short poem posted on a barren Bay St. Louis lot where a home had once stood. Shreds of an American flag drooped from a dead tree next to the sign:

> *I know my flag is tattered*
> *In need of loving care*
> *But I can't take it down*
> *Till State Farm pays its share*

The raw emotions relayed by the signs hardened into a pervasive suspicion as stories of unmet promises began to circulate through the community. Many of the angry homeowners were like my friend "Annette," who initially filed a claim for her lost home with no misgivings. Her insurance company was no fly-by-night operation, but a national icon that spent millions annually bombarding the public with pledges of reliability.

"I'm not worried," she said over coffee in my kitchen, a few weeks after the storm. "It's gonna be a hard road, but I'll make it."

In the first week of October, she met a representative from her insurance company at the former site of her home. The company had sent no ordinary adjuster, but an engineer to ascertain if the destruction was from wind or flood. Like most houses on the coast, Annette's had probably been a victim of both natural forces. Her homeowner's policy only covered wind damage. The engineer inspected the property, implying the company would cover damages in full. That evening, she slept with complete peace of mind in the tiny travel trailer that had become her temporary home.

For the next three months, Annette hung on to that afternoon's assurance, continuing to make mortgage payments on her empty lot. Then she received a letter from her insurance company offering to settle her policy worth over $150,000 for around $10,000.

"I was so damned angry," she bristled later. "I'm usually pretty easy going, but that pushed me over the edge."

Like several generations of American homeowners before them, Annette and thousands of other Gulf Coast residents had placed firm faith in their insurance companies. In the decades after World War II, lenient lending terms encouraged home ownership; however, insuring the property was an obligation of the mortgage. At first, the system presented few problems. Homeowner's insurance was easily obtained, inexpensive, and was usually included in the monthly house notes.

Then insurance companies began to shy away from covering catastrophic risks like earthquakes, floods, and windstorms. In 1968, the federal government stepped in with a nationally available flood insurance program. Individual states sometimes offered earthquake and wind coverage—available from state-sponsored "pools." The coverage was generally more expensive, but managed to keep the mortgage machine humming in higher-risk areas of the country. Mississippi began its own state wind pool in June of 1970, after many insurers fled the coast in the wake of Hurricane Camille.

By 2005, many people in the Mississippi coast area carried two or even three policies to cover their homes from hurricane losses. Often, they had a federal flood insurance policy, a state wind-pool policy, and a "standard" homeowner's policy—which excluded both windstorm and flood. Those who were still covered for windstorm under policies written by national companies considered themselves lucky.

In the months after Katrina, that good fortune often turned out to be another illusion. Like Annette, most people hadn't read the fine print in their homeowner's policies that mentioned "anti-concurrent causation."

Congressman Gene Taylor explains the provision for the policy in a 2007 editorial (*USA Today*):

> After Hurricane Katrina, insurance companies paid for wind damage as far inland as Tennessee, 300 miles from the Gulf Coast, but denied wind damage claims in coastal areas where five hours of destructive winds were followed by the storm surge.
>
> State Farm instructed its adjusters that "where wind acts concurrently with flooding to cause damage to the insured property, coverage for the loss exists only under flood coverage." Other companies implemented similar policies.
>
> Homeowners who paid high premiums for decades were left with unpaid claims for wind damage. While denying their own claims, companies were generous with taxpayers' money, paying federal flood insurance claims in full without proving how much damage was caused by flooding.
>
> When insurers did order damage assessments, the reports were rigged. One engineering firm was fired and then rehired by State Farm only after promising to rewrite reports that found wind damage. Managers at another firm changed the on-site assessments of engineers who concluded that damage was caused by wind.

Gene Taylor and Mississippi attorney general Jim Hood blasted the insurance companies for passing on the responsibility for coverage to the federal flood program—a tactic that ultimately cost American taxpayers billions.

At least insurance companies didn't play favorites: both Taylor's and U.S. senator Trent Lott's Mississippi homes were destroyed, and, like hundreds of their constituents, they were forced to contend for insurance settlements while juggling the logistics of putting their lives back together. The benevolent slogans branded in the minds of millions became objects of derision on the coast.

"Like a good neighbor?" said activist Ana Maria Rosato. "With neighbors like that, move to a different country. *You're in good hands?* To get strangled. *We're on your side?* You'd better jump the fence."

Eighteen months after the storm, Rosato left her career in the California political arena and returned to her hometown of Bay St. Louis to help her mother rebuild. Moved by the insurance hardships she witnessed, the feisty writer took on industry giants in a blog called "A.M. in the Morning." Later in 2007, she began working with Gene Taylor, eventually joining the congressman's insurance reform team.

"Insurance isn't sexy," Rosato said. "And nobody gives a hoot until you need it. But Katrina was a real eye-opener. Insurance companies bamboozled the American people." As an example, she points to the exemption the industry currently enjoys from federal antitrust legislation, something Taylor and his team would like to eliminate.

In testimony before a congressional committee, Taylor asked, "Is it really fair that State Farm can call up Allstate and call up Nationwide and call up USAA and say, you know what? If you don't pay claims, then I don't have to pay claims. Under the current law, that is allowed. It's wrong as all get out and it should be illegal."

As accusations leveled by lawmakers and policy holders were widely publicized throughout the country, suddenly some insurance companies found themselves enmeshed in a public relations nightmare. In Bay St. Louis, protesters marched on Highway 90, brandishing signs taking an insurance company to task. The harsh sentiments elicited honks of endorsement from passing motorists. Armed guards with holstered pistols were posted outside the offices of one local insurer, a stern reminder to any irate customer tempted to lose composure.

Yet in an August 2006 press release, the Insurance Information Institute (III), a "nonprofit, communications organization supported by the property/casualty insurance industry," proudly trumpeted the findings of a survey. "One year after Katrina, nearly 95 percent of homeowners insurance claims have been settled in Louisiana and Mississippi . . . and the vast majority of homeowners in both states say they are satisfied with their insurance company."

The survey was performed by Ipsos Public Affairs—who, according to their Web site, are "The Social Research and Corporate Reputation Specialists." Three hundred fifty-nine insured homeowners from Mississippi were polled. Of those, fewer than half (47 percent) had suffered damage to their homes caused by hurricanes in 2005. Less than a year after Katrina, a mere 5 percent of those Mississippi residents polled remained displaced from their homes. To some, that sampling didn't seem an accurate representation of those most seriously affected by Katrina. At the time of the storm's first anniversary, thirty-six thousand Mississippi families still lived in FEMA trailers.

Mississippi state senator David Baria called the III press release "industry pablum." Baria, a Waveland resident, won his coastal district seat in 2007 by campaigning heavily for insurance reform. He pointed to the seemingly impressive figures found in the release that touted the $5.2 billion paid to 334,800 Mississippi homeowners. "Using some easy division," he said, "you can see that the average claim payment was in the neighborhood of $15,600. I cannot imagine that most of the people who were paid that amount were happy with it."

Yet while insurers faced accusations of misconduct, the Mississippi Windstorm Underwriting Association was quietly taking care of business. Joe Shumaker, manager of MWUA, explained that the wind pool insured over sixteen thousand customers when Katrina struck. Most of the policies were written for properties near the beachfront, south of Interstate 10. In the weeks following the storm, it became obvious to the wind pool executives that few, if any, of those property owners would have escaped damage. Instead of waiting for their scattered customers to contact them, within two weeks MWUA opened a claim for every policy they carried.

Shumaker said, "We told our adjusters, if you get there and there's no damage, then say, hallelujah! Shake their hands." He added that of those sixteen thousand policy holders, over 98 percent of claims were settled with no dispute. Of the few complaints filed, none had gone to trial as of 2008.

"Insurance has a great role to play," Shumaker said in defense of the industry as a whole. "They have the responsibility for putting America back on its feet. There's a lot of good out there that's not always told."

Charlie Lucas sees it a bit differently. The Bay St. Louis resident, who lost family members as well as his home, wasn't a wind-pool customer. He recounted that his insurance company sent three different adjusters at his insistence before one would concede to the obvious damage. The first adjuster even declined to go onto the roof to examine it. "That sorry-ass outfit," Lucas said. "I had insurance with my company for forty years and my daddy before that. If they'd paid their claims like they should have, they'd have still come out ahead and no one would have bad-mouthed them."

THE THIRD STORM
I notice when I whine to friends on the "outside" about the skyrocketing insurance rates on the coast, they offer little sympathy at first. One told me outright, "What do you expect? You live smack in the middle of a hurricane zone."

But when I start to quote actual premiums, condescension turns to shock. One homeowner insured for a hundred thousand dollars pays over four thousand dollars a year. A local art gallery shells out thirty-three thousand dollars, an Old Town coffeehouse, twenty-eight thousand. The owners of a three-room bed-and-breakfast saw their wind coverage alone rise in one year from ten thousand dollars to twenty-eight thousand. Their accountant advised them to close, and they followed his recommendation.

—Notes from my journal, April 2008

Wendy McDonald drew a hand across her brow when I mentioned the word "insurance"—she suddenly seemed to be fighting off a headache. In the three years since the storm, the director of Bay-Waveland Habitat for Humanity had overseen the construction of dozens of houses with a program that makes home ownership affordable. I took notes as Wendy

Bay St. Louis businesses have been besieged by years of constant construction, their woes compounded by astronomical insurance rates.

explained how rising insurance rates were making it difficult to fulfill that mission on the Mississippi coast. Then she made a statement so startling, I stopped typing and asked her to repeat herself.

"Yes," she affirmed. "You heard me correctly. One hundred percent of the time—in the case of every home we've built here—the monthly insurance payment totals more than the amount of the actual mortgage payment."

That financial punch was felt by more affluent homeowners as well. Friends of mine who planned to rebuild a storm-resistant house fronting the beach in Waveland surrendered when the best quote for a homeowner's policy came in at $18,000 a year for $450,000 worth of coverage. Renters didn't escape the crunch either, as landlords were forced to pass along enormous rate increases.

Small merchants groaned under a twin burden. Laboring to keep shops open when tourist traffic had evaporated, they were brought to their knees by already expensive premiums that sometimes tripled overnight. The local coffeehouse calculated that they had to sell seventy cups of coffee a day just to cover their insurance. Big business wasn't immune either. After Hancock Bank—with almost $7 billion in assets—restored its original office in Bay St. Louis, they were unable to obtain insurance for the stately historic building. Ironically, one arm of the financial institution actually sells insurance.

For those who wanted to throw in the towel and move on, sales of their real estate holdings were stymied—once again by insurance rates. Purchasers balked once they discovered what their annual premiums would cost, sometimes even walking out of closings.

Recognizing fundamental flaws in the current system, Taylor tackled the monumental task of a national overhaul. His team formulated one possible solution, "multi-peril" insurance, a proposal that would incorporate an optional wind risk feature into the federal flood insurance plan. Both wind and water damage would be covered. Although the plan was drawn up to be self-supporting and not rely on taxpayer subsidies, it met resistance from critics who claimed that it'd be cumbersome, costly, and inefficient.

Taylor's insurance team countered that since 55 percent of Americans live within fifty miles of a coastline, the issue wasn't simply a Gulf Coast problem. Their belief was borne out in 2006, when insurers began dropping policies by the thousands in states like Florida, Texas, New York, and Massachusetts.

As federal insurance reform legislation stalled, rising rates in south Mississippi became community fodder for fury. One spring afternoon in 2008, I sat in a local salon while a timer ticked off the minutes for the color percolating in my hair. I idly brought up the topic of insurance, and the large room instantly ignited with a burst of hostile comments. While scissors flashed in fury, tales flew between mirrored stations, with clients, beauticians, and a manicurist competing to tell the most impressive horror story.

The retired accountant getting her hair trimmed probably won. She told of a $10,000 quote she'd gotten to insure her new $600,000 house. Certain there'd been some mistake, she informed the agent that she'd already obtained windstorm coverage from the state pool. The agent coolly replied that the quote didn't include wind.

Jan, the owner of Hairworks, checked her own insurance bills. Before the storm, she'd paid almost $2,400 for $123,000 coverage on the historic cottage. In 2007, the bill had shot up another $1,500. The policy covered neither wind nor flood damage.

Resentment swelled when the salon coalition began comparing our own rates with those of friends who had moved to different parts of the state. We discovered that those of us who had stayed on the coast seemed to be paying premium prices for insurance that didn't cover any hurricane-related risks.

"Hey, shouldn't we be getting a big *discount* instead of paying more?" demanded a woman with foil in her hair.

State senator David Baria asked the same question of Mississippi insurance commissioner Mike Chaney in 2009. Baria later detailed the curious conversation.

"He [Chaney] initially said that insurance companies decide which areas they consider to be 'high risk.' I asked him what risks make the Mississippi Gulf Coast a 'high risk' area, and he responded 'wind and water.' I reminded him that those risks are already excluded from most homeowners' policies and yet our policies are more costly per $1,000 for less coverage.

"He really didn't have much of a response, other than to say that the amount of premium is an issue decided by the insurer. When I pointed out that he has the authority to approve or deny the premium, he responded that they [the companies] had to make a profit or they would cease writing policies in Mississippi."

That explanation didn't satisfy Baria, who would like an investigation to explain why his constituents on the coast are paying more for minimal coverage. Yet the state has yet to take an aggressive stance on insurance reform. In his first months in office, the senator introduced seven bills aimed at benefiting the insurance consumer. None made it out of the committee process. Among the common sense proposals was one mandating insurance discounts to homeowners who incorporate hurricane-resistant features in their houses. Another would require companies to give an explanation for any claim denial. A third was a regulation that would prohibit the state insurance commissioner from receiving gifts from insurance companies.

When asked why none of the bills was successful, Baria answered, "The insurance lobby is very powerful."

Judy is one of the citizens Baria represents. The single nurse lives in Waveland and doesn't understand why something can't be done to make life on the coast a little easier.

Katrina left Judy with the brick shell of a house. After the rebuilding, her insurance company of twenty-three years dropped her wind coverage and relegated her to the state windpool. They offered no discount for the reduced coverage. Several months later, they informed her that the rates for that basic policy—which now excluded any hurricane risks—would be increased up to 90 percent. Judy's total insurance note had shot up from $1,500 a year to over $4,000. Her house is valued at $103,000.

The first year, Judy took money from her savings to pay the bill. But as her retirement approached, the sixty-year-old found it frightening to deplete her life savings. Like some other coast homeowners who have fulfilled their mortgage obligations, she made the difficult decision to drop most of her coverage. Now, she carries only flood insurance on her home.

"It's an awful risk, but I simply can't afford it," she said. "All I can do is pray that we don't get anything like Katrina again."

BAY POLAR

Teri Lucas: "One of my neighbors told the Red Cross volunteers that I'd lost my parents in the storm, so they kept coming over to check on me. They'd ask, do you need anything? Do you just want to talk? Once, four or five of them stopped by in a single day. I said to my husband, I must not be doing so good. No, he said. You're not."

When I moved full-time to Bay St. Louis in 1995 and began to meet older residents who'd spent their lives in the town, I was often amused at the frequency with which Hurricane Camille was mentioned. I'd try not to yawn when someone would suddenly veer off any given topic and launch into a story about their narrow escape from death, or the incredible hardships of the aftermath.

Jeez, I'd think to myself, *that happened twenty-five years ago, why on earth are they still talking about Camille? Get over it already!*

In 2008, I found myself sitting at a kitchen table with family in South Carolina. Midway through the lunch, I realized that I'd mentioned Katrina at least a dozen times. I only caught the trend when my nephew stifled a yawn and narrowed his eyes as if assessing me for mental illness. I pinched my own arm under the table, furious at myself for dragging my muddy mental baggage into a holiday gathering. Yet a few moments later, "Katrina" popped out of my mouth again, as distracting as a belch in the middle of a Sunday sermon. Eyebrows were raised. My nephew gave his young wife a significant glance. I could read his silent message: *Why on earth is she still talking about Katrina? It happened almost three years ago. Get over it already!*

I was beginning to understand that humans never quite get over a significant tragedy. Like dye in water, the event colors every fiber of a life. And the pigment of pain seems especially vivid when an entire community experiences a common calamity.

Individual misfortunes usually elicit support from those unaffected by the tragedy. After a death in the family, neighbors will ring the doorbell, bearing casseroles and condolences. A house fire will inspire fellow church members to take up a collection and provide temporary housing.

Yet after Katrina, no person in the community had escaped the consequences of catastrophe. Those crippled by anguish were forced to lean on other limping souls. Like a beaten brigade after a losing battle, we staggered off the field in our comrades' arms, the weak supporting the wounded.

The combat comparison is more than a metaphor to Dr. Raymond Scurfield, who served on an army psychiatric team in Vietnam. Now a professor of social work, Scurfield teaches at the University of Southern Mississippi Gulf Coast. He lives in Long Beach, a coastal town about ten miles east of Bay St. Louis. Long Beach was mauled by the storm, as was the beachside university. When Scurfield hiked to his office the next day, he found a lifetime of painstaking research ruined and spread willy-nilly

The stretch of beach where Deb Gross's cottage and several other businesses—including the Good Life bar—once stood. Photograph by Joe Tomasovsky.

across the campus. Scurfield's personal Katrina experience and his extensive expertise in post-traumatic stress led him to draw several parallels between combat veterans and hurricane survivors.

According to Scurfield, both groups often undergo a loss of faith, wondering how God could permit something so dreadful to happen. Or they lose confidence in government when a bureaucracy "that doesn't function well in normal times" becomes gnarled and tangled during crisis.

Survivors commonly became disoriented when they returned to a home that suddenly seemed an alien place. A sense of feeling forgotten is another similarity—one frequently encountered by Gulf Coast residents who'd been through the storm. Scurfield recounted attending a Katrina

conference at a prestigious university that drew hundreds of experts from
around the country.

"During the thirty-minute opening speech, Mississippi was not mentioned a single time," he said.

Physical triggers can set off anxiety. Some veterans abhor the sound of
firecrackers that remind them of gunfire, while hurricane survivors may
become jittery during a bad thunderstorm. Amazingly, even emotions
brought on by an event with no connection to the original trauma can
induce stronger than normal reactions. For instance, losing a loved one
has the power to bring up every loss a hurricane survivor experienced,
magnifying the grief exponentially.

The full catalog of post-traumatic stress symptoms is a large one. Once while researching the subject, I printed out a list of thirty-seven different indicators. The little Internet test instructed me to check off the symptoms I'd experienced. When I'd finished, there wasn't a blank space on the page. I could have even added a few others, like "aggressive avoidance" and "post-traumatic procrastination." The list read like a litany of mental distress and included "increased anger, nightmares, mood swings, memory problems and dissociation."

I learned that dissociation is very common in people exposed to extreme trauma. The term refers to a state where perceptions are altered and normal thought patterns become disrupted. Everyday reality transforms into a dream. *Sign me up*, I thought as I read. It sounded like an accurate description of my life during and after Katrina.

Dr. Deborah Gross experienced an incident where dissociation actually affected her vision. Two days before Katrina, the psychiatrist had evacuated from her beachfront cottage in Bay St. Louis where she lived and maintained her practice. She shoehorned as many belongings as she could into her car, then said farewell to her beloved home and headed to her fiancé's house in Jackson, Mississippi.

The couple later shopped in a Jackson grocery store, stocking up on nonperishables in case they lost electricity. On one shelf, a row of cans caught her eye. "Pea cheese," the labels advertised. Intrigued, she reached for a can, thinking that it'd be something new and interesting to try. Holding it in her hand, Deb squinted again at the label. It now read something completely different. "Peaches."

She placed the can in the cart and tugged on her fiancé's arm.

"Robert," she said. "In the foreseeable future, don't let me drive."

Deb never saw her home again. When she and Robert were able to return to the coast, she was unable to even recognize the spot where the building had stood. Her fiancé followed her as she clambered over the rubble, dispensing tissues while she sought some small reminder of her past.

Over the next two years, the psychiatrist documented her own manifestations of PTS, as she struggled with crying bouts, panic attacks, and memory loss. Deb once discussed her growing concerns about memory loss with a scientific researcher. Her scientist friend informed her that psychological trauma can actually cause physical damage to the brain. "Hey," he said. "If we bopped our lab rats over the head, they wouldn't know how to get through the maze either."

Deb took a job away from the coast and tried to settle into her new community, yet like many who moved elsewhere for reasons of sorrow or practicality, she often felt alienated. Surrounded by unmarred landscapes and people who—although sympathetic—simply couldn't relate, many "expatriates" experienced survivor guilt, an anxious suspicion that they hadn't suffered, lost, or sacrificed as much as others on the coast.

One neighbor of mine who'd lost her home relocated to Jackson for her job. On a visit back to the Bay, she drank a cup of coffee on my porch and lamented: "Like a marriage, I was committed to this town for better or for worse," she said. "We had many years of wedded bliss. Now it's been hurt in an accident and paralyzed, but just maybe—with lots of intensive therapy—it'll be OK. By moving to another city, I feel like I've abandoned my duty and run off with the drummer from a rock and roll band."

For those of us who remained behind, the communal crack-up provided an odd comfort: our neighbors and friends could empathize en masse. Yet the inescapable, daily sight of ruin and debris added to our misery. Long-standing marriages dissolved overnight. Drug and alcohol abuse, suicide, child abuse skyrocketed. One local pharmacist estimated that prescriptions for antidepressants shot up at least 25 percent after the storm—at a time when the town's population had declined significantly. My own doctor joked that antidepressants should be added to the water supply.

Depression was sometimes accompanied by chronic fatigue, yet another PTS symptom. I compared it to the utter exhaustion I'd experienced while working on a ship as a young woman. After a few days at sea, I would no longer notice the motion of the vessel, yet my body unconsciously compensated for each wave, constantly striving to maintain balance. Mild activity in rough seas would leave me feeling like I'd run a marathon. I began to understand that trying to keep a mental balance in the post-Katrina world wore on my community in much the same way.

The sense that we faced endless and unexpected travails was heightened by some bizarre attacks from strange quarters. We were still sifting through the rubble for our dead when proclamations began to appear in the national news claiming that Katrina was a punishment from God. A wild array of sources, including frothing ministers, antiabortion groups, politicians, and even Al Qaeda named a variety of sins that were supposedly to blame for the destruction. While most charges were aimed at flamboyant New Orleans, one Alabama state senator asserted that God had not overlooked the iniquities of Mississippi.

Senator Hank Erwin wrote, "New Orleans and the Mississippi Gulf Coast have always been known for gambling, sin and wickedness. It is the kind of behavior that ultimately brings the judgment of God . . . Warnings year after year by godly evangelists and preachers went unheeded. So why were we surprised when finally the hand of judgment fell?"

The concept that a personal God had directed the devastation fired off already touchy tempers in some survivors. A petite, mild-mannered friend, whose home had been destroyed, exploded in fury after hearing a seemingly innocuous comment.

"If one more person tells me how blessed they were not to lose their house," she fumed, "I'm going to smash their face! What are we? *Unblessed?*"

Another ugly trend surfaced as blame began to be cast toward Katrina survivors for choosing to live in a vulnerable area. I once cried while reading a series of mean-spirited comments on a Web site that featured an article about our town's recovery efforts. As people around the country lambasted Gulf Coast residents for trying to rebuild, their wagging judgmental fingers seemed pointed directly at me.

Later, I was visiting another state when a man voiced that same venom to my face. He almost wound up a victim of my own PTS symptoms (numbers 1 and 26), increased anger and extreme irritability.

He begins with a self-congratulatory pat on the back and lets it drop that he is leaving the following week for Mississippi, to spend a week building a house for someone who'd been left homeless by Katrina. But before I even have a chance to applaud him, he starts on a rant about how people on the Gulf Coast "deserved what they got."

"People down there knew it was only a matter of time, they should have moved out years ago. They should have had their insurances paid or moved

somewhere else if they want to whine. I don't feel sorry for them, I'm no bleed-
ing heart liberal."

I think that if I tell him that I live on the Mississippi Gulf Coast, it will
embarrass him. I am wrong.

He looks me right in the eye and knows I'm itching to deck him. He's old and
out of shape and I'm sure I can break his nose before he knows what's happening.
A friend who's a bleeding heart liberal saves me from assault charges by gently
putting her hand on my arm and pulling me away.

"But hey," the jerk says from a safe distance. "I'm not king of the world."

"Good," I answer.

Although relatively rare, the misplaced blame seemed to compound
the symptoms of stress already shouldered by the community. The saving grace for myself and other survivors in Bay St. Louis was something
Wendy McDonald calls the "little piston."

"When someone was going down," she said, "someone else was always
there to step up. Nobody had to do it on their own, there was always somebody to lift the load, saying, *here, let me do that for you.*"

The miraculous "little piston" went to work soon after the storm and
somehow managed to keep the sputtering engine of community running. Survivors gathered given the slightest opportunity. Communal
dinners, city meetings, and church functions often acted as group therapy sessions, as neighbors shared stories of loss and residents embraced,
reunited after long separations. Our Second Saturday Artwalk morphed
from a social event to a psychological shindig, another chance to celebrate resilience.

The opening of the new bay bridge in May 2007 became a milestone
of recovery. Over seven thousand people converged in Bay St. Louis, all
rejoicing at our literal and symbolic reconnection with our neighbors to
the east. Of the many photographs taken on that jubilant occasion, my
favorite is one of my beaming friend Prima Luke. The T-shirt she wore
sported a lighthearted, yet ironic message. *Build a bridge—and get over it.*

Humor had become our brightest buoy, with laughter lifting us above
the swells. Understanding humor's healing power, minister Jean Larroux
coined a phrase for the community-wide mental disarray.

In this photo taken a year after the first BridgeFest celebration, Prima Luke stands atop the new bay bridge wearing yet another shirt from her whimsical collection. Prima was the chef at the popular Dock of the Bay restaurant for twenty-one years before the storm.

"Bay Polar," he said. "That's what we call it when you laugh and cry in the same sentence. It's what happens when you come here, it's the way it feels."

Some of our artists dug for any levity that might be mined from the loss. For the first post-Katrina holiday season, one couple sent out a photo greeting card that showed them embracing, with the sad ruins of their Waveland house looming starkly in the background. Beside them is a life-sized drawing of Rhett Butler holding Scarlett O'Hara in his arms. The large caption above the *Gone With the Wind* cartoon reads: *Oh, Fiddle Dee Dee. Let's worry about this mess tomorrow.*

Strangers thrown together would banter to lighten the mood. Once while standing in line at the liquor store (increased alcohol consumption—symptom number 8), I overheard several sweaty women in grimy clothes anxiously discuss an approaching storm. One woman bemoaned the threat, predicting that it'd be "the end of the world."

"If it's going to be the end of the world," groused another, "it'd better happen before I finish cleaning all the damned mud out of my house." The gloom dispersed instantly as everyone in the store laughed.

Uncomfortable housing situations were also fair game for dark humor. After living for over a year in a FEMA trailer with a miniscule lavatory, Ernie, the owner of the Good Life, grinned wickedly while describing the plans for his new dream house. "It's going to have a three-thousand-square-foot bathroom," he announced.

Living in Jackson, Deb Gross noticed a lightening of her own spirit as the months turned to years. While her memories of her former life were "like a knife in the heart" during that first year of aftermath, she noticed a slow emergence of happier recollections. The psychiatrist found herself reminiscing about the fishy smell of the salt air and the luminous light on the coast. She returned to Bay St. Louis in May 2008 to marry Robert in St. Rose de Lima Catholic Church, where before the storm, she'd joyfully sung in the choir.

"I was afraid that the loss would overwhelm the gain," she said. "But I was so happy all day long, I couldn't even talk to anyone. I just held Robert's hand and looked at everyone in that church of my heart."

Gain despite loss. It's not mentioned in the traditional psychological model for disaster. The accepted phases that a community undergoes after a traumatic event are Heroic, Honeymoon, Disillusionment, and Recovery. Dr. Scurfield pointed out that—based on recent research and his own experience—he's convinced of another phase called "Post-Traumatic Growth."

"For the vast majority of Katrina survivors," Scurfield said, "there were some positive outgrowths to come out of the experience. Post-Traumatic Growth usually manifests with enhanced relationships of some kind. I call the ones I've experienced and observed the Three F's: Family, Friends, and Faith. The faith can be enhanced in a higher power or in the inherent goodness and interconnectedness of humanity."

Considering my own life, I saw many signs of that growth. My understanding of community had transformed from the thought that it was merely a pleasant social accessory to the knowledge that those bonds served to sustain survival during crisis. While my relationship with Joe had shifted from romantic to familial, our friendship had become a bedrock of good will. My faith had expanded far beyond theological bounds. I'd seen terrible things happen to very good people, yet tragedy had been revealed as an opportunity to magnify light in the darkness.

I'd watched others around me change in a heartbeat from ordinary people to extraordinary heroes, willing to sacrifice their lives for others. I'd witnessed the evolution of complacent housewives who turned into courageous warriors, battling to provide normalcy for their children amidst the carnage. Some who'd found their livelihoods stripped away tackled challenging new careers they would never have imagined before the storm. Each day on the coast presented me with more evidence of the indestructibility of hope and the human spirit.

Yet despite the positive forces set in motion by Katrina, I remained haunted by the sense that I simply wasn't "getting over it." Dr. Scurfield inadvertently hit this personal land mine during our interview when he said, "The most important thing to remember about post-traumatic stress is to give credit to the power of the trauma. In varying degrees, the impact will last a lifetime—even in perfectly normal people."

I kept typing furiously into the laptop as he continued, but had to fight off a sudden and powerful urge to weep. Several minutes later, when the kitchen table interview was completed, the gentle-spoken professor saw me to the door of his house and gave me a hug.

As I drove the coast road heading back to the Bay, I thought about the shame I'd been living with for over three years. *Get over it already*, I'd told myself, time and again when I'd experienced depression and sleeplessness and crying jags over insignificant setbacks. I'd come to see myself as flawed and weak, unable to subdue the raw emotions that often bushwhacked me, ones that brought back the horror and fear of an event that had happened long ago.

The beach to my left glowed golden in the sunset, but tears obscured my vision as Dr. Scurfield's parting comments reeled through my head.

"Time heals all wounds—it's a myth. Else all old people like me would be paragons of mental health. Time helps assuage some of the piercing pain that comes in the immediate aftermath, but that pain never goes away.

"At first, there's some compassion from others. But you're expected to recover and move on. If someone is still beset by nightmares three years later, the tide starts turning. People's acceptance and understanding seem to recede and the blame shifts onto you. Others think that something's the matter with you and eventually, you accept that blame, take it on yourself."

I pulled the car over for a minute and rolled down the window. The humid air smelled a little fishy, and luminous light bathed my eyes like a balm as more tears of relief streamed down my face. I realized that I had embraced that blame and the awful shame that was its companion. With a few simple words, Ray Scurfield had exonerated me from guilt and offered a cleansing absolution. I'd never quite get over it and that was "perfectly normal." But while I was marked for life, I now could see the beauty manifested in that intricate, mysterious tattoo.

PART EIGHT
Storm Journal

SOMETHING WONDERFUL
IS ALWAYS HAPPENING . . .

For the third Katrina anniversary, Bay St. Louis planned a festival instead of a memorial service. "New Day in the Bay" had a bright logo and a catchy subtitle—"A Celebration of Our Can-Do Community." By showcasing dozens of major recovery projects like new schools and community centers, New Day would encourage residents to look forward instead of mourning the past.

But the universe has a sharp sense of irony: a few days before the event, a hurricane named Gustav charged into the Gulf. As residents began to evacuate, town punsters came up with another name for the festival. "New Day in the Bay" turned into "Doomsday in the Bay."

—Notes from my journal, August 2008

MIDMORNING, MONDAY, SEPTEMBER 1, 2008   The windows of my kitchen had not been boarded over, so I looked towards the back corner of the yard where the thick bamboo grove bowed towards the ground, humbled by the power of the gale. In the adjoining room, my neighbor Gary shouted into his cell phone, straining to be heard over the racket of the storm. When he signed off, he walked into the kitchen, stepping over the towels we'd spread on the floor to sop up puddles. My new roof had already begun to leak.

"I just heard from a friend who's down by the front," Gary said. "I'd like to tell you what's happening, but first you have to promise that you won't flip out."

Too late! And I already knew exactly what was happening. I was in the middle of a freaking hurricane, despite the vow to myself to never ride out another.

I brazenly lied to Gary. "I'll be fine," I said. "I want to know what's going on."

"He says that the water at the front is only five feet from the top of the railroad bridge," Gary said.

The official surge prediction for Gustav was twelve feet, less than half of Katrina's. But since the storm was just winding up, Gary's news meant that the estimates for a maximum could be way off, *just like they'd been during Katrina.* In my mind's eye, I could see the massive pilings of the railroad bridge rising high above the beach. Imagination painted an impossible wall of water over the bridge footings. A few more mental brushstrokes gave the picture a chilling detail—breaking waves that smashed violently onto the tracks.

I peered out toward the street, expecting to see water streaming over the asphalt, *just like in Katrina.* My stomach squeezed and if I'd eaten breakfast, more than bile would have been forced up into my throat.

"The storm isn't even hitting here," I whined, as if logic could change reality. "It's coming in a hundred miles to the west."

"We're in the northeast quadrant," Gary explained, "so we're actually getting the brunt of it. On the radio they said that high tide this afternoon could push in even more surge." Watching my face pale, he added a chipper tagline. "But they think we're seeing the worst now." He punched me lightly on the shoulder for encouragement. "Come on, let's go play some gin rummy, I'm tired of solitaire."

Gary's dog, Booger, led the way to the guest side of my house. The small white ball of fluff was the carpenter's inseparable sidekick, and the two lived nearby in a travel trailer. The evening before, when I realized I wouldn't be able to evacuate in time, Gary had offered to be my storm companion. I was relieved at their presence. Hurricanes are like scuba diving—the buddy system considerably ups the odds of survival.

Gary had moved into the guest apartment and set up a command station in that kitchen with a battery radio and a deck of cards. He'd taken the precaution of stashing his pack of cherished belongings in the bathroom of the building's center hallway, the most protected part of the house. While making my own storm preparations the night before, I'd remembered the story of a friend who'd hidden her grandmother's punch bowl set in the dishwasher before she'd evacuated for Katrina. The house had been utterly destroyed, but cleanup crews later found the dishwasher blocks away. The punchbowl set was still inside, with nary a chip. I had tried to jam my computer into my own dishwasher, but it wouldn't fit, so I'd stashed it in my dryer instead.

Gary and I pulled up chairs to the table, and he began shuffling the deck of cards. When I admitted I'd forgotten the rules to gin rummy, he reeled off a complicated refresher course. Too distracted to follow, I eased my anxiety by petting the dogs beneath the table. Booger had settled on the floor next to Jack and Buster, both of whom outsized her exponentially.

Buster was the new kid on the block; he'd only been part of my family for a few months. The bashful stray had wandered the neighborhood at will until Jack brought him home to live on my porch. Buster became Jack's best bud and had even managed to win over my normally scrappy terrier, Frieda. When seventeen-year-old Frieda died from a seizure a few weeks later, the tawny dog soon graduated from a bed on the porch to one in the house. I was delighted to find that despite his shy demeanor, Buster was a steady storm comrade.

None of the dogs seemed disturbed by the strident tornado warnings issuing from the radio like machine gun fire. The announcers blasted out the alarms, issuing two new ones for every one that expired. Other than a freak surge that topped Katrina's, a tornado was the one thing that might reduce my house to matchsticks. As if he'd read my morbid thoughts, Gary dumped a box of matches onto the table.

"Surely you know how to play poker," he said. "We'll use matches instead of money—that way you won't go broke."

In that dim room with the branches of the oaks thrashing outside the windows, I tried to focus on the cards in my hand. Gambling seemed appropriate. I'd made the decision to stay in the Bay with my eyes wide open, knowing that several times a decade, I'd have to face the threat of hurricanes. The past two years of tame weather had lulled me into a blissful state of denial. Now, the surge was climbing up the railroad bridge, my computer was in the dryer, and Gustav beat at the door like a blustering loan shark, bent on collecting exorbitant interest on my false sense of security.

I lost the first few hands of poker; then as my heart rate gradually returned to normal, good fortune smiled. Gary dealt me a full house. I bluffed by acting befuddled, and he bet enough matches to start a forest fire. I was scraping the large pot over to my side of the table when Joe burst in through the kitchen door.

He'd run across to check on us and shook the rain from his coat as we exchanged the latest news. Robyn had evacuated New Orleans the day before to take refuge with him, and both were weathering the storm in his house with full electricity. I'd lost power the evening before, so I felt a stab of jealousy. Although Joe offered to bring over a meal later, I declined, since my gas stove still worked and I had a cooler full of thawing food from my freezer. Hoping for another easy mark, I tried to persuade Joe to play a few hands of poker with us, but he pulled up the hood of his raincoat and struck back out into the storm.

While I dealt out another hand, I thought of friends who had sensibly evacuated. Hugh had texted me from his safe haven in Pensacola. Lori was well north of the coast in the new house she was building. Kat had taken refuge with friends in Columbia, Mississippi. We'd spoken the evening before, and Kat had expressed shock over my decision to stay.

I explained that I'd planned to take cover with my friends Julie and Tommy in their recently completed house ten miles north. Before I left, I decided to download files from my older computer to a new one I'd just gotten. Late in the afternoon, a confident—and incompetent—computer tech I'd reached by phone had assured me that the transfer would only take an hour. The process had taken nine hours and couldn't be aborted. By then, it was well past dark. Gary and Booger were settling into the guest

The completion of the new bridge that spanned the Bay of St. Louis was only one element of the recovery that New Day would have celebrated.

apartment while the first real bands of the storm were windmilling over-head. I resigned myself to staying put and invited Buster and Jack into the loft bed with me. They quickly fell asleep, but I could not. The winds howled across the roof while I replayed the fiasco of the day before—when "New Day" had turned into "Run Away."

It had seemed a splendid idea. While other coast communities would be grieving losses on the weekend of Katrina's third anniversary, irrepress-ible Bay St. Louis would throw a party celebrating the future. The New Day concept kindled enthusiasm among both residents and city officials. It appeared that everyone was ready to put the past behind us and focus on the profusion of positive assets. Bay St. Louis was creating a stronger and more beautiful city; the festival presented an opportunity to strut our stuff and buck up community morale.

New Day had provided my first experience as an event coordinator. I'd been offered the job by the Hancock County Chamber of Commerce, a client of the new public relations business I'd begun eighteen months before. No one seemed to mind that I was a novice at festival production, and several seasoned professionals volunteered to help. The event's highlight would be a Civic Showcase, with more than seventy booths displaying their ongoing projects. Over a hundred local artists assembled a show with the theme of rebirth. The New Day team scheduled tours of historic sites, several bands, a frolic area for kids, and even an old-fashioned horseshoe tournament.

The festival was slated for Saturday, August 30—the day after the third Katrina anniversary. On Tuesday, August 26, I started getting e-mails and calls from vendors worried about Gustav. Some computer models predicted that the storm would move into the Gulf by Saturday, then intensify and strike in our vicinity on Monday, September 1. I held tight to my belief that early predictions were invariably wrong. But Gustav refused to change course, and each day I watched as the little hurricane icon marched across the map in lockstep with the predicted path. Before the storm even reached Cuba, vendors cancelled by the dozens and spin-off events folded.

On August 29, city leaders conferred and took a "plucky, but prepared" stance, deciding not to cancel the event. Mayor Eddie Favre announced that "while we're watching Gustav very carefully, we want to maintain a sense of normalcy for as long as possible. The city has already undertaken preparations—cleaning drains, gassing up city vehicles, alerting residents—all the things that we'd do under normal emergency circumstances.

"But Saturday evening, the New Day celebration will be a time for citizens to take a break from preparations made earlier in the day. As a community, we can come together, relax for a few hours, appreciate the many positive aspects of our life here and look towards our future."

Yet it became difficult for anyone in the community to maintain a sense of normalcy when media outlets fastened on the irony angle: on the anniversary of Katrina, another potentially devastating hurricane roared toward the coast. The post-traumatic trigger was pulled again and again as Katrina's name was mentioned more frequently than Gustav's.

To complicate matters, on Friday, the governor's office issued a mandatory evacuation for those in FEMA trailers and to residents in flood hazard zones.

By Saturday afternoon, Old Town seemed like Ghost Town. A few hardy groups had set up booths, and their tents billowed with the winds of squalls that were racing overhead. Scattered pods of residents walked empty streets, pausing to exchange evacuation plans with neighbors. Many hugged, not knowing when they'd have the chance again—we all remembered the long and anxious separations caused by Katrina.

Surveying the sorry scene, I wanted to cry. Dozens of volunteers had worked hundreds of hours in a wasted effort. I took the defeat personally and apologized to everyone I came across—the mayor, city councilmen, the police chief. They all laughed good-naturedly and talked about luck of the draw.

Pulling his hand from the pocket of his shorts, the mayor shook my hand. "We'll do it again!" he said. "But maybe not during hurricane season . . ."

When I offered an apology to chamber director Tish Williams, her mother overheard. Myrt Haas pulled me off to the side, and the dauntless matron gave me a sound rebuke.

"You stop that right now!" she commanded. "Do you think you're God? Did you personally steer Gustav in this direction? Now hold your head up, look people in the eye, and thank them for participating."

Still following Myrt's advice a few hours later, Kat and I performed with our band at the local coffeehouse. Only a few stalwart souls sat at the tables arranged before the outdoor stage at the Mockingbird Café. Rogue gusts snatched at our sheet music and threatened to topple mike stands. One friend compared us to the dance band on the Titanic.

Yet I was cheered as we sang, working from a set list that seemed to bizarrely befit the occasion. Kat grinned all the way through "Stormy Monday." The sparse audience joined in with a rousing rendition of "You Are My Sunshine." Harmonies fused our spirits as well as our voices when we sang "Solid Ground," a Katrina ballad written by Kat's daughter, Molly Fitzpatrick. The message of the chorus had never been more meaningful and seemed to spit directly into Gustav's spinning eye.

When the rains fall and the waters rise
And the winds come and blow me down
When the earth moves right before our eyes,
We will lead each other back to solid ground . . .

TUESDAY, SEPTEMBER 2, 2008   Gustav had crashed the party on Saturday, slept over Sunday night, and by Monday morning had raised enough hell to attract the attention of national media. We were hoping for peace by early Tuesday, but the ruffian refused to leave. That morning, while squalls still buffeted the town, I turned my video camera on a sleep-deprived Gary. "Gustav," he groused. "The storm that wouldn't end."

At least my electricity had been restored; it had been out less than ten hours. Joe was one of many residents in town who never lost power in the storm. I'd later hear a story from friends who had evacuated to Natchez, over two hundred miles north of the coast. The power in that antebellum city had been severed by Gustav, yet when the couple returned home to the Bay, they discovered not a clock in their house had lost a minute. I felt pride in the reliability of our power on the coast—it seemed to symbolize a hardened storm stance.

I inspected my own house for damage and could find none except for the few places where water had breeched the new roof. There had been no flooding in my yard, so the moldy boxes from Katrina that remained beneath my house were uncompromised and still reproachfully calling for my attention.

By late morning, the squalls had become more isolated. Gary and Booger headed back to their trailer, while Jack and Buster jumped into the back of my wagon, eager to take a tour of the town. I planned to go by the homes of friends who had evacuated, make a quick check of the properties, and phone the owners—I hoped with good news.

Taking Citizen Street towards the beach, I passed Augusta's new cottage, recently completed with the help of volunteers. Her little red truck wasn't in the drive, so I assumed she'd taken refuge with relatives elsewhere. This would be a good report—all appeared to be in good order. Augusta's home was one of dozens that had been constructed in my immediate neighborhood by volunteer forces. I often marveled that, even three years after Katrina, those good Samaritans had not forgotten us. Almost every week, I'd spot a new house going up, the construction site teeming with laboring teenagers and adults.

Between Augusta's home and the beach stood seven other new or renovated houses. Gustav hadn't seemed to faze any of them. I was beginning to believe we'd skated by unscathed from the storm when I took a left on Beach Boulevard. I was only able to drive for two blocks toward Old Town before a barricade blocked my way. A sizable length of the temporary road that ran along the bluff had been pulverized by the surge and had avalanched down the eroded bank. I might have been disheartened, but sighed with relief at the sight of the newly constructed pier for St. Stanislaus College, a venerable prep school facing the beach. Beyond the ruined road, the new pier stretched proudly out into the Mississippi Sound and seemed to be unharmed.

The long expanse of beach that runs beneath the pier is where I usually walk my dogs, and they whined in recognition, yearning to be let out for a good run. I ignored their pleas because I couldn't even see the sand. It was covered with thickets of torn marsh grasses, sprinkled with sodden gray lumps. As I eased myself down the crumbled bank to get a better look, a small striped snake slid beneath my foot. I leapt back and saw dozens of them writhing in the mats of tangled vegetation.

A bystander up on the road called out to warn me about the snakes. Although he identified them as a harmless swamp variety, I'd already retreated and had no plans to disturb them further. After thanking him, I asked about the gray forms on the beach.

"They're dead nutria rats," the man said. "Guess this whole mess got washed out of the Louisiana swamps. You know, those nutria are a real problem there, they've taken over and are tearing up the levees." He pointed up the coastline and wrinkled his nose. "There are hundreds of dead ones between here and Bayou Caddy. It's gonna smell pretty bad in a day or two."

Gustav had apparently raped the barrier islands and the Louisiana wetlands, leaving us even more vulnerable to future storms. I thought of the U.S. Army Corps of Engineers, spending millions of taxpayer dollars to rebuild those defenses, yet easing the way for Mississippi developers to fill wetlands. The conflicting goals put forth by a single government agency seemed embodied by the endless snarls of refuse that covered the beach.

My dogs didn't care about politics. They wagged their tails, eager to chase after snakes and rodent corpses. Still pensive, I ignored them, got back into the car, and backtracked toward Main Street. The streets had been hazardous even before the rains of Gustav. Most roads in Old Town had been torn asunder in the last two years, with the object being to replace every sewage, water, and gas pipeline in Bay St. Louis.

When I'd first heard that the city's entire underground infrastructure would need replacement, I couldn't understand how Katrina could have affected pipes beneath the streets. Later, in one report I'd read, a team of scientists said that "from half a continent away, we made an unusual seismic observation of a killer hurricane on Aug. 29, 2005 as Katrina bore down on New Orleans and the Gulf Coast. By using an array of 150 seismic stations in Southern California and a signal processing technique called beamforming to identify the seismic signal, we recorded a signal strength 1,000 times greater than that generated by volcanic tremor."

I asked Buddy Zimmerman, who'd worked for twenty-three years as assistant director of the city's public works department, about the possibility of Katrina's thundering surge causing seismic damage to the underground utilities. That possibility hadn't occurred to him, but he said that after the storm, over three dozen manhole covers had been missing from the streets. Since the gaping holes presented a huge safety issue, Zimmerman immediately assigned a crew to retrieve the covers. He gave directions to search within a hundred-foot radius of the openings.

Zimmerman said, "At the end of the day, they'd only found *one* and that was 350 feet away from where it belonged, lying on the beach. My theory is that the surge pressed in from above, creating an enormous pressure on air trapped in the pipes. That could have created an explosive effect that just blew those covers to kingdom come. You can imagine what that would do to the pipes themselves." He paused. "Those manhole covers are solid steel. They weigh over a hundred pounds each."

I drove slowly down the broken roads, avoiding the patches of flooding, when a mail truck turned into the road ahead of me. I did a double take

and hit the brakes. The entire coastal region had been shut down for the major blow, and postal service had already resumed? Determined to catch a photograph, I forgot my caution, wheeled the car around, and chased the vehicle for several blocks. Finally, I zipped into a driveway a few houses ahead of the postman and was waiting when he pulled up to the mailbox and reached out his arm. He laughed when I asked for a picture, a little unsure about why I found his routine job so remarkable on this day. The image represented a big score for my Perfect Pictures game and I thought it deserved bonus points for the timing, just one day after a storm.

On Blaize Avenue, I checked out the *This Property Is Condemned* building. Its shabby looks hadn't changed much since Katrina, but the building was no longer a target for the wrecking ball. Earlier in the year, the Bay St. Louis Little Theatre had acquired it and was planning a full restoration. Local volunteers had cleaned it out, tidied the grounds, and propped up a sign facing the street. The piece of roofing tin had been painted red and lettered with white: *"The Show Must Go On!"*

A few doors down, I stopped for a Coke at C. J.'s neighborhood grocery and overheard a few locals rating Gustav as "a good old-fashioned storm." I understood what they meant. Most hurricanes barely create a blip on the radar of coast lives—rather like blizzards or ice storms up north, or minor earth tremors in California. They are natural events that disrupt everyday life—annoyances, not assassins. While a storm like Gustav might create mayhem in places like Baton Rouge and Natchez, the coast could handle an "old-fashioned" storm with poise. We regarded Katrina as a mutant, an obscene abnormality. We were building back with her in mind, but hoped it would be generations before another perfect storm would test our new mettle.

Driving in front of the old city hall, I examined the grand shoofly oak next to it. I didn't see any downed limbs, and the elaborate white wooden deck—the shoofly itself—blossomed unscathed from around the tree's enormous trunk. A few months ago, I'd used the oak as a model for a public awareness campaign that encouraged coast residents to replant trees. In a series of photographs, several local celebrities had posed, literally hugging their favorite trees. Mayor Favre had chosen the shoofly oak, and the image showed the mayor wearing a nice shirt over his shorts, attempting to wrap his arms around the tree's impressive girth.

During the shoot, I explained that later in the day, I'd be heading home to visit my parents in North Carolina. The mayor's easy smile snapped shut and he glowered at me.

"Your home?" he said with incredulity. "Your *home*?"

I read the meaning of his question with clarity.

"North Carolina is the place I grew up," I stammered. "Bay St. Louis is my home. *This* is my home."

His point made, the mayor's smile returned. He embraced the tree and leaned against it, waiting for me to snap the shot.

Passing the oak, I turned onto Main Street, and a large "OPEN" flag was the first thing I saw. I stopped the car again, laughing. The owner of the chocolate shop walked over, and I asked if he'd had any customers that day.

"No," said Dwight. "But you know me. I have to be here in case any show up."

I took his picture as he stood by the fluttering flag and drove on. Shops open, mail delivered, electricity restored. I knew that many homes had flooded and we'd be cleaning up for weeks, but we'd weathered our first storm since Katrina with composure intact.

I'd only driven half a block before I pulled over again, stopping in front of my darling "Monkey House." The historic cottage that had served as my gallery and home for almost ten years was in sad shape. Although she'd been gutted after Katrina, she awaited major structural repairs before restoration would begin in earnest. There was little traffic, so I let the dogs loose, and they followed me onto the porch. Jack sniffed obsessively at the doors of his old home, and I wondered what memories he could scent. I patted the front wall of the cottage, stroking her with affection. She'd survived for over 150 years and deserved some praise. Then I tilted my head back to look up at the large sign that hung on the eave of the house. It faced any passerby heading toward the beach, proclaiming a simple message.

Another sign had borne the same statement for almost a decade on a building closer to the beach. It had been braced like a billboard on the flat rooftop of Serenity Gallery, announcing "Something Wonderful Is Always Happening in Bay St. Louis." With a single line, that sappy sentiment had summed up my feelings about the town.

Yet, after Katrina, I'd discovered that it'd just been another illusion. In a conversation with the gallery founder, Jerry Dixon, I mentioned that the sign had seemed to personally welcome me to the Bay when I'd first moved into town.

"Oh no, darling," Jerry said. "The sign never said 'Bay St. Louis.' It didn't say *where* something wonderful was happening—it left that part to the reader's imagination." Jerry even brought me a photo of the sign to prove it, and I could see that the word "Happening" was trailed by three tiny ellipses. My imagination had actually concocted the name of the town.

Yet, my imaginary version of the sign still seemed on target. Even though Katrina had sucked huge parts of the town into the sea, some miracle magnet continued to attract magic. Each day, I witnessed evidence of its work. Why would I want to call another place "home"? But I still had to defend that decision on a regular basis. *Why do you stay?* Every resident of the coast hears that same persistent question, asked by well-meaning friends or family who live in other, presumably safer parts of the country.

Kat and I had recently shared a meal and pondered the strange phenomenon of perpetual inquiry. Friends who blithely reside on major fault lines on the West Coast and in the Midwest had asked why we stayed. A family member who sees steam rise daily from the towers of a nearby nuclear plant questioned my resolve to live on the coast. Acquaintances in the Northwest were curious about our decision, although Yellowstone could become a supervolcano at any moment and pulverize three states. Considering the odd terrorist or psycho and the looming possibility of an economic meltdown that would cause the total collapse of society, it seemed clear to Kat and me that everyone alive faced some catastrophic risk on a daily basis. But the people of the coast lived with less illusion. That clarity of vision—although hardly comforting—seems to make our colors more vivid, our landscapes more endearing, and the lines of love between us stand out bold and strong.

"Well," Kat said. "When the world ends, I want to be in Bay St. Louis. We've had plenty of practice. And I know that here, we'll take care of each other, even in the very worst of times."

The rain had started up again, a last gasp from Gustav, which had moved on to the north. I opened the back door to the car and the dogs jumped in without command. I took another look up at the sign. Like our town, it had been patterned on the old, but the new one was quite different. Yet the conviction of both remained the same: *Something Wonderful Is Always Happening . . .*

ACKNOWLEDGMENTS

I've never given birth to a book before and every romantic notion I'd held about writing was shot to smithereens during the four years of extended labor. I cried bitterly, laughed hysterically, whined piteously, and tried to procrastinate delivery for as long as possible.

Head midwife Ann McCutchan is an author, professional writing coach, and friend. She patiently held my hand over the last two years, shouting with the power of a drill sergeant. "PUSH!" she'd order, again and again. "BREATHE!"

The minute I wrote the book's last sentence, I called her. "It's out of the womb!" I screeched.

Ann paused as if she were counting the fingers and toes of the final manuscript before she let out a sigh and then said, "Damn, this baby has a big head!"

To Ann and the many other midwives who helped bring this big-headed baby into the world, I offer cigars and huge swathes of gratitude. This book about community came into the world only with the constant support of my own extended tribe of neighbors, family, and friends.

To everyone who generously dredged up painful memories to share their stories, thank you. May the tears you shed while recounting your experiences be compensated with the knowledge that you've offered inspiration, understanding, and comfort to others. I'm also indebted to others who contributed information to this book, including state senator David Baria, Dr. Raymond Scurfield, Buz Olsen, and Ana Maria Rosato.

To the hundreds of people around the world who took the time to write me words of encouragement after reading some of these essays on my blog, I'd like you to know how your letters helped steel me to continue writing in the face of my own grief. To my cadre of literary friends who offered their services as readers through the years, I am grateful for your candid input, which strengthened the work considerably. Special thanks and big hugs go to: Meg Bowen, Julian Brunt, Jeannie Deen, Julia Denton, Nan Ebright, Mary Minor Ferguson, Kat Fitzpatrick, Minrose Gwin, Thomas Harrison, Lucy Keenan, Carole and John McKeller, Nan Parati, David Sallis, Dawn Ruth, and Jo Rusin.

The list of those who worked tenaciously on my behalf to bring these writings to publication is long: Malcolm White and the Mississippi Arts Commission validated my writing efforts early on with a literary fellowship and major moral support. The Pirate's Alley Faulkner Society heartened me by awarding honors to two of these essays in their William Faulkner–William Wisdom Creative Writing Competition, while cofounder Rosemary James offered excellent advice. I'd also like to thank Gotham Book Executive Editor Lauren Marino, who critiqued a sample of the book on behalf of the competition and astonished me by offering encouragement. Lisa Eveleigh, Ayse Erginer, and the staff at *Southern Cultures* humanities journal at UNC Center for the Study of the American South afforded me the stellar opportunity to share the story of the Bay Town Inn with a wider audience. The very patient and professional staff at University Press of Mississippi—especially Assistant Director and Editor-in-Chief Craig Gill—have garnered my lifetime loyalty and gratitude for gently guiding this fledgling author through the publishing process.

The news organizations on the Gulf Coast deserve both credit and respect for exceptional coverage that continued despite grueling post-storm conditions. Four years later, they labor tirelessly to give residents the information they need to rebuild their lives. To my friends and colleagues at the *Sun Herald*, the *Sea Coast Echo*, and WLOX, I'm proud to know you! Special kudos go to MSNBC and the editors, journalists, and photographers who worked diligently to bring the oft-neglected story of Bay St. Louis and Waveland to the world. Their "Rising from Ruin" series sensitively covered an amazing array of aspects of the disaster and its effects on our towns.

Artist, writer, and friend Kat Fitzpatrick not only buoyed me during the desperate times; she also conjured the poem that provided the title to this book. I hope we're still singing harmonies when we're little old ladies. And to Molly Fitzpatrick, many thanks for sharing your song "Solid Ground."

Hundreds of Hancock County residents participated in a charity walking event across the new Bay of St. Louis bridge in the spring of 2008. Thanks to all those who helped us get to the point where we're able to give again!

I'll never forget the first time I heard it, after a survivors' dinner in my home. Your clear, sweet voice rang out, bringing us all to our knees and tears to every eye.

I never took a formal photography class from Joe Tomasovsky, but I understand from experience that his thousands of former students must consider themselves very fortunate. His clarity of vision not only provided poignant images for this book, but taught me to choose my writing target carefully and stay focused on the bull's-eye.

Thank you, Mom and Dad, for always believing in me. A big shout-out goes to niece and soul-daughter Anna Hirshfield, whose bright spirit and faith in me never flagged.

Larry Jaubert, I can never repay you for the nurturing and guidance that saw me through the final months of writing the manuscript. You wiped away more tears than I thought possible to shed and never ran out of tenderness or tissues.

Dr. Deb Gross reminded me that those who offered emotional support to survivors will probably never be recognized for their role in recovery. I'd like to change that now. To all of you who have vicariously lived through the pain with us, thank you for loving our wounded selves and smoothing our paths.

I'd also like to thank Dr. Deb for sharing one of the best insights I've ever heard, applicable to the survivor of any trauma.

My friend and fellow psychiatrist Donna Sudak says some variation of the following when people say they feel they should "just get over stuff":

"I hope you don't get over such a thing—what would that say about you as a person? And what would be the cost? I hope for you that your life becomes so big and so meaningful that it can contain such a thing."

RESOURCES

This book is based on my notes, memories, interviews with numerous people, and personal research. I've listed several Web site addresses below to facilitate further reading if a particular topic has piqued your interest. By doing so, I'm not endorsing any particular organization or Web site. Please keep in mind that Web site addresses are subject to frequent change, so as time passes, some links may become inactive.

References to local news stories may be searched on these sites: Biloxi *Sun Herald*—www.sunherald.com, *Sea Coast Echo*—www.seacoastecho.com, and WLOX TV—www.wlox.com.

To view more photography by Joe Tomasovsky, go to: www.joetomasovsky.com.

Cover artist H. C. Porter's Web site is: www.hcporter.com.

Find more music by singer/songwriter Molly Fitzpatrick at: www.myspace.com/mollyryanfitzpatrick.

To find information about artists mentioned in the book (and many more from the Mississippi coast), access: http://www.hancockarts.org/.

THE TIES THAT BIND
The Web site for the Hancock County Historical Society contains an amazing archive of Bay St. Louis images, as well as those from other sites in the county: http://www.hancockcountyhistoricalsociety.com/.

THE DETHRONING OF CAMILLE
One respected resource on this storm is *Hurricane Camille: Monster Storm of the Gulf Coast*, by Philip D. Hearn, published by University Press of Mississippi: http://www.upress.state.ms.us/books/388.

Some of the artists belonging to The Arts, Hancock County pose with Debbie Woodward (second row, third from left). Woodward, manager of the Northrup King Building arts center in Minneapolis, spearheaded an effort to help local artists after Katrina. She is one of many from around the country who worked closely with The Arts, Hancock County to resuscitate our wounded arts community. Photograph by Joe Tomasovsky.

WIND IN THE WILLOW

The full transcript of New Orleans mayor Ray Nagin's speech is available at: http://edition.cnn.com/2005/US/09/02/nagin.transcript/index.html.

THE LONG ROAD HOME

More of Michael Homan's eloquent writings can be found on his personal blog: www.michaelhoman.blogspot.com. Go to the archives section and select "September, 2005" to read more about his escape from New Orleans. To watch the very cool movie his daughter Kalypso made about Katrina, go to: http://kalypsotheodyssey.com/?page_id=154.

To read more about the Phoenix Fire Department's frustrations, go to: www.firehouse
.com/node/44344.

One of the most riveting accounts of the Causeway camp was written by a doctor who
worked desperately to save lives there. His name is Dr. Scott Delacroix and the article
is titled "In the Wake of Katrina—a Surgeon's First-Hand Report." You can access
it online at a site called MedScape: www.medscape.com. You'll have to register with
them to read the article, but it's free and well worth the effort.

TAKE IT ALL

The final Bay St. Louis report from the Mississippi Renewal Forum is available for
download at: http://mississippirenewal.com/info/plansReports.html.

The MSNBC site, "Rising from Ruin," featured comprehensive coverage of Katrina's
impact on Bay St. Louis and Waveland. The site can be accessed at: http://
risingfromruin.msnbc.com/stories.html.

MSNBC stories specifically about Paradise Properties by reporter Mike Stuckey can be
found at:
http://www.msnbc.msn.com/id/13561785/ and http://www.msnbc.msn.com/
id/16430798.

Two other MSNBC stories by Mike Stuckey cover the modifications to wetlands fill
regulations in Mississippi:
http://www.msnbc.msn.com/id/15305378/ and http://www.msnbc.msn.com/
id/17132172/.

Patrik Jonsson covered Hancock County poststorm development issues for the
Christian Science Monitor in this 2008 article:
http://www.csmonitor.com/2008/0521/p01s02-usgn.html.

GRAPES OR GIANTS

While I'm not endorsing any particular church or volunteer group, below are links
where readers can find out more about some of the organizations recognized in
this book.

Meet Dr. Carol Currier, who volunteered in Bay St. Louis with other team members of
the Loudon Medical Group in Virginia: http://risingfromruin.msnbc.com/2006/01/
bay_st_louis_mi.html.

To find out more about Lagniappe's ministry on the coast, go to: http://www .lagniappechurch.com/.

This link will take you to the Bay-Waveland Habitat for Humanity site: http://www .habitatbaywaveland.org/.

The Web site for St. Rose de Lima Catholic Church is: http://www.strosedelima-bsl .org/1.html.

To find out more about the history and work of the Bucks-Mont group, go to: http:// www.bucksmontkatrinaproject.org/.

THREE STORMS

A video record of Mississippi attorney general Jim Hood's testimony before Congress in 2007 may be found at: www.youtube.com.

A video record that includes some of the testimony from the August 2007 town hall meeting hosted by Congressman Gene Taylor may be found at: http://www.youtube .com/user/USRepGeneTaylor.

The full text of Gene Taylor's *USA Today* editorial may be found on his official Web site. Go to http://www.taylor.house.gov/ and click on the "Insurance Reform" tab. The site also contains extensive information about the coast insurance crisis.

Ana Maria Rosato's blog address is: http://www.aminthemorning.blogspot.com/.

Video records of Congressman Gene Taylor's testimony before Congress is available on Youtube at: www.youtube.com.

CNN's Kathleen Koch investigated the insurance crisis following Katrina in "The Town That Fought Back." A complete transcript of the show may be found at: http://transcripts.cnn.com/TRANSCRIPTS/0702/25/siu.02.html.

The Insurance Information Institute's press release about the insurance satisfaction survey may be found in full at: http://www.iii.org/media/updates/archive/ press.760032/.

To download the actual survey go to: http://www.ipsos-na.com/news/pressrelease .cfm?id=3168. Click on "Topline Results" to download the PDF file.

Mississippi state senator David Baria's Web site address is: http://davidbaria.com/.

The address for the Mississippi Windstorm Underwriting Association is: http://www
.msplans.com/mwua/.

BAY POLAR
Raymond Scurfield, www.usm.edu/gc/health/scurfield.

The Jackson County Community Services Coalition site contains the "test" I took,
listing PTSD symptoms. Go to www.jccsc.org/uploads and look for "Stress and the
5 Common Reactions."

An article detailing Alabama state senator Hank Erwin's comments can be found at
WorldNetDaily, http://www.wnd.com/news/article.asp?ARTICLE_ID=46568.

SOMETHING WONDERFUL IS ALWAYS HAPPENING . . .
The findings of a scientific team regarding Katrina's seismic strength called "When
Katrina Hit California" are available at: http://www.acoustics.org/press/151st/
Gerstoft.html.